Music, Imagination, and Culture

Music,
Imagination,
and Culture

NICHOLAS COOK

CLARENDON PRESS · OXFORD

Oxford University Press, Walton Street, Oxford OX2 6DP
Oxford New York
Athens Auckland Bangkok Bogota Bombay
Buenos Aires Calcutta Cape Town Dar es Salaam
Delhi Florence Hong Kong Istanbul Karachi
Kuala Lumpur Madras Madrid Melbourne
Mexico City Nairobi Paris Singapore
Taipei Tokyo Toronto
and associated companies in
Berlin Ibadan

Oxford is a trade mark of Oxford University Press

Published in the United States by
Oxford University Press Inc., New York

First published 1990
First published in paperback 1992

British Library Cataloguing in Publication Data
Cook, Nicholas, 1950–
Music, imagination and culture.
1. Music—Philosophical perspectives
I. Title
780'.1
ISBN 0-19-816303-7 (pbk)

Library of Congress Cataloging in Publication Data
Cook, Nicholas, 1950-   .
Music, Imagination, and Culture/Nicholas Cook.
Bibliography: p.
Includes index.
1. Music—Philosophy and aesthetics.
2. Music—Psychology.   I. Title.
ML3845.C67   1990   89–3352
781'.11—dc20
ISBN 0-19-816303-7 (pbk.)

7 9 10 8 6

Printed by Interprint Ltd, Malta

Contents

Acknowledgements

My thanks go to Alexander Goehr, who acted as midwife to many of the ideas presented here (others I simply filched from him); to Patricia Williams, who originally encouraged me to turn these ideas into a book; to several anonymous referees, whose comments helped to bring about the transition; to Charles Covell, who persuaded me to read Wittgenstein and Scruton; and to Louise. Finally I am grateful to the staff of OUP for making the production process not just (comparatively) painless but actually enjoyable.

Acknowledgement is also due to the following for kindly permitting me to reproduce copyright materials:

Ex. 1: *Journal of the Acoustical Society of America* and Diana Deutsch

Ex. 9: Boosey and Hawkes Music Publishers Ltd.

Ex. 29: Academic Press Ltd., John Sloboda and David Parker

Exx. 37–8: Universal Edition (Alfred A. Kalmus Ltd.)

Ex. 48a: Stiftsbibliothek St Gallen

Introduction

The main theme of this book is the difference between how people think or talk about music on the one hand, and how it is experienced on the other.

It is of course a general phenomenon, and not one confined to music, that words and images rarely if ever express quite what they are meant to. They distort the experiences that they are intended to represent, either through carrying false or unintended meanings with them or through leaving unexpressed the finer shades of what was intended. But in the case of music the problem of experience and its representation is so pressing and so specific that some theorists, like the ethnomusicologist Charles Seeger, have questioned the degree to which words can be regarded as capable of expressing musical experiences at all. They have done so on the grounds that there is a basic incompatibility between words and rational reflection on the one hand, and the experiencing of music on the other—an incompatibility whose source lies in the quite distinct logical structures of verbal and musical consciousness. And it is not only theorists who have such doubts. People who go to concerts must sometimes be upset by the lack of correspondence between the manner in which they experience a piece of music and the manner in which it is described in the programme-note; for programme-notes often dwell on the aesthetic importance of large-scale tonal structures or motivic relationships that are in practice inaudible to most listeners. To be told that the beauty or significance of a piece of music lies in relationships that one cannot hear is to have the aesthetic validity of one's experience of the music thrown into doubt; and the manner in which music is described by professionals can only create in the untrained listener a sense of inadequacy, a feeling that though he may enjoy the music he cannot claim really to understand it.

I suppose any work of intellectual enquiry is motivated by a sense of perplexity. What I find perplexing, and stimulating, about music is the way in which people—most people—can gain intense enjoyment from it even though they know little or nothing about it in technical terms. To write music, to understand its techniques, or even to play an instrument requires time, application, and specialized knowledge. But when music is heard, the results of all this are somehow synthesized into an immediate and intrinsically rewarding experience that does not, as a precondition, depend upon the listener having any kind of trained understanding of what he hears.

In saying this I am not denying that a musical education can open up new dimensions in the experience of music: it would be surprising if this were not the case. It is, after all, possible to get more out of most arts and crafts if one knows something about the techniques involved in them. The connoisseur of Chinese ceramics sees more in them than other people because he knows about the different types of glaze, the different shapes of pot and their origins, and so forth. Someone who knows nothing about these things may like one pot or dislike another, to be sure, but his appreciation and enjoyment are hardly likely to be as intense as those of the expert who understands the tradition within which the potter was working, or the constraints imposed by a particular body or firing technique. So it is not the enjoyment of the musical connoisseur who knows something about classical harmony and form that is perplexing: it is the degree of involvement that people who know nothing of these things feel in music, and their ability to respond to the music in an appropriate and meaningful manner. Glenn Gould (ed. 1987: 42) in fact believed that the critical responses of listeners who know nothing of music in technical terms 'usually have an intuitive edge' over those of trained musicians, who can always think of something to say in defence of whatever preconceived opinion they may have regarding anything that they hear. To this extent I would maintain (in opposition to Schenker) that music is an essentially democratic art: while it may not eradicate the distinction between the connoisseur and the layman, it does seem to render the distinction less important than it is in other arts.

It will not do, then, to explain the discrepancies that exist between the experience of music and the language of programme-notes or books on theory simply in terms of the inadequacy of untrained listeners' perceptions. And in any case, music is full of things which even trained musicians find hard or impossible to hear in terms of their structural organization; serial structures are merely the most obvious example of this. What is more, people who can follow a piece in technical terms do not necessarily do so when they listen to it in the normal way, that is to say for pleasure. Anybody who has had a training in Western art music should be able to follow the unfolding of a classical sonata form without too much trouble (that is, to observe the first subject, the modulation to the dominant, the second subject, and so forth); but experiments have shown what introspection might lead one to suspect, that people who have this ability do not by any means invariably choose to exercise it, unless they have some particular reason for doing so or are specifically asked to. And one might conclude from all this that the conventional theory of music, in which sonata forms, tonal structures, and thematic relationships play so large a part, is no more than a theory of unheard forms, imaginary structures, and fictitious relationships.

In this book I document some of the discrepancies between the listener's experience of music and the way in which it is described or explained in theoretical terms, and I argue that for purposes of critical evaluation it is important to distinguish the one from the other. But I do not see these discrepancies as being necessarily indicative of the inadequacy of musicians' ways of thinking about music. The reason for this is that when musicians criticize music or formulate theories about it, they are not trying to describe the phenomena of music in strictly factual terms or to account for them in a neutral or objective manner; they are not, in other words, trying to be psychologists or social scientists. On the contrary, they are working within a musical culture, which is to say that they are operating within the framework of presuppositions or (if you like) prejudices that constitutes a culture. And they are doing so as musicians, that is, they are in some sense involved in the production of music, and their criticism and their theorizing are an integral part of the productional process. To take a concrete example, some knowledge of Schenkerian theory is nowadays widely regarded as an important part of professional musicianship; and the value of Schenkerian theory lies not in its validity as a neutral or objective account of musical phenomena, but in its effectiveness as a means of interpreting musical structure that leads to better performance, better teaching, and better musicology. For it is obvious that a Schenkerian analysis is far from being a scientifically accurate account of how people actually experience music under normal circumstances. The large-scale linear or harmonic structures on which it is based are not things which people normally hear when they listen to music; rather, they represent ways of conceiving pieces of music as integrated wholes. A performer who has grasped an extended piece in Schenkerian terms may be able to bring to his performance a higher degree of large-scale rhythmic or dynamic shaping just because he has a reflective awareness of the music's structure that exceeds anything that is ordinarily experienced by the listener. In other words, the value of a Schenkerian interpretation of a piece lies precisely in the extent to which it diverges from the listener's everyday experience.

A Schenkerian analysis is not a scientific explanation, but a metaphorical one; it is not an account of how people actually hear pieces of music, but a way of imagining them. And at the core of this book lies the proposition that a musical culture is, in essence, a repertoire of means for imagining music; it is the specific pattern of divergences between the experience of music on the one hand, and the images by means of which it is represented on the other, that gives a musical culture its identity. Indeed, what I offer might be described as a psychology or sociology of musical imagination to the extent that it deals with the manner in which musicians represent music, and the manner in which these representations are embodied in the various productional activities in which musicians are professionally engaged. This is not, however, a work of social science, attempting to avoid making culture-specific or ethnocentric assumptions and so aiming to achieve a validity that transcends cultural or aesthetic boundaries. On the contrary, as a work of musicology, it interprets musical imagination in terms of a quite specific cultural and aesthetic stance; and any aesthetic interpretation takes certain beliefs or interests for granted, simply by virtue of being an aesthetic interpretation.

Aesthetics is not an ancient discipline: it takes its name from Alexander Baumgarten's *Aesthetica*, which was published in 1750 and argued, in Carl Dahlhaus's words, for 'the emancipation of sensuous perception' (1982: 6). Until then perception had generally been regarded as no more than a transitional stage in the acquisition of knowledge, a means of arriving at ideas: by contrast, as Dahlhaus explains, 'Baumgarten would show that perception was no preliminary, no shadowy, murky beginning of knowledge, but a kind of knowledge itself. . . . Then, since perception had the character of knowledge and the capacity of existing on its own, there would be in any perception achieving completeness, fulfilling its assigned possibilities, a multiplicity that coalesced, a variety of perceptions that shaped itself into a whole.' It was in achieving this completion and wholeness that the perception marked itself out as an aesthetic one. In this way the idea that to perceive something aesthetically is to perceive it as an integrated whole is axiomatic to the entire enterprise of aesthetics; as Dahlhaus goes on to say, 'The notion of the whole is one of the few to survive intact the transformation of esthetics from a theory of perception to metaphysics and on to psychology.' The field of musical analysis, nowadays increasingly important, is also predicated upon it; analytical methods as distinct from each other as Schenker's, semiotics, and set theory share as their common aim the demonstration of the manner in which musical elements combine with one another to form integrated compositional structures. In this book I argue that the structural wholeness of musical works should be seen as a metaphorical construction, rather than as directly corresponding to anything that is real in a perceptual sense; but I take for granted an even more fundamental assumption of the aesthetics of music, namely that the significance of music lies in what we perceive as we listen to it.

This is an interpretative assumption, and not the expression of a necessary truth. John Baily has attacked as ethnocentric the more or less exclusive emphasis of most music psychology on the manner in which sounds are perceived rather than the manner in which they are produced; as he says (1985: 238), it is general in Western or Westernized cultures for music to be regarded as 'primarily a sonic phenomenon; study of the motor control of musical performance may be interesting but it is ultimately irrelevant to the central issue, which is the perception of musical sounds'. And he goes on to cite the *kalimba* (thumb piano) music of Africa as an example of a music which is organized in kinaesthetic terms—that is, in terms of patterns of fingering—rather than in terms of the sounds that result; he also quotes Gerhard Kubik's statement that 'The organization of African music is motionally rigorous, right down to the tiniest areas. Whereas in Western music the movements of a musician playing his instrument generally have meanings only in terms of the sonic result, in

African music patterns of movement are in themselves a source of pleasure, regardless of whether they come to life in sound in their entirety, partly, or not at all.' (p. 241.) Now it might of course be replied that we have a different word for aesthetically interesting patterns of movement: we call them dance. But why in that case are we led to think of *kalimba* music as music at all? The answer is that in approaching it as music, and not as dance, we are expressing our own aesthetic interest in the sounds that arise from the performers' patterns of motion: we are, that is, making music of what the performers do, regardless of the terms in which they might conceive of their actions, or of their own interest or lack of interest in the resulting sounds.

As a matter of fact there is really no need to assume that, if it is indeed the case that the rational organization of *kalimba* music lies solely in its patterns of motion, then other aspects of the music can have no significance for *kalimba* players. In Chapter 4 I discuss the mistaken assumption that significance can be ascribed only to such aspects of music as are made the object of rational control. In the West we rationalize the sounds of our musical productions, and the manner in which they are experienced, to a rather high degree; we do not, on the other hand, rationalize their physiological, psychological, affective, moral, or social consequences in the same way. But this does not mean that our music has no such consequences. It simply means that we are not in the habit of thinking reflectively about them. In other cultures it is the other way round; the fact that such cultures do not rationalize the perceptual aspects of their music does not mean that such aspects have no significance in such cultures—it simply means, as I said, that culture-members are not in the habit of thinking reflectively about them.

At the same time, there is no doubt that to approach another culture's music from an aesthetic viewpoint is to interpret it in an ethnocentric and therefore partial manner. It is not just that, as Bell Yung (1984: 514–15) points out in connection with Western analyses of Chinese zither music, an exclusive concentration on the perceptual aspect of the music can lead to an unbalanced interpretation of it. Yung is referring to the importance of the motions described by the zither player's hand as he plays—motions which do not correspond in any simple manner to the sound of the music, and which can be followed and appreciated only by other players or connoisseurs who are present at the performance. And here the social context of the music comes into play. For the Chinese zither, or *qin*, was traditionally the instrument of the scholar; it was played in order to concentrate the mind and achieve a certain type of self-control. Virtuosity and acoustic gratification were disdained; what mattered was not the sound of what was played, but the moral and intellectual qualities that it embodied. While a scholar might play before a few like-minded friends, the concept of public performance was altogether foreign to this tradition. But nowadays there are professional *qin* players who give concerts before audiences that may have little or no knowledge of the instrument and its tradition. This means that, whereas the sounds themselves may be the same as they were in the *qin* music of the past (though more probably they are not, since public performance encourages a more virtuosic performance style), they are perceived in terms of a quite different social context. Even if today's listener hears the same sounds, he orientates himself differently towards them. And the same applies to any kind of functional music, whether intended for secular or religious ceremonial, for therapeutic purposes, or as an accompaniment to work: no such music can be experienced in an authentic manner when a recording of it is played in a London or New York apartment. It is for this reason that Alan Durant (1984: 5) maintains that however hard a contemporary Western listener who hears a recording of such music may try to experience it in terms of its original social function (for instance by studying sleeve-notes or reading books), 'what is gained is in no way the restoration of an original, fundamentally social experience of ritual or assembly. On the contrary, what is produced is an importantly new (in this sense "original") phenomenon of representation, in the projection—frequently for private, domestic consumption—of scale, ambience of ceremony, or mass performance.'

To approach music aesthetically—to interpret it in terms of a specific interest in sound and its perceptual experience—is not, then, to transcend Western cultural values, but rather to express them. As a study of the manner in which we imagine music and think about it, this book takes as its starting-point the aesthetic that is embodied in late twentieth-century Western institutions of musical production, distribution, and consumption—an aesthetic which is essentially consumer-orientated in that music is treated as a kind of commodity whose value is realized in the gratification of the listener. This represents a distinctly restrictive approach to music—and not just the music of other times and places. As I have explained, it leads to an unbalanced interpretation, if not downright misinterpretation, of ritual, religious, and easy-listening music—all of which are intended not so much to be listened to, as to be experienced within a larger social context from which they derive much of their significance. Again, it finds little use for a great deal of Renaissance and baroque music, whose interest lies in the playing rather than the listening. And it is not even adequate as an approach to twentieth-century art music. Schoenberg's work reflects the idea that music's ultimate significance lies not in the effect it makes on an audience, but in the integrity with which it expresses the composer's personal vision; to this extent Adorno's critique (trans. 1973) of Schoenberg's music, which focuses on its ethical rather than its perceptual qualities, is indispensable for a balanced and sympathetic understanding of Schoenberg's achievement. Stravinsky's serial compositions, such as the Variations 'Aldous Huxley in memoriam', are constructed in the manner of finely chiselled, geometric sculptures in pitch and time; while a work such as this can be experienced simply as a succession of sounds, it is evident that the composer's aesthetic attention was directed as much to the imaginary musical object delineated by the sounds as to the sounds themselves. It may be impossible for the listener to grasp this musical object without an analytical reading of the score.

Audibility, in short, is not everything in music. Dahlhaus writes that 'an undogmatic theory of art must recognize that the criterion of audibility, of complete realization by perception, is not a natural law of aesthetics but a postulate of historically limited scope. By rigorously restricting the concept of music or of "music proper" to the perceptible, one curtails historic reality for the sake of a dogma not older than the eighteenth century.' (1983: 54.) One cannot reasonably demand that music must, by definition, yield all its meaning in perception. It would obviously be narrow-minded to deny the aesthetic validity of Machaut's palindromic chanson *Ma fin est mon commencement*, or to refuse to recognize it as music, simply because of the impossibility of grasping its structure in purely perceptual terms; it is equally narrow-minded to reject a piece of serial music (as people actually do, or at least used to do) on the grounds of its consciously adumbrated organization, without giving it a hearing first. If, however, such a work were to yield nothing of interest in perception—if, in Dahlhaus's words, it remained 'a surplus intention which does not attain phenomenality' (1987: 225)—then one would have good reason for rejecting it, or even for failing to recognize it as music; for without the criterion of perceptual gratification there would be no means of drawing a distinction between music on the one hand and numerological speculation, theatrical activity, or mere mechanical exercise on the other. Consequently, while a musical composition may not be exhausted in perception, some degree of meaningful or gratifying perceptual engagement with it is a prerequisite if one is to approach it as music at all.

To this extent the aesthetic viewpoint, as I have defined it, is a necessary, though not sufficient, component of any study of music that is carried out in musicological terms, rather than purely sociological or psychological ones. And if this is so, then it follows that no work of musicology can in a fundamental sense transcend the musical preconceptions of its author or the cultural circumstances that give rise to these preconceptions. On the contrary, it will express them; it will be, to use Dahlhaus's derogatory term, dogmatic. I would prefer, however, to think of such preconceptions not as dogmas, but as axioms. Or to put it another way, the musicologist may not be able to transcend his basic convictions about the nature and purposes of music, but he can at least do his best to explore their ramifications.

1 *Musical form and the listener*

1.1 MUSICAL AND NON-MUSICAL LISTENING

Music is an interaction between sound and listener.

There have been many attempts to define what music is in terms of the specific attributes of musical sounds. The famous nineteenth-century critic Eduard Hanslick regarded 'the measurable tone' as 'the primary and essential condition of all music' (trans. 1957: 105). Musical sounds, he was saying, can be distinguished from those of nature by the fact that they involve the use of fixed pitches, whereas virtually all natural sounds consist of constantly fluctuating frequencies. And a number of twentieth-century writers have assumed, like Hanslick, that fixed pitches are among the defining features of music (Radocy and Boyle 1979: 170–2). Now it is true that in most of the world's musical cultures, pitches are not only fixed, but organized into a series of discrete steps (Dowling and Harwood 1986: 90–1). However, this is a generalization about music and not a definition of it, for it is easy to put forward counter-examples. Japanese *shakuhachi* music and the *sanjo* music of Korea, for instance, fluctuate constantly around the notional pitches in terms of which the music is organized. And there is other music in which discrete pitches do not even have a notional role—African percussion music, say, or some contemporary electronic music. Such examples show that it is perfectly possible to have musical organization without restricting what is organized to fixed pitches: and so an alternative strategy, which would admit such instances, is to define music as organized sound. But this definition is unacceptably broad. It includes musical scales: these are certainly organized sounds—and fixed pitches at that—but we would not want to regard them as music (Serafine 1988: 66). It also includes such communicational systems as Morse code and spoken languages. So, as Roman Ingarden says (1986: 54), we cannot maintain that 'a particular order of co-present and successive sounds and sound-constructs of a higher order . . . are sufficient to distinguish a musical composition either from acoustic signals or sounding phenomena in nature'.

If it is not possible to arrive at a satisfactory definition of music simply in terms of sound, this is probably because of the essential role that the listener, and more generally the environment in which the sound is heard, plays in the constitution of any event as a musical one. A practical illustration of this is provided by the works of John Cage. Cage gained notoriety in the early 1950s as the composer of 4′ 33″, an entirely silent piece which is normally performed by a pianist (though it can be adapted for performance by other instrumentalists too). The pianist sits at a closed piano; opens the lid to begin the performance; and closes it some four and a half minutes later. The effect of this piece in live performance (it hardly makes sense to envisage a recording of it) is to create an expectation of musical sound which, in the event, remains unfulfilled; this results in a distinctly heightened sensitivity on the listener's part to the environment of the performance, and, in particular to any small sound events that may occur—for instance the creaking of a seat, a stifled comment, or a yawn. In other words, though 4′ 33″ specifies no sounds as such, it creates a musical event out of whatever there is to be heard, and it does so through creating in the listener an openness to the qualities of sounds, heard for their own sake, such as is normally lacking in people's awareness of their acoustic surroundings. One of Cage's character- istic anecdotes from his book *Silence* (1966: 276) expresses the aesthetic viewpoint underlying this in a particularly clear fashion:

I have spent many pleasant hours in the woods conducting performances of my silent piece, transcriptions, that is, for an audience of myself, since they were much longer than the popular length which I have had published. At one performance, I passed the first movement by attempting the identification of a mushroom which remained success- fully unidentified. The second movement was extremely dramatic, beginning with the sounds of a buck and a doe leaping up to within ten feet of my rocky podium. The expressivity of this movement was not only dramatic but unusually sad from my point of view, for the animals were frightened simply because I was a human being. However, they left hesitatingly and fittingly within the structure of the work. The third movement was a return to the theme of the first, but with all those profound, so-well-known alterations of world feeling associated by German tradition with the A–B–A.

Cage's tone is facetious: the passage reads as a take-off of Nathaniel Hawthorne's similar, but distinctly more solemn and literary, experience at Sleepy Hollow.[1] Yet the point he is making is a serious one: anything can be heard as music, Cage is saying, if the listener chooses to hear it that way. From this point of view, composing music becomes not so much a matter of designing musically interesting sounds as such, as of creating contexts in which sounds will be heard as musically interesting. This idea is reflected not just in avant-garde art music, but also in the broad and inclusive range of sounds that is to be heard in contemporary pop music; listeners, it seems, will tacitly accept virtually any sound as being potentially musical, provided that it appears in an appropriate context.

It is in keeping with the liberalism of John Cage's outlook that he expresses his point inclusively: anything can be music if it is heard as music. What he says, however, has an exclusive corollary: nothing can be music if it is not heard as music. For instance Mozart, when played in factories, supermarkets, or airport waiting-lounges, is rarely heard as music, and it is the circumstances of listening rather than the sounds as such that are responsible for this. Sometimes, it is true, the actual sounds are modified for the purpose: much 'canned music' is physically reprocessed in such a way that the dynamic contrasts between loud and soft passages are diminished. This is done so that the music remains audible at all times without, however, obtruding upon the attention, and properly speaking it is such reprocessing that defines 'Muzak' as such (Muzak is simply the trade name of the leading company engaged in this business). But any music can be used in this manner, without resorting to physical reprocessing; James Parakilas says that many American college students specifically choose classical music to study by, and comments:

Classical music is no longer itself when it is used as background music. It becomes like 'easy-listening' popular music, valued more for its geniality than for its genius. But the change that comes over it is a change in the listening, not in the notes. The performance that a student puts on the

---

[1] See Marx 1967: 11 ff. In view of Cage's interest in Japanese philosophy, it is presumably no coincidence that his description is reminiscent of the Japanese custom of 'listening intently to the sounds of nature just as if they were produced by musical instruments', as illustrated in Hiroshige's print 'Listening to insects on Dōkan-yama hill' (Kikkawa 1987: 86–7).

cassette player while studying may be a performance that thrilled Philharmonic subscribers. (1984: 15.)

There is a good deal of hard evidence that music heard in this manner—heard rather than listened to—has an influence on the mood of its listeners; hence its widespread use in industrial or office environments as a means of enhancing productivity.[2] Now many people regard such uses of music as somehow objectionable. This may be partly because they feel that the music is being used for purposes of manipulation. But there is another factor, at least in the case of classical music. Many people are irritated when they hear Mozart in the supermarket, not because they find the sound intrusive or unpleasant, but because they feel that it is in some sense a betrayal of Mozart's music to hear it and yet not to give it the attention that it deserves. The surroundings, in other words, devalue the music: they cause it to be heard in such a way that it ceases really to be music at all, and becomes indistinguishable from Muzak.

The same kind of moralistic reaction can be found in the case of contemporary avant-garde music. Here again it is the circumstances of listening rather than the sounds themselves that are decisive in determining the listener's response, for the same person may react to the same piece of contemporary music quite differently under different conditions. A passage from Karlheinz Stockhausen's *Mikrophonie II*, for instance, may be accepted without demur as the sound-track for a science-fiction movie; heard on the car radio it may be ignored, or the radio may be retuned to another station; whereas in the concert-hall the music may be angrily rejected. Throughout the twentieth century, the most characteristic response to avant-garde music on the part of its detractors has not been a cool indifference, but a hot-blooded denial: 'that's not music!' is the pronouncement not of somebody who is simply uninterested in the new music, but of someone who feels that his basic musical values are being challenged by it. Indeed it can happen that this response is elicited not by the new music itself, but simply by the way that its composers talk about it.

Everyone who attends concerts of contemporary music—and this is perhaps especially true of music written by university-based composers—will be familiar with the kind of programme-note

---

[2] See e.g. Radocy and Boyle 1979, ch. 8.

that explains the particular principles of pitch formation or rhythmic construction that are being exploited in a new composition, and tells the listener what to listen out for at any given point. Such programme-notes are liable to elicit the 'that's not music!' reaction even before a single note of the music has been heard. The reason is evidently that many music-lovers object to being told what to listen for, at least when it is done in so specific a manner: and this response is simply a contemporary version of a response that goes back to the nineteenth century. When Schumann encountered Berlioz's *Symphonie fantastique*, he wrote,

At first the program spoiled my own enjoyment, my freedom of imagination. But as it receded more and more into the background and my own fancy began to work, I found not only that it was all indeed there, but what is more, that it was almost always embodied in warm, living sound. (trans. 1971: 246–7.)

Many people were not as open-minded (or open-eared) as Schumann, however: critics such as Hanslick and Adorno have repeatedly denied the validity of programme music on precisely the grounds that Schumann mentions—namely, that the programme intrudes upon the listener's freedom of imagination, simply telling him what he is meant to feel at any given point. This is what is shared by programme music and the kind of contemporary music (or at least the kind of contemporary programme-note) that I have mentioned; and in both cases the response elicited—'that's not music!'—is one of moral outrage, not of simple taxonomic classification. It is the kind of response that is generally provoked when deep-rooted, and probably unconscious, values are being threatened—as when, for example, people are given the wrong sort of food to eat, or the fundamental tenets of democracy are questioned.

Such situations as these, then, reveal that many people (and not simply musicians and aestheticians) have deeply entrenched convictions regarding the extents and limits of what can be properly defined as music. At first sight, however, these convictions may appear contradictory. In the case of programme music and new music, what is being complained about is the excessive degree to which the listener is being told what to think— here he must visualize a particular image, there he must feel such- and-such an emotion or observe the hexachordal invariance of two serial transforms. In the case of the supermarket music, on the other hand, the complaint is that the listener is turned into a totally passive recipient, on whom the music has certain predetermined effects without his conscious attention being involved at all. But there is a feature that is common to both situations, and this is the elimination of the listener's freedom to decide what he will hear and how he will hear it—his freedom of imagination, as Schumann put it.

It is precisely in terms of the listener's imaginative activity that critics have generally sought to draw a line between music and non-music. One of the first to do so was Hanslick. As he put it, it is for the imagination, and 'not for the organ of hearing as such, for the "labyrinth" or the "tympanum", that a Beethoven composes' (trans. 1957: 49); and this places an aesthetic responsibility on the listener. His seminal work, *The Beautiful in Music*, is more than anything else a polemic against what he saw as the inadequate manner in which most people listen to music. The average music-lover, Hanslick says, responds only to the sensual qualities and emotional suggestions of music. For such listeners music is no more than a series of psychological effects: accordingly 'a good cigar, some exquisite dainty, or a warm bath yields them the same enjoyment as a symphony, though they may not be aware of the fact.' (trans. 1957: 91.) This 'objectionable mode of hearing music' has nothing to do with beauty because it does not involve an imaginative awareness of the composition as a work of art. Aesthetic value in music, then, means experiencing a piece of music as a kind of beautiful object through 'the voluntary and pure act of contemplation which alone is the true and artistic method of listening' (p. 97). In saying this Hanslick was not arguing, as people sometimes maintain, that music has no emotional effect. What he meant was that the aesthetic beauty of a piece of music depends not upon the emotions that the music stimulates, but upon the objective properties of the composition itself. Hence, he said, 'the most essential condition to the aesthetic enjoyment of music is that of listening to a composition for its own sake. . . . The moment music is used as a means to induce certain states of mind . . . it ceases to be an art in a purely musical sense.' (pp. 100–1.)

Hanslick's ideas, and even some of his words, are echoed in the more wide-ranging distinction that R. G. Collingwood drew some eighty years later between what he called 'Art proper and Art falsely so called'. Collingwood (1938: 276) describes false art as being

aimed ultimately at producing certain states of mind in certain persons. Art falsely so called is . . . the utilization of 'language' (not the living language which alone is really language, but the ready-made 'language' which consists of a repertory of *clichés*) to produce states of mind in the persons upon whom these *clichés* are used.

False art, in other words, predetermines its listeners' (or viewers', or readers') responses, and to the extent that much so-called art does this Collingwood concludes that 'most of what generally goes by the name of art nowadays is not art at all, but amusement.' (p. 278.) But like Hanslick, he also makes it clear that whether a piece of music is perceived as art or as amusement depends as much on the listener as on the music itself: the aesthetic satisfaction we get out of music, he says, 'is something that we have to reconstruct in our own minds, and by our own efforts; something which remains for ever inaccessible to a person who cannot or will not make efforts of the right kind, however completely he hears the sounds that fill the room in which he is sitting.' (p. 141.)

Stuart Hampshire (1969: 174–5) makes a similar distinction between art and entertainment in music, and goes on to spell out in some detail what this might mean in terms of the listening process:

Music is understood as art if, and only if, the listener is intellectually active in listening to it. If he remains intellectually passive and attends only to the surface play of sound, he is treating the music only as entertainment. . . . The listener creates the impression in his own mind by tracing the structure of the work for himself, using his own natural imagery and his musical memory. If no parallel working of the listener's mind is interesting, the work has failed as a work of art.

But this account glosses over some awkward issues. In particular, what exactly does it mean to reconstruct the music in one's mind, or to trace the structure of the work using one's own natural imagery? Does this mean that to listen to music properly it is necessary to have some kind of professional training, so that one can follow the musical structure in more or less the terms in which the composer conceived it? Hampshire's description of the imagery as 'natural' suggests otherwise, but it is hard to know in what natural sense one can trace a composition's structure, and in practice many critics have taken it for granted that some kind of training is necessary if music is to be appreciated properly. For Hanslick, adequate listening depended upon what he called 'the preparatory knowledge for the aesthetic appreciation of musical beauty' (trans. 1957: 99), while Theodor Adorno considered a technical understanding of music to be a prerequisite for its appreciation at the highest level—a level which he considered unlikely to be achieved by anyone other than a professional musician.[3] Similarly, Dahlhaus speaks of the inability to read music as an impediment to adequate musical hearing, and refers to 'the "qualified" hearer, whose aesthetic judgment rests on a sufficiently adequate factual judgment.' (1983: 25.)

The emphasis that Adorno and Dahlhaus both place on acquired knowledge makes their accounts of musical listening rather different from that of Stephen McAdams. For McAdams (1984: 319) it is the freedom and creativity of the listener's interpretation of the music that is most important:

The will and focus of the listener play an extraordinarily important role in determining the final perceptual results. Musical listening (as well as viewing visual arts or reading a poem) is and must be considered seriously by any artist as a creative act on the part of the participant. . . . Perceiving is an act of composition, and perceiving a work of art can involve conscious and willful acts of composition. What this proposes to the artist is the creation of forms that contain many possibilities of 'realization' by a perceiver, to actually compose a multipotential structure that allows the perceiver to compose a new work within that form at each encounter. This proposes a relation to art that demands of perception that it be creative in essence.

Despite these differences of emphasis, however, Adorno, Dahlhaus, and McAdams are in agreement with each other—as also with Collingwood and Hampshire—that the active participation of the listener plays an essential role in the constitution of the musical artwork.

---

[3] Adorno trans. 1976: 4–5. Elsewhere, Adorno writes that 'The basic musical concept . . . alone lends dignity to good music. . . . The cultivation of such logical consequence, at the expense of passive perception of sensual sound, alone defines the stature of this perception, in contrast to mere "culinary enjoyment".' (trans. 1973: 12.) (His reference to culinary enjoyment is reminiscent of Hanslick's talk of cigars, dainties, and warm baths; the baths, incidentally, are echoed in Aschenbrenner's statement (1981: 109) that to hear music 'uncritically, without a power of discriminating its inner quality, is to enjoy only a warm musical shower'.) Some further quotations regarding the listener's active participation in what he hears are given in Cone 1974: 122.

It is not only in the field of musical aesthetics—indeed not primarily in it—that the importance of this principle has been recognized. One of the more significant developments in literary criticism during the last twenty years or so has been the emergence of what is generally known as 'reader-response criticism'. The essence of this approach is that the literary process is, as Wolfgang Iser puts it,

a dynamic *interaction* between text and reader. We may take as a starting-point the fact that the linguistic signs and structures of the text exhaust their function in triggering developing acts of comprehension. This is tantamount to saying that these acts, though set in motion by the text, defy total control by the text itself, and, indeed, it is the very lack of control that forms the basis of the creative side of reading. . . . Thus author and reader are to share the game of the imagination, and, indeed, the work will not work if the text sets out to be anything more than a set of governing rules. The reader's enjoyment begins when he himself becomes productive, i.e., when the text allows him to bring his own faculties into play. There are, of course, limits to the reader's willingness to participate, and these will be exceeded if the text makes things too clear or, on the other hand, too obscure: boredom and overstrain represent the two poles of tolerance, and in either case the reader is likely to opt out of the game. (1978: 107–8).

When he speaks of the text being too clear, Iser is referring to pulp literature or propaganda, in which the work is, as it were, used up in a literal reading of the text (pp. 29, 152); this is the literary equivalent of supermarket music, in that it denies the reader the opportunity to take part in the imaginative constitution of the literary work. In other words, literature as such arises from the gaps between the literal significations of the text; 'whenever the reader bridges the gaps,' Iser says, 'communication begins.' (p. 169.)

A particularly important aspect of this approach to literature, and to art in general, is that it implies that criticism can play an essential part in the constitution of the artwork, rather than being restricted to the essentially redundant role of evaluating what already exists in its own right. For if literary significance emerges from the interaction between text and reader, then this means that the reader's knowledge, interpretative framework, and expectations all contribute towards the constitution of such significance. And literary criticism can obviously have an important role to play in adding to the reader's knowledge, suggesting interpretations, and creating expectations; in this sense the critic is in some degree the creator of the literary experience about which he writes. To be sure, critics did not wait for the advent of reader-response criticism to act in such a manner: one only has to think of Bradley's Shakespeare or Leavis's Milton to appreciate the extent to which earlier critics have influenced the way in which literary texts are read. What reader-response criticism has done, however, is to establish a framework for rationalizing the role of literary criticism, and to provide a set of tools for analysing the interaction of text and listener.

The aesthetician Roger Scruton (1979) has developed a theory of architectural perception which is based on a distinction (also made by Iser) between literal perception on the one hand, which aims at the factual identity of objects, and imaginative perception on the other, which involves voluntary interpretation.[4] An essential aspect of this is that seeing and interpreting are not two different processes that occur in succession. To see an architectural façade as being made up of certain geometrical shapes, for instance, is as much an act of perception as seeing that it is grey or that it is constructed out of ashlar blocks, and the way in which one interprets the overall form of the façade will affect the way in which the details themselves are seen. But—and this is Scruton's central point—while this kind of architectural perception is a genuine variety of perception, this does not preclude it from having the attributes of rational thought. One may decide to see the façade in terms of one given geometrical composition or another; and it is possible to argue someone into seeing a building in a particular way by marshalling appropriate reasons for doing so. In other words, experiencing a building as architecture is a matter of rational judgement: and that, according to Scruton, is where the critic has a role to play in the education of the viewer to see a building in architectural terms. Viewed thus, the critic plays an active and essential part in the constitution of the architectural

---

[4] Philosophers sometimes reserve the term 'perception' for a direct, sensory response to a stimulus, referring to any higher-level, interpretative response as a 'cognitive' one. But this distinction has been undermined by the realization that almost all perceptual responses are to some degree interpretative (i.e. involve perceptual construction). In this book I use the term 'perception' in the same inclusive sense that Scruton does. What becomes important, then, is to distinguish between the different kinds of perception involved in music and the extent to which they can be affected by critical interpretation or reflection.

phenomenon: in Scruton's words, 'The relation of a building to an historical, spiritual or moral interpretation is a critical achievement; it is *created* by the critic.' (1979: 123.)

What makes Scruton's approach particularly relevant in the present context is that at a number of critical points he bolsters his argument about the nature and scope of imaginative perception through drawing parallels with music. Indeed, he specifically justifies the role of the music critic in just these terms:

> To be 'active' a perception must exhibit that kind of conscious participation that is involved in the perception of an aspect: it must involve an engagement of attention, an interest in surface, a transference of concepts from sphere to sphere (as in metaphor); in the limiting case it may itself be a voluntary act. All those features of 'activity' are exhibited in the perception of musical movement. The voluntary character of this perception provides one of the foundations for structural criticism of music. It is because I can ask someone to hear a movement as beginning in a certain place, as phrased in a certain way, and so on, that the activity of giving reasons in support of such analysis makes sense. Much of music criticism consists of the deliberate construction of an intentional object from the infinitely ambiguous instructions implicit in a sequence of sounds.[5]

The kind of synthesis between sensory perception and rational interpretation that Scruton describes—in short, imaginative perception—is evidently what the pioneering music analyst Heinrich Schenker had in mind when he prefaced his final work, *Free Composition*, with a quotation from Goethe's *Theory of Colours*: 'we never benefit from merely looking at an object. Looking becomes considering, considering becomes reflecting, reflecting becomes connecting. Thus, one can say that with every intent glance at the world we theorize.' (trans. 1979: 3.) Accordingly Schenker's detailed analyses of specific compositions (of which a good deal will be said in the pages that follow) are intended to create not so much an abstract knowledge of the work under analysis, but a more fully adequate perceptual understanding of the music.

When, for instance, Schenker presents a structural graph of the

---

[5] Scruton 1983: 108–9. See also Evans 1985 for a detailed application to music of an approach similar to, and partly dependent on, Scruton's. Evans says that 'when we succeed in conveying an insight via a fruitful metaphor, what we have done is not merely to reflect on the aesthetic object but to engage in it.' (p. 90.)

D minor Fugue from Book I of Bach's *Well-Tempered Clavier*, and comments that 'One can hear this fugue correctly only if one keeps in mind the indicated relationships which the fundamental line and the bass arpeggiation establish' (trans. 1979: 143), his words should be taken quite literally: except in this way, he is saying, the music cannot be perceived properly at all (cannot, that is to say, be perceived as music rather than just as sounds). Obviously this requires something more than a casual interest in music. Indeed, Schenker inveighed against the 'dilettante', as he called him, who expects to be able to appreciate everything in music instinctively and without any kind of application.[6] As he wrote, 'the uncorrupted instincts of which [the dilettante] is so proud have no value whatever for art itself as long as they remain untrained, unrefined, and unable to move on the same level as the artistic instincts of the masters, who alone have true artistic instincts in the first place.' (trans. 1987: i, p. xix.) Schenker, then, was not in the least interested in explaining how people ordinarily perceive music; what he wanted to do was to demonstrate how music *ought* to be heard. Indeed, what lay at the heart of Schenker's work—and here there is an obvious link with his elder compatriot Hanslick— was his conviction that virtually nobody knew how to listen properly to the master-works of the past. So it is really quite inappropriate to see Schenker, as many psychologists and some music theorists have seen him, as a musical equivalent of the linguist or psycholinguist who explains how people, in fact, use language; he viewed himself as a critic in the same sense as Bradley and Leavis were—that is to say, as someone with an essential role to play in the aesthetic process. And it is to this role that the contemporary analyst Edward T. Cone refers when he writes that 'the greatest analysts (like Schenker at his best) are those with the keenest ears; their insights reveal how a piece of music should be heard' (1962: 36).

There is, then, a widespread consensus of opinion among twentieth-century aestheticians and critics that listening to music is, or at any rate should be, a higher-order mental activity which combines sensory perception with a rational understanding based on some kind of knowledge of musical structure. Quite what form

---

[6] Schenker's dilettante is reminiscent of Fontenelle's 'Sonate, que me veux-tu?' which, in Dahlhaus's words, 'implied, with an arrogant gesture, that anything not immediately clear to a man of common sense . . . was not worth understanding' (1982: 24).

this knowledge might take, however, is not so clear: not all aestheticians and critics would willingly go along with the view of Adorno, Dahlhaus, and Schenker that professional technical knowledge is the prerequisite for a fully adequate aesthetic perception of any composition. Possibly the best way to throw light on this problem is to trace the process by which a literal perception of musical sound is transformed into an imaginative— and hence, according to this consensus of opinion, more aesthetically adequate—perception of it, as more musical knowledge and rational thought is brought into play. The following discussion centres on musical form, not only because this is the most obvious example of an imaginative synthesis of musical sound, but also because of the extreme importance that aestheticians, critics, and theorists of Western music have attributed to it throughout the last two hundred years or so.

1.2   EXPERIENCING MUSIC AS FORM

I

Even in the simplest possible contexts, musical perception is not so literal as to be in one-to-one correspondence to the input signal. When we hear a single tone, according to Creel, Boomsliter, and Powers,

what we experience is a form which we impose. Its raw material is memory of the past portion of the stimulus and expectation of its future. The auditory input itself is, at any given instant, a single stimulus which, standing alone, has no pattern or meaning. Investigation of larger sound patterns in language and music has led to evidence that the sensation of tone is itself an imposed form. (1970: 534.)

And if the sensation of tone is itself a psychological construct, it stands to reason that it should be subject to such basic perceptual principles as the Gestalt law of closure. Experiments have shown that this is indeed the case. As Watkins and Dyson explain,

An alternation of tones and gaps is heard to be continuous if suitable noise bursts are inserted in the gaps. It is as though the auditory system fills in the gaps with a suitable tone. Furthermore, suitable filling in also occurs if the tonal segments are part of a longer frequency glide, so that illusory glides are heard in the gaps. The closure idea accounts for this by attributing the physical absence of the tones to masking by the louder noise. (1985: 82–3.)

Larger contexts, too, can affect the perception of tone quality. Anton Ehrenzweig describes the effect of reversing a tape recording of violin music. The violin loses its brilliance as the result of the melodic and harmonic context of the music being disrupted, the result being an effect of 'often astoundingly poor' tone quality; rather than sustained tonal sonority, he says, one hears only 'a multitude of little smears, grunts, and squeaks'.[7]

The same Gestalt principles that operate in the perception of individual tones also operate in the perceptual synthesis of successive tones that gives rise to the experience of a musical line; Diana Deutsch (1982a) summarizes a large number of laboratory experiments in which stimulus tones have been shown to be grouped by listeners on the basis of Gestalt principles. In a typical experiment of this sort, listeners are played two simultaneous sequences of tones through headphones, one sequence to each ear; each sequence makes little sense in itself, but the aggregate of the two sequences results in a very clear musical pattern—in Ex. 1,[8] for

Ex. 1

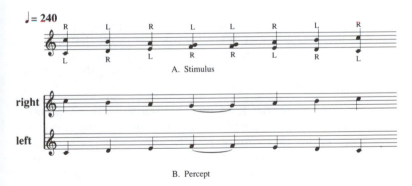

♩ = 240

A. Stimulus

right

left

B. Percept

[7] Ehrenzweig 1953: 100, 99. Randall (1972: 125), speaking from the perspective of the computer synthesist, also emphasizes the role of melodic context in the experiencing of violin tone.
[8] Taken from Deutsch 1975.

instance, the aggregate consists of two continuous scalar motions. When asked to say to which ear each tone was presented, listeners tend to group the tones according to frequency proximity rather than in terms of their physical source; in this case they hear one scalar motion as being presented to one ear and the second to the other. (The same effect, incidentally, was exploited by Tchaikovsky in the last movement of his 'Pathétique' Symphony.) Here, then, perceptual grouping is taking place according to Gestalt principles operating in the frequency domain.

When one hears a scale—when one perceives tones as grouped in this manner—is one perceiving literally or imaginatively? Roger Scruton would argue the latter. His argument goes like this. To hear a sequence of tones as a scale is to hear them not as a series of individuals, but as a single moving line. And what is this line that moves? In Scruton's words, 'We may find ourselves at a loss for an answer to that question: for, literally speaking, nothing *does* move. There is one note, and then another; movement, however, demands *one* thing, which passes from place to place.'[9] The solution, of course, is that to hear a moving line is to perceive sound imaginatively. Musical lines have no material existence; they only exist in terms of the metaphor of space, a metaphor which Scruton considers to be so deeply entrenched in the experience of music as to constitute one of its defining properties. And so he concludes:

It seems then that in our most basic apprehension of music there lies a complex system of metaphor, which is the true description of no material fact. And the metaphor cannot be eliminated from the description of music, because it is integral to the intentional object of musical experience. Take this metaphor away and you take away the experience of music. (1983: 106.)

At the same time, the kind of imaginative synthesis Scruton describes is by no means peculiar to music, at least at the very basic level of perception that is involved in hearing a scale. For instance, there is a close visual analogue to the perception of musical motion at this level. This is the Phi phenomenon: if two lights in a

---

[9] Scruton 1979: 81. Dahlhaus (1982: 80) makes a similar point: 'musical motion seems to lack any moving agent or substance. For it would be a questionable hypothesis to claim that it was a tone that moved in tonal space. A higher tone following a lower one is "another" tone rather than "the same" tone in another place. The first tone, when the melody proceeds, does not change its position, but is replaced, displaced by a second tone.'

darkened room are switched on and off in alternation, they create the impression of a single light that is being swung back and forth between the two locations (Sloboda 1985: 159). Indeed, as every first-year student of psychology knows, it is a quite general characteristic of perception that it involves interpretation rather than a literal response to the sensory attributes of stimuli: thus to regard the perception of a musical scale or the Phi phenomenon as instances of imaginative perception is, in effect, to render the term coextensive with what psychologists refer to as 'perceptual construction'. This devalues the notion of imaginative perception, because it eliminates what Scruton himself sees as its defining properties, namely that it is voluntary and that it is amenable to rational argument.

If the role played by imaginative perception in the experience of music is to provide the foundation for criticism, as Scruton suggests it should, then these properties are crucial: and in this respect none of the instances of musical listening that I have discussed so far can be considered as exemplifying imaginative perception. One does not *choose* to hear violin music played backwards as a series of smears, grunts, and squeaks; equally one cannot choose to hear violin music that way under normal circumstances, however hard one tries. And in the case of the scale illusion experiment, Deutsch (1982a: 129) says:

It appears that the initial division of the stimulus configuration into groupings is often outside the listener's voluntary control, though ambiguous situations may be generated where attention focusing can be effective. In contrast, once a set of groupings is established, voluntary attention focusing plays a prominent role in determining which of these is attended to.

In other words, the listener can choose whether to attend to the upper or the lower line, but he is generally unable to control the grouping of the various tones into lines. Yet the ability to decide what goes with what must be the basis for any way of hearing music that embodies rational judgements about musical structures such as those yielded by Schenkerian analysis.

The level of perceptual synthesis with which I have so far been dealing corresponds to what Iser refers to as the 'autocorrelation' of textual signs, by which he means 'the interconnection between the textual signs prior to the stimulation of the individual reader's disposition' (1978: 120). But there is in music, as in literature, a level at which imaginative perception—in the full sense—comes into play; and this is the level at which musical lines are heard not simply as texture, but in terms of form.

II

How many lines are there in the central section of Chopin's Prelude in F sharp major (Ex. 2)? The music is written in four parts, except in the last two bars of the section, where there are five or even six notes at once. But that is not the same as saying that there are four (or five or six) musical lines in the sense that a listener will hear it that way.

What does one hear? One hears the highest notes as forming a continuous line, indeed as the tune; this is in part because of a general psychological tendency to focus on the top line of any musical texture (Sloboda 1985: 172), but also because the contour and rhythm of this line have a degree of large-scale interest and significance that is lacking in the other parts. Nevertheless most listeners will probably not hear the passage simply as consisting of a tune plus a generalized harmonic accompaniment. Other parts from the middle or bottom of the texture come into prominence from time to time: the tenor part coalesces, so to speak, into a continuous line in the middle of the first bar of Ex. 2, and then retreats into obscurity; the lowest part does the same in the second bar. Chopin has so designed the texture that melodic activity in one of the lower parts generally coincides with held notes in the main tune, and this means that the listener experiences the music as being made up of several interweaving lines even though it may be hard or impossible for him to focus on more than one line at any given time (Sloboda 1985: 169); his attention is led from one part to another according to the degree of activity in it. The result is that any listener is likely to hear the passage in the way I have described, even if the pianist makes no particular effort to bring this out.

This is not so true, however, of the opening of Schumann's 'Einsame Blumen' from *Waldscenen* (Ex. 3). Unless the performer makes a special effort, the listener is likely to hear the first four bars simply as a tune plus accompaniment, so that the upper parts are grouped as shown in Ex. 4a. But this is musically quite different from what Schumann wrote, even though the notes are the same.

Ex. 2

What the pianist is required to do—as Schumann has indicated through the direction of the note-stems—is to project the grouping shown in Ex. 4*b*; this can be done partly by playing the lower melodic part rather louder than the upper one (in order to counteract the natural tendency to focus on the top line of a musical texture) and partly by giving each line a different

Ex. 3

articulation. But why should it matter that the music is heard this way, as an imitative dialogue between two melodic lines? The reason is that the musical continuity of the passage—the coherence of its movement through time—depends in part upon this contrapuntal structure. The harmonic pattern of the passage, considered in isolation, is decidedly strange; in particular, the series of four consecutive chords with C as their root (C minor in bars 2–3, and C major in bars 4–5) lacks any intrinsic harmonic logic. The chords sound sensible in this context because of the movement of the two melodic lines which they support; and the logical relationship between the two lines also makes sense of a number of dissonances which would otherwise seem unmotivated or arbitrary. For instance, the seventh chord in the second bar is better regarded as not really a seventh chord at all, but a first-inversion C minor chord with a suspension; and it is only likely to be heard this way if the D is taken to be a continuation of the melodic line of the opening bar. Consequently the listener who hears this passage as consisting of a single tune plus accompaniment—perhaps because it is badly played—will hear the music as harmonically clumsy, or at least strangely inconsequential.

In 'Einsame Blumen', then, the manner in which the listener

Ex. 4

(a)

(b)

hears the music as grouped into continuous lines has a more than local significance, because it affects his perception of the music's temporal extension; this is not the case in the Chopin prelude, where the shadowy lines of the left hand have a purely textural significance. Nevertheless the contrapuntal aspect of 'Einsame Blumen' has no consequences for the larger structure of the piece as a whole; the composition consists of a series of contrasted sections, some of which are not contrapuntal at all. There are, however, some compositions, such as fugues, in which the perception of line is a function of the music's overall form.

One does not *have* to perceive a fugue in such a way, of course; it is possible to hear, for example, Bach's D major Fugue from Book I of the *Well-Tempered Clavier* (Ex. 5) simply in terms of imitative texture. This would mean that one noticed the distinctive opening figure recurring at different points—sometimes higher, sometimes lower—and with the imitations being sometimes further apart from each other (as at the opening) and sometimes closer together (bars 11, 13, 20, 23–4); one would experience the music as a closely knit fabric, with the changes in the distance of imitation contributing to the tensional shape of the composition. But one would have no sense of the piece consisting of four continuous lines, with the interaction between them generating the temporal extension of the composition as a whole; and this is as much as to say that one would not be hearing it as a fugue.

Ex. 5

What then does it mean to hear this piece as a fugue?[10] It means that one hears the opening bar, the entry of the first voice, as being already pregnant with the subsequent entries, and indeed with the entire composition. Thus the second entry, in bar 2, is already implied in the first bar; bar 3, on the other hand, represents an extension of the structure, in that it postpones the implied entry of the third and fourth voices. (If one is hearing the piece as a fugue, that is, then bar 3 will *sound* like an extension.) The third voice enters in bar 4, and this illustrates another distinction between a simple textural perception of the music and hearing it as a fugue.

[10] Cf. Patricia Carpenter's description (1967: 80) of hearing a Bach fugue as a musical object.

For it is obvious in the score that the D on the second beat of bar 4 belongs to two separate voices, because the note is written twice; but of course it can only be played once. Simply judging by the sound, then, there is no way in which one could tell that this D marks the entry of the third voice at all. In the same way, there is nothing in the sound of the music to indicate that the A on the second beat of bar 5 marks the entry of the final voice; and this time the score is hardly more clear, because the direction of the note-tails makes it look at first sight as if there were a single melodic line, F♯–G♯–A–B–C♯–D–C♯–B–C♯–A, at the top of the texture. But this is not what one hears if one is hearing the piece as a fugue; rather one hears a new voice entering at both these points, because that is what makes sense within the larger context of the fugue as a whole. Ex. 6 clarifies these bars by showing each voice on a different stave.

Ex. 6

This initial section is followed by an episode, during which the thirty-second-note figure from the opening appears on the first beat of the bar, in the lowest voice (bars 9, 10, and 11). At bar 11 one of the upper voices imitates this figure a quarter-note later—or at least that is what one would hear if one were simply listening in a note-to-note manner. In terms of its formal structure, however, this is not at all a correct description of the passage. The thirty-second-note figure on the second beat of bar 11 marks the beginning of the second group of fugal entries; in other words it plays an essential role in the music's architectural form. But the appearance of the same figure on the first beat of the bar is not essential at all; it is no more than, so to speak, a pre-echo of the structural entry a beat later. (Ex. 7 demonstrates this by showing how the figure on the first beat of bar 11, and the equivalent figure in bar 13, can be eliminated without detriment to the larger musical form.) If one is to hear the music in formal terms, then, one must hear the structural and non-structural appearances of the thirty-second-note figure in quite different ways. It is true that this cannot be done straight away on a first hearing: the fact that the figure on the second beat of bar 11 is the structural one only becomes clear in retrospect, because of its relationship to the subsequent entries. The same does not, however, apply to bar 13: by then the context is established, and so an attentive listener should be able to tell that the figure on the first beat is not a structural one, even at a first hearing. In this way the experience of the thirty-second-note figure actually changes during the course of the passage, in accordance with its function within the larger musical form.

In bar 20, and again in bars 23–4, the same figure appears in stretto, giving in both cases a continuous thirty-second-note texture. These two passages have different formal functions from those I have described so far, and they therefore represent further ways in which the figure can be heard. In neither passage does the figure play an important structural role; it is really no more than motivic decoration applied to a cycle of fifths. Bars 20 and 23 are still contrapuntal in texture; the left-hand part of bar 20 is to be understood as in (a) rather than (b) of Ex. 8. But the counterpoint is of no formal significance. In bar 24, by contrast, the counterpoint disappears, and the fact that this happens is itself significant in terms of the music's form. The two voices do not interact; they simply move in parallel tenths, so that the passage may be considered as essentially a single line which happens to be coloured by the addition of tenths. And then, in bar 25, the texture switches completely, from the continuous thirty-second-note pattern of bar 24 to a dotted-note pattern.[11] Here the texture is completely homophonic: Bach uses only four-part chords, as if to preserve the

---

[11] This is derived from the 2nd half of the fugal subject, just as the thirty-second-note pattern comes from its first half, so that bars 24–5 represent in a sense an expansion of the opening bar of the piece. If a listener is aware of this, it will heighten his sense of the fugue's formal closure.

Ex. 7

Ex. 8

fiction that the music is written for four voices rather than for one player at a keyboard, but musically speaking there is no reason why the chords should not have been thickened out by adding one or two extra notes to them. In other words, there is no counterpoint in the final four bars of the piece; and this makes it an entirely appropriate conclusion for a composition whose formal extension up to this point has been created by means of counterpoint. All this, again, will be heard if the composition is being experienced in terms of fugal form rather than just imitative texture.

The description I have given of what it means to hear a four-part texture as a fugue may perhaps seem over-idealized, in that it involves experiencing each part as an independent voice. For is it possible for anyone to hear four contrapuntal voices all at once? Mursell records that he was once told by a distinguished musician that 'no human being, however talented and well trained, can hear and clearly follow more than three simultaneous lines of polyphony.'[12] Actually this formulation is a little problematical, because it is hard to be sure precisely what meaning to attach to the phrase 'hear and clearly follow'. Does it mean the ability to sing back the notes of each line after hearing a piece a few times? (If so, some people cannot hear and clearly follow even one line!) If, on the other hand, it means sensing the multiplicity of the lines, then there seems no good reason for the restriction to three; a six-part fugue surely sounds more sonorous than a three-part one. Maybe it means the ability to count how many lines are present at any one time. Fortunately it does not much matter, because the ability to hear a fugue as such does not depend on the listener's capacity to discriminate each voice from the others all the time in the manner that Mursell describes. What is important in hearing a fugue is that the linear elements that are heard should be experienced in terms of a formal structure defined by the interaction of all the voices. In this way hearing music as fugue—or for that matter as any other musical form—means interpreting the sound of the music as a token of something that exists in some sense independently of the sound; it means not so much hearing the sound as hearing the composition through the sound.

It may seem paradoxical to make a distinction between a musical composition and the noise it makes. But such a distinction has been made by many musicians, critics, and philosophers. For instance, the distinguished harpsichordist Ralph Kirkpatrick (1984: 41) writes of the *Well-Tempered Clavier*:

most of the time Bach is using the keyboard not to suggest itself, but to suggest something that lies beyond it. If one listens to four- and five-voice fugues only in terms of the sounds that the keyboard instrument is making, one hears . . . a rather unsatisfactory succession of not very interesting chords.

And this is just a specific instance of what Collingwood regarded as

---

[12] Mursell 1937: 204. He identifies the musician as Professor Edwin Stringham.

a general principle, for according to him 'any concentration on the pleasantness of the noises themselves concentrates the mind on hearing, and makes it hard or impossible to listen.' (1938: 141.) In saying this Collingwood is using the word 'listen' to refer to imaginative perception, and 'hear' to literal perception.[13] He summarizes his argument on this point as follows:

A piece of music is not something audible, but something which may exist solely in the musician's head. To some extent it must exist solely in the musician's head (including, of course, the audience as well as the composer under that name), for his imagination is always supplementing, correcting and expurgating what he actually hears. The music which he actually enjoys as a work of art is thus never sensuously or 'actually' heard at all. It is something imagined. (p. 151.)

And Sartre, in his classic text *The Psychology of the Imagination*, heightens the paradox when he says of Beethoven's Seventh Symphony that 'In the degree to which I hear the symphony it is *not here*, between these walls, at the tip of the violin bows.'[14] Consequently if a fire breaks out and the concert-hall is evacuated, he continues, 'we cannot conclude that *the* Seventh Symphony has come to an end. No, we only think that the *performance* of the symphony has ceased.'

To hear a symphony as a symphony, to hear a fugue as a fugue—in short, to hear any music as form—is then to hear it as repeatable, and hence as independent of its realization in sound on any particular occasion. But we do not just hear the Seventh Symphony as 'a symphony', as an exemplar of a type; we hear it as an individual composition. A historical attitude is implicated in this. In the eighteenth century, as Dahlhaus explains (1983: 13, 22),

---

[13] This usage goes back to Hanslick (trans. 1957: 92) and has been adopted by a number of writers since then. Among them is Eric Blom, according to whom of all the various ways of attending to music, 'The most primitive form is hearing. . . . Within certain genteel limitations the possibilities for betraying a mere aural function unconnected with any mental process are infinite. For that is what hearing, in the sense in which I use it here, amounts to. . . . Listening . . . is . . . a total absorption in the music, not merely a soaking up by the ear, but its penetration through that channel to the brain.' (ed. 1977: 738–9.) Mursell (1937: 220) also mentions this usage, ascribing it to Vernon Lee; it appears, too, in Stravinsky's conversations with Robert Craft (1979: 130). And Ortega y Gasset (quoted in Cooper 1961: 94) associated hearing, defined thus, with romantic music and listening with 20th-cent. music—a distinction equivalent to that proposed by Blume between classic and romantic music (1972: 155–6), though Blume does not use the terms 'hearing' and 'listening' to make it.

[14] 1972: 224. Sartre is not using the word 'hear' in Collingwood's specific sense.

one of the criteria for a work's success was that it fulfilled the functions and illustrated the attributes of the genre to which it belonged: it is in terms of this attitude to composition that we can understand the production in the eighteenth century of large numbers of symphonies, fugues, and other works whose style is generally derivative and whose merit lies in their conformity to the established principles of their genre. Such works were not intended or expected to endure beyond their own time. Like present-day pop music, they were ephemeral: and so it was the symphony or the fugue, as a genre, that existed independently of the occasion or the sound of the performance, rather than the particular music through which the genre was realized in any given instance. But all this changed about 1800. It was now the particular qualities of the individual composition and its originality that were considered to be important, and as a result the imitation of existing models fell into disrepute (except as a pedagogical exercise). It is in this sense that we think of Beethoven's Seventh Symphony not as 'a symphony', but rather as a unique work of art in its own right.

In doing so we make the assumption that the basis of musical culture, and the focus of musical listening, must be the individual composition. This assumption is deeply embedded in current thinking about music; the entire discipline of structural analysis is predicated on it. But it is by no means a universally valid principle. As Dahlhaus says (1982: 11), the conception of music as

an *opus absolutum*, a work in itself, freed from its sounding realization in any present moment, suffused only around 1800 into the consciousness of 'connoisseurs and amateurs'. Even up to the present time this idea is foreign to listeners who restrict their musical experience to popular music.

For in popular music—perhaps Dahlhaus is thinking of jazz rather than pop music as such—the element of improvisation is such that 'the piece' is sometimes little more than a show-case for the performance; indeed, the same could be said of some of the brilliant variation sets of the early Romantic period, in which nobody really hears 'the piece' as such (rather, one hears Hofmann or Holliger). The same applies, too, when listeners queue to attend not Beethoven's Seventh Symphony, but Karajan's performance of it. In each of these cases the focus is on the unrepeatable qualities of the musical event; the music that is heard is, in this sense, irremediably tied to its context. And this is as much as to say that the music is being heard primarily as performance and not as form.

III

To hear music as form, then, is to hear it as in some important sense logically distinct from any external context. In a recent book, Alan Durant has traced the evolution of various contemporary musical forms from their origins in ceremonial circumstances, and he comments that when these forms are displaced from their original contexts 'it is repetitions, contrasts and permutation of materials which become of focal interest, rather than surrounding relations of occasion, patronage and commerce, or means of distribution.' (1984: 42.) Or to put it another way, musical form defines an independent and repeatable context within which the events of a musical composition can be heard as meaningful. These events gain a kind of objective identity by virtue of their relationship to this context: when a theme is repeated in a symphony, one's experience of the repetition is not a subjective one ('I feel like I did before') but an objective one ('this bit is like the previous bit', or more simply 'here's the same bit again'). The second ricercar from Stravinsky's Cantata illustrates this particularly well, because during the course of it something that is at first heard as a singular, contextually embedded gesture is transformed by stages into a formally constituted musical object. This is simply an effect of repetition. The ricercar is mainly atonal, but it is punctuated at regular intervals by a cadence in B major (Ex. 9). At its first appearance this cadence sounds simply like an archaizing gesture, perhaps serving an illustrative function in relation to the text (which dates from the fifteenth or sixteenth century). But as the cadence is repeated, one begins to hear it not as a passing effect, but as a formal element signifying the articulation of the movement into a series of sections. (If one has previous knowledge of the movement, of course, one may hear it in that way from the start.) The effect is that, as one listens, one refers each cadence directly to the others, 'seeing' them much in the manner of the rows of engaged columns favoured by Renaissance architects as a means of articulating flat surfaces.

To 'see' musical events that are temporally remote from each other as constituting an objective structure—that is, to perceive

Ex. 9

them as relating directly to each other—is of necessity to have a spatial, and most likely a visual, awareness of them. Accordingly Dahlhaus (1982: 12) states:

Nothing would be farther from the truth than to see in the tendency to spatialization a distortion of music's nature. Insofar as music is form, it attains its real existence, paradoxically expressed, in the very moment when it is past. Still held firm in the memory, it emerges into a condition that it never entered during its immediate presence; and at a distance it constitutes itself as a surveyable plastic form. Spatialization and form, emergence and objectivity, are interdependent: one is the support or precondition of the other.

In other words, music becomes form and not just sound to the extent that it is experienced spatially and not just temporally. Again, this is an idea which has the support of musicians as well as aestheticians.[15] Indeed, Dahlhaus's words echo something that Schoenberg once said to Josef Rufer:

[15] See e.g. Ligeti 1965: 15–19. A discussion of Ligeti's views, with further references, may be found in Bernard 1987: 210.

Music is an art which takes place in time. But the way in which a work presents itself to a composer . . . is independent of this; time is regarded as space. In writing the work down, space is transformed into time. For the hearer this takes place the other way round; it is only after the work has run its course in time that he can see it as a whole—its idea, its form and its content.[16]

And this statement is borne out by another musician, Thomas Clifton. Clifton attempted to make a phenomenological description of the manner in which he experienced Webern's Bagatelle No. 1 for String Quartet, Op. 9, and concluded, 'If, in saying that I experience the Bagatelle, my language makes any sense at all, it is because I experience the *whole* Bagatelle as present.' In which case, he added, 'What have I been talking about, if not a visual experiencing of the sound-structures of this Bagatelle?' (1976: 82, 86.)

But it is in Schoenberg's own writings, and by implication in his music, that the most rigorous development of this concept of musical space is to be found. In his essay 'Composing with twelve tones' Schoenberg writes (ed. 1984: 220; the capitalization is his):

THE TWO-OR-MORE-DIMENSIONAL SPACE IN WHICH MUSICAL IDEAS ARE PRESENTED IS A UNIT. Though the elements of these ideas appear separate and independent to the eye and the ear, they reveal their true meaning only through their co-operation, even as no single word alone can express a thought without relation to other words. All that happens at any point of this musical space has more than a local effect. It functions not only in its own plane, but also in all other directions and planes, and is not without influence even at remote points.

The implication of this highly influential idea is that at the highest formal level an entire composition should be considered to be a single Gestalt: that is to say, an integrated structure in which the perception of individual parts is determined by their relationship to the whole. And this means that form can be regarded as a mechanism whereby the Gestalt principles of grouping that I discussed earlier in this chapter are transferred from the very simple contexts of perceiving a tone or a scale to the extremely elaborate perceptual context that is constituted by an entire composition. In particular, the Gestalt principle of closure is explicitly seen by

[16] Quoted in Rufer 1969: 49.

analysts such as Leonard B. Meyer (1973) and Lerdahl and Jackendoff (1983), who have been particularly concerned with the perceptual aspects of musical analysis, as being fundamental to compositional organization; and in a more general sense, most musical analyses can be viewed as attempts to demonstrate specific ways in which the overall structure of a composition lends significance to its smaller-scale events. Each individual composition, in other words, provides a unique context within which sound can be heard as musically meaningful.

Now perceptual grouping at the lowest level of musical organization—hearing a tone, hearing a scale—is more or less involuntary and is unlikely to demand the acquisition of any specific knowledge through musical training.[17] At the intermediate level of perception represented by the first few bars of 'Einsame Blumen', it is to some degree possible for the listener to decide what he wants to hear, and it is possible to modify the way someone hears such a passage by discussing it with him and suggesting how it should be heard. And at this level there is no particular difficulty in hearing the music as being grouped in one way or another. But it does not follow that the same is true of the level at which an entire piece is considered as a structural unit; for at this level, that of form, music is not only highly complex in its organization but also extends over considerable periods of time. Schoenberg (ed. 1984: 103) was himself acutely aware of the perceptual difficulties that had to be overcome if a listener was to grasp a composition's formal structure:

In general, music is always hard (not even relatively hard) to understand—unless it is made easier by repetition of as many minute, small, medium or large sections as possible. The first precondition for understanding is, after all, memory. . . . If, then, in music, a figure is so constituted, so lacking in character, for example, or so complicated, that I cannot recognize and remember it, then correct understanding of all that follows—all that results from it, follows from it—is impossible.

But this raises the possibility that, if it is indeed hard to hear music as form, then many listeners may not in fact succeed in doing so. According to Adorno, 'it is only the coarsest vulgarities and easily remembered fragments—ominously beautiful passages, moods,

---

[17] See, however, Sloboda (1985: 161–2) for evidence that musical training affects performance in the scale illusion experiment when there are conflicting cues.

and associations—which find their way into the comprehension of the public.' (trans. 1973: 9.) Moreover, the idea that responding adequately to music is hard, if not beyond the capability of many listeners, is one of the basic premises of Hanslick's aesthetics:

Without mental activity no aesthetic enjoyment is possible. But the kind of mental activity alluded to is quite peculiar to music, because its products, instead of being fixed and presented to the mind at once in their completeness, develop gradually and thus do not permit the listener to linger at any point or to interrupt his train of thought. It demands, in fact, the keenest watching and the most untiring attention. In the case of intricate compositions, this may even become a mental exertion. Many an individual, nay, many a nation undertakes this exertion only with great reluctance. The monopoly of the soprano in the Italian school is mainly due to the mental indolence of the Italian people, who are incapable of that assiduous fixing of the attention so characteristic of northern races when listening to and enjoying a musical *chef-d'œuvre*, with all its intricacies of harmony and counterpoint. (trans. 1957: 98.)

Nowadays, of course, we shy away from making such generalizations about racial aptitudes. But that is not the only problem with Hanslick's argument. For if it were indeed the case that many individuals and even entire nations are incapable of appreciating music aesthetically (a view with which Schenker concurred), then the purview of musical aesthetics would shrink to the point that one might reasonably begin to question its relevance or interest. Or to put it another way, it would mean that the enjoyment which many individuals and entire nations derive from music has nothing to do with aesthetic listening as defined by Hanslick and Schoenberg. One would have to look for alternative explanations of what it is that such people find so enjoyable about music—or else simply accept it as a fact, as did Hanslick, that for most people music means no more than a warm bath does.

Through the descriptions offered in this section I have been trying to define what it means to hear music as form—to hear it, that is, in what aestheticians and critics have generally regarded as the most fully adequate manner. In what follows, however, my aim is to establish the extent to which such formal perception is actually implicated in the enjoyment which large numbers of people, with or without musical training, routinely derive from listening to music. And this can only be done on the basis of empirical data regarding the perception of form. The next section provides some such data, and considers various operational definitions of formal perception in which the general principles I have outlined are given specific applications.

1.3   THE PERCEPTION OF FORM: SOME TESTS

I

In classical architecture pilasters, cornices, and other architectural details are used as a means of articulating the visual form of a façade. Such details can be used to project or highlight the underlying geometric composition of a building; they can even be used to create an architectural interest where otherwise there was none, as for instance when engaged columns are used to give rhythmic articulation to a plain surface. In the same way, musical forms can be seen as being defined by specific features which project the underlying structure of the composition, or which even create structural organization where otherwise there was none. The clearest illustration of such form–defining features in music is perhaps offered by the ways in which pieces of music end. In general, musical endings are treated quite differently from any other point in a composition, because they are designed with the specific intention of communicating finality to the listener. Most musical endings could be described as some kind of 'gesture to infinity'. In terms of pitch, this normally means that they move towards a vanishing-point, as in the stock nineteenth-century close on the tonic; occasionally it means the opposite, as in the total chromatic spread with which Schoenberg concluded his *Erwartung*. As regards dynamics, it means that they either fade away to nothing or build up to a climax; tension either dissipates or reaches a maximum. Alternatively a sonority may be introduced which has not previously been heard; the pizzicato chords at the end of the first movement of Beethoven's Quartet Op. 18 No. 2 are an example of this, and so is Debussy's habit of terminating his piano pieces with a single extremely low note. On a larger scale, the endings of Schoenberg's *Verklärte Nacht* and Stravinsky's *Les Noces* each represent a kind of music quite different from anything that has appeared earlier in the piece: and each is highly effective as a means of creating the sense of an ending.

Sometimes the special way in which endings are designed leads to a kind of contradiction between the ending and the rest of the work. For example, Charles Rosen writes that by the end of the nineteenth century 'the final appearance of the tonic chord in many works of Strauss, Reger and others sounded like a polite bow in the direction of academic theory; the rest of the music has often proceeded as if it made no difference with what triad it ended.' (1976b: 40–1.) In such works the traditional tonal ending is being used not because it is tonal (as Rosen suggests, there may be little or no large-scale tonal organization in such works), but because it is traditional: in other words, it has become simply a conventional sign of finality. Nor is such historical sedimentation restricted to endings. Historical forms such as the classical sonata can be seen as a kind of conventionalized 'plot' in which tonal relations are associated in a stylized manner with recognizable themes and with dynamics, texture, and instrumentation—aspects of music which are highly significant in determining the way in which listeners respond to musical structure.[18] The use of these stereotyped gestures or associations is particularly characteristic of classical genres such as the symphony or concerto, which were intended for mass audiences and were therefore designed to be readily accessible; indeed Schoenberg, presumably thinking of these more public genres, speaks of their 'exaggerated intelligibility', adding that 'The ceremonious way in which the close of a composition used to be tied up, bolted, nailed down and sealed would be too ponderous for the present-day sense of form' (trans. 1978: 128).

Nevertheless, such empirical data as are available suggest that the ceremonious nailing-down of the close which Schoenberg describes is in fact a necessity if most present-day listeners are to perceive the finality of a musical close. In an informal series of tests,[19] subjects who were played the first movement of Beethoven's G major Sonata Op. 49 No. 2 frequently predicted that the music would continue for another minute or more when the

---

[18] See Rosner and Meyer 1986: 36 for some psychological data bearing on this. A musicological discussion of textural signs, with further references, will be found in Levy 1982.

[19] I carried out these tests between 1982 and 1984 at the University of Hong Kong. The subjects were freshman music students, who as a result of local educational conditions generally combine a fair level of practical proficiency (mainly as pianists) with a rather low level of music-theoretical knowledge. Further details may be found in Cook 1987d.

performance was broken off just before the final two chords. As soon as they heard those chords, of course, they realized that the movement had ended; and this shows how effectively these chords (a perfect cadence played louder, and its bass lower, than anything earlier in the movement) signal the conclusion. But by the same token it also shows that, as far as these listeners were concerned, the conclusion was not implied by anything that had come before— the recapitulation, for instance, or the coda. Furthermore, and despite Schoenberg's frequent statements regarding the importance of repetition in clarifying formal structure, a majority of the listeners failed to observe the repetition of the exposition, or else believed the repeat to be a modified one. This result confirms an earlier test[20] in which subjects were played the first movement of Webern's Symphony Op. 21. Despite the fact that they had a relatively high degree of musical training, only half of these listeners observed the literal repeat of the exposition; the others heard the entire passage as being through-composed. This reflects what is probably a quite general experience; any music teacher is likely to have encountered the surprise expressed by untrained listeners when they discover how much repetition, and therefore how little distinct material, there is in a great deal of familiar music.

Listeners perform much better in tests such as these when they have been specifically told what to listen for. The listeners who failed to spot the repeat of the exposition in the Beethoven sonata when it was first played to them all observed it when they heard the movement again: this time they had been told to keep track of the various sections of the piece and to identify them with a letter name (A, B, C, and so on), which they were able to do without undue difficulty. The directions that were given, in other words, modified the way in which the music was heard. And if subjects are not only asked to observe the formal features of the music that they hear, but also given some specific instruction in the conventions governing these forms, it becomes possible to achieve quite impressive results even with people who otherwise have little in the way of musical training. This, at any rate, is the finding of Alan Smith (1973), who subjected a group of seventh-grade American

---

[20] This test (details also in Cook 1987d) was carried out in conjunction with Alexander Goehr. It took place during 1979 at the University of Cambridge; the subjects were 2nd- and 3rd-year music students, who were simply required to write down their impressions of the music as they listened to it. No specific instructions were given as to what to listen for.

students to several hours of training in the formal properties of classical minuets and sonata forms before administering a series of tests to them. In these tests the students were played recordings of minuets and sonata movements which they had not previously heard; the recordings were incomplete and the students had to indicate the point in the form at which each recording terminated. The result was that they achieved a high success rate; Smith concludes that 'Musically unsophisticated seventh grade students can be taught to keep track of the unfolding forms of unfamiliar minuets and sonata-allegro movements.' (p. 208.)

This test shows how people *can* perceive musical forms; it does not show how people normally *do* perceive them. In fact Smith performed another test which illustrates this distinction particularly clearly. Again he required his subjects to identify the formal point at which recordings were terminated, but this time the subjects were fourth-year and graduate music students. As Smith explains (pp. 212–13), these students

did not know they would be asked to identify the termination point of the first selection. They were told only to 'listen carefully to this piece of music. It is the first movement of an early Haydn symphony and it begins with a slow introduction'. The results were no better than might have been expected had the subjects all guessed. However, during two sequent selections the subjects, who now knew what was expected of them, performed well. From this it appeared that musically sophisticated subjects can keep track but normally do not do so unless specifically asked.

This clearly raises questions regarding the aesthetic relevance of this kind of conscious tracking: it is hard to believe that following the unfolding of form in such a manner can be an important source of listening pleasure if people who have the ability to do it don't normally bother to, and Smith admits that 'a skeptic might reasonably argue that tracking is no more than busy work and therefore not a defensible behavioral objective for a music curriculum.' (p. 211.) Nevertheless he concludes:

For the present the individual must discover his own answer to the question of the educational worth of tracking in light of the almost unanimous advocacy by musicians, music educators, and aestheticians that listening should be active and should concentrate on formal matters.

Smith's appeal to the musical authorities is, however, weakened by the fact that the conception of form on which his tests are based is considered by most present-day theorists and analysts to be an altogether inadequate one. Essentially he treats the classical forms as stereotyped patterns in which keys, themes, or sections are repeated or alternated with one another; each of these patterns corresponds to one of the established forms—the sonata allegro or rondo, the various types of concerto pattern, and so on—so that the listener's task is to observe the repetitions or alternations in the music, and to match them with the appropriate pattern. But Charles Rosen (1976a, 1980) has argued persuasively that surface patterns of the type Smith refers to really make no sense seen simply as patterns: what makes sense of them is the tonal drama that lies behind them. Essentially Rosen sees the tonal forms of classical music as being based on the idea of preparing and resolving a dissonance, an idea which classical composers extended from the note-to-note level of strict counterpoint to the level of form. Thus he regards the modulation to a contrasted key area that characterizes any sonata form as 'essentially a dissonance raised to a higher plane, that of the total structure' (1976a: 26); and this dissonance receives its final resolution through the statement of all the thematic material in the tonic. The creation of a large-scale dissonance and its resolution are, then, what makes sense of sonata and the other classical forms; the various surface patterns are simply the consequences of this underlying formal process, different ways in which the tonal drama can be projected. Seen from such a perspective, Smith's entire programme seems strangely wrong-headed; and certainly one wonders what his seventh-graders made of a style of music that forces its productions into as complicated and yet arbitrary a mould as sonata form must have appeared to them.

Rosen's interpretation of the classical forms is merely a specific application of a general analytical and theoretical approach to musical form. This approach is particularly associated with Schenker, according to whom 'all forms appear in the ultimate foreground; but all of them have their origin in, and derive from, the background.' (trans. 1979: 130.) By this he means that the various surface patterns represented by the traditional forms can only be understood when interpreted in terms of the basic linear-harmonic structures that they elaborate; they are entirely without significance when considered by themselves, and for this reason he sometimes speaks of them as being illusory. For Schenker real musical form only exists in the specific influence of the fundamental structure over every detail of a composition. And it follows from this that form is not so much something to hear as a way of hearing things.

This is easier to illustrate than to explain. The second chord of the Sarabande from Bach's Second English Suite, shown in Ex. 10*a*, is a striking and expressive dissonance but has no special structural function; it is perfectly possible to imagine the piece beginning as in Ex. 10*b*, and though the effect is certainly weaker

Ex. 10

than the original the damage is purely local in nature. But the same chord has a very different effect when it appears in Schumann's song 'Auf einer Burg' (Ex. 11, bar 35). Here it stands out as a significant structural point, even on a first hearing (and this is something on which I have found music students, at least, to be agreed). Schumann's chord itself is identical to Bach's: why then does it have so different an effect? The answer, of course, lies in the context. Specifically, it is with this chord that the linear processes that have been building up since bar 29 reach breaking-point; the dissonant C and E have been 'prepared' by these processes, and the movement of the bass to D initiates a II–V–(I) cadential pattern in which the tension built into the chord is rapidly dissipated. (Ex. 12

Ex. 11

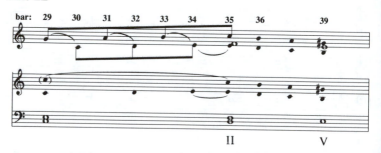

Ex. 12

illustrates this schematically.[21]) The different structural contexts of the two compositions, then, mean that the identical chord is heard in quite different ways. From a Schenkerian point of view it is precisely in this influence of the total context over the perception of the parts that real musical form is to be found.

II

The concept that form is the influence of the whole over the perception of the parts provides a quite different paradigm for experimental investigation from that adopted by Smith. It is also a more plausible approach from the point of view of the untrained listener, in that it does not depend on his having a specific

---

[21] 'Auf einer Burg' comes from the Eichendorff *Liederkreis*; the beginning of the next song in the cycle supplies the tonic resolution. A fuller analysis may be found in Cook 1987a, from which Ex. 12 is adapted. The 2nd stave in Ex. 12 is to be read as a reduction of the top stave, which in turn is a reduction of the corresponding passage in the song.

knowledge either of conventional formal patterns or of analytical nomenclature. For Smith, hearing a piece of music as a sonata means the same as hearing that it is a sonata; it involves factual knowledge. But for Rosen and Schenker, hearing a piece as a sonata means hearing everything that happens in it in the light of its larger tonal context; a reflective awareness of the manner in which the music is organized need not necessarily be involved at all. And, conversely, a listener might be able to tell that a piece was, as a matter of fact, a sonata, but not be able to hear it as one. Now this means that testing this kind of formal perception is not a matter of finding out what people are consciously aware of when they listen to music. Rather, it is a matter of determining the extent to which aspects of the music's organization affect their aesthetic responses. And of these aspects, one of the easiest to investigate is tonal closure.

Western composers of the tonal period (approximately 1700–1900) almost invariably began and ended their compositions in the same key. A 'Symphony in D minor', for instance, will not be in D minor all the time in any literal sense; tonal contrast is necessary both for variety and for purposes of large-scale tensional shaping. Nor is it likely that all its individual movements will be in D minor; the third movement of Beethoven's Ninth Symphony is in B flat major, whereas the symphony as a whole is in D minor. In fact this symphony does not even begin in D minor, but in A minor. What then does it mean to call it a 'Symphony in D minor'? It means that D minor has a special function in relation to the entire composition: it represents the 'home' key, in the sense that the other keys through which the music passes are to be understood in relation to this overall tonic. (The opening A minor, for instance, is to be understood as merely an approach to D minor, which is strongly established as the tonic thereafter.) Schoenberg coined the term 'monotonality' to express this conception, commenting that

according to this principle, every digression from the tonic is considered to be still within the tonality, whether directly or indirectly, closely or remotely related. In other words, there is only *one tonality* in a piece, and every segment formerly considered as another tonality is only a region, a harmonic contrast within that tonality. Monotonality includes modulation—movement towards another *mode* and even establishment of that mode. But it considers these deviations as regions of the tonality, subordinate to the central power of a tonic. Thus comprehension of the harmonic unity within a piece is achieved. (ed. 1969: 19.)

He even drew up a chart, reproduced in Ex. 13, in which the relationships between the regions of a tonality (here C major) are presented in spatial terms.[22] The implication of this chart is that the way a given key is experienced in the context of a particular composition depends upon its distance from, and its specific relationship to, the overall tonic.[23] In particular, distance from the tonic is associated with a heightening of tension, and the return to the tonic with relaxation; in this way the closed tonal plan of most eighteenth- and nineteenth-century compositions, which begin in the tonic key and then move through other keys before finally returning to the tonic, represents an arched-shaped tensional contour in which the return to the tonic creates a sense of finality.

An example of such a formal structure in miniature is provided by the third of Liszt's *Fünf kleine Klavierstücke* (Ex. 14). The initial part of this piece—up to bar 16—is in F sharp major; there is then an abrupt shift to A major. However, the sense of the overall tonic does not altogether disappear during this A major episode, for the B major triad over a C♯ bass at bar 22, which leads directly to the final close in F sharp major, creates a sense of home-coming or resolution: in other words, the piece concludes in a satisfyingly final manner—rather than just stopping—because one perceives the continuity of the F sharp tonality at the beginning and the end of the piece. That, at any rate, would be the standard theoretical interpretation of this composition's tonal structure, and there is no doubt that it is easy, for a musically trained person at least, to hear the music in this manner.

Despite this, tests which have been more fully reported elsewhere (Cook 1987e) suggest that such tonal closure does not have any very clearly defined effect on listeners' responses in the normal way. In these tests pieces of music whose durations varied from less than thirty seconds to around six minutes were played in

---

[22] Taken from Schoenberg ed. 1969: 20.

[23] There have been a number of more recent attempts to model structural representations of pitch in spatial terms (for an overview of these see Shepard 1982); such spatial models, which are based on empirical data, sometimes closely resemble Schoenberg's chart. There is, however, a methodological problem as to the relevance of the data on which they are based to the perceptual processes involved in normal listening; for a discussion of this see Cook 1987b.

Ex. 13

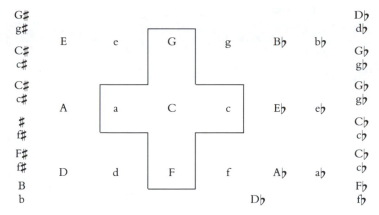

two different versions: in each case one version was the original one, which began and ended in the same key, while the other version had been modified so that it ended in a different key from that in which it began. For instance, *Kleines Klavierstück* No. 3 was altered so that it ended in the rather inconvenient key of D sharp major; Ex. 15 shows how. The result of this alteration is that while bar 16 remains perfectly coherent—the music simply continues in F sharp major instead of moving to A—there is now a lack of coherence, or closure, between the beginning and the end of the piece. If the general approach to tonal form which I have described above is correct, then, the ending of the altered version of Liszt's piece ought to result in a diminished sense of completion as compared to the ending of the original version.

But the tests provided no clear confirmation of this. In the case of this particular piece, a small (and not statistically significant) majority of listeners preferred the original version to the altered one. On the other hand, there were some cases in which there was a small (and again not statistically significant) preference for the altered version over the original piece; there was, for example, a general preference for a version of Brahms's Intermezzo Op. 117 No. 3 in which the final section of the piece (from the upbeat to bar 76) had been transposed up a minor second from the composer's original score! Such a result is unlikely to indicate any preference for lack of tonal closure as such; more probably it is to be explained in terms of the local effects of the two versions of bars 76–7, or of

Ex. 14

ordering effects (there was a tendency for listeners to prefer whichever version of a piece they heard second over the one they heard first, regardless of the presence or absence of tonal closure). In other words it seems that, despite the fundamental importance

Ex. 15

that musicians customarily attach to it, tonal closure lacks psychological reality for the listener—at least when, as in this intermezzo, it extends over a duration of several minutes. Only in the case of the shortest piece of music that was used in these tests was there a statistically significant correlation between tonal closure and the listeners' responses, regardless of the order in which the different versions were played: and this was not a complete composition, but a single theme (the opening ten bars of Brahms's Haydn Variations).

These tests, then, indicate that tonal closure has psychological reality for the listener only when the time-scale involved is very small—much smaller than is the case in most tonal compositions. Yet tonal closure—or, more generally, the organizing function of the overall tonic—is the basis of the traditional forms of eighteenth- and nineteenth-century music, as the music analyst or theorist views them. Sonata form, for instance, may be viewed as resulting from a single, closed, tonal gesture (the movement from one key to a contrasted one and back again) which is progressively divided and subdivided into functionally differentiated segments. Ex.16 shows this schematically: the tonal gesture that constitutes

Ex. 16

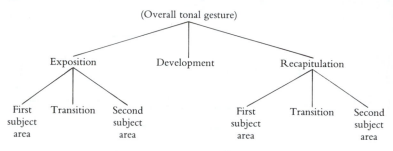

the movement as a whole is divided into three principal formal areas, which are in turn subdivided into contrasted thematic areas, together with transitions between them. And at every level it is tonality that is the organizing principle. The exposition represents the move away from the initial tonal area, whereas the recapitulation represents its re-establishment; at the next level the function of each theme or thematic group is to express a tonal area, and it is indeed the association with tonality that defines a given segment of the music as being thematic. In other words a sonata, as the analyst or theorist sees it, is a closed and hierarchically organized structure whose fundamental principle is that of tonality.

But if listeners do not perceive tonal closure in movements lasting several minutes, how can they possibly perceive this kind of formal organization? Certainly the students who listened to the first movement of Beethoven's Op. 49 No. 2[24] did not experience the music as being organized in any such manner, even when asked to keep track of the various sections of the piece and to identify each with a letter name. While they were generally accurate in the sense that they observed repetitions and recognized which material was being repeated, the way in which they categorized the

[24] See above, pp. 44–5.

materials bore little affinity to the analytical interpretation of sonata form offered above, and indeed varied widely from one listener to another.[25] Where listeners attempted some kind of hierarchical categorization (such as labelling sections as A, A′, B, B′, and so forth) they were as likely as not to couple materials associated with different tonal areas, or to associate thematic materials with transitional ones; and in any case, many listeners did not distinguish the sections hierarchically at all, simply labelling the first section as A, the next as B, and so on.[26] Someone who hears the music this way is perceiving it not as a sonata but as a kind of extended rondo-like form, in which materials recur in various patterns but in which there is no overall formal closure. (It is in the nature of a rondo form that it has no internal reason not to continue indefinitely: ABACADAE . . .) And this, of course, explains the students' failure to anticipate the ending of the movement until they heard the final pair of chords.

Such discrepancies between the way in which theoreticians and analysts think of compositions on the one hand, and the way in which listeners respond to them on the other, are by no means restricted to tonal structure. The tests based on Webern's Symphony, mentioned earlier, yielded very similar results, and here the musical structures involved are serial rather than tonal. The first movement of this work treats time like space: not only is the series itself used both forwards and backwards—that, after all, is one of the normal features of serialism—but other aspects of the music are reversed with it too. The movement consists of a number of sections which are played first forwards and then backwards, with not only the pitches but also the rhythms and instrumental colours recurring in a reversed order, as if the music has been reflected in a mirror; these sections are contained within larger sections, so that viewed analytically the composition has a highly

[25] A similar phenomenon was observed by Francès in an experiment which required listeners to identify occurrences of the principal themes in movements by Beethoven and Schubert (1984: 211–13). Results were rather poor; Francès notes in particular that subjects often perceived more than 2 themes, and sometimes as many as 4 or 5.

[26] Though there was much disparity in the particular identifications of sections that were made, the listeners had in common a limit of 5–6 distinct classes of material; those who made more detailed identifications in the earlier part of the piece would compensate by making less detailed identifications thereafter. The similarity of this apparent limit to Miller's measure of unidimensional channel capacity (1956) is consistent with the apparent absence of hierarchical organization in the students' discrimination of the different sections of the music.

symmetrical, hierarchically organized structure. The music, in other words, is conceived not as a series of psychological effects, but as an objective, quasi-spatial structure. It would be hard to imagine a piece better calculated to create the experience of 'surveyable plastic form' that Dahlhaus describes.

And yet the listeners' reports of what they experienced as they heard Webern's music revealed little evidence of this; one might have guessed from what they wrote that they had been listening to Schoenberg's *Erwartung* or Richard Strauss's *Ein Heldenleben* rather than Webern's Symphony. Not only did they fail to observe the palindromic structure of the music—and subsequent discussion made it clear that this was a failure to observe, not just a failure to report—but the very language in which the subjects expressed their experience was directed at the psychological response rather than the musical object giving rise to this response. They would speak, for example, of the music 'straining' or 'collapsing' or 'grinding to a halt', and while these terms are objective in the sense that they describe something that 'the music' did, they emphasize the affective quality of the response.[27] Moreover, the subjects sometimes reported large-scale processes in the music that are simply contradicted by what is visible in the score: one listener talked of a continual gathering of tension throughout the entire exposition, and another of a gradual clarification of the texture, despite the fact that the exposition actually consists of a single section that is played twice. It would of course be possible to argue that these listeners were simply not listening properly to the music. But to do so is just to give a particular, prescriptive definition of what it means to 'listen properly'; the fact remains that when people—even people as musically well qualified as the students taking part in these tests—listen to music that is highly organized in objective terms, there are striking discrepancies between the structure of their experiences and the structure of the music itself, as one would analyse it on the basis of the score. I would agree, then, with Kathryn Bailey's remark that Webern's Symphony consists of 'two quite different pieces—a visual, intellectual piece and an aural, immediate piece, one for the analyst and another for

---

[27] Leo Treitler (1967: 88) says much the same about Carpenter's account of the way in which a Bach fugue is experienced as a musical object (c.f. n. 10 above); in other words, he implies, Carpenter's very language controverts her argument.

the listener' (1983: 195). And I would suggest that, while this may be an extreme case, it is an extreme case of a general phenomenon.

Thomas Clifton expressed all this more trenchantly. 'For the listener,' he declared, 'musical grammar and syntax amount to no more than wax in his ears.' (1983: 71.)

III

There is, of course, an irremediable problem with any experiment that is intended to show how people normally listen to music. The problem is simply that people do not normally listen to music under experimental conditions. The tests I have been describing attempted to be as naturalistic as possible, in that subjects were given no specific instructions as to what they were to listen for, but were merely asked to write down their impressions as they listened. But one does not normally write down one's impressions as one listens to music, and to do so makes one listen in a rather different manner from normal; indeed, doing this is a good music-educational exercise for the precise reason that it forces one to listen in a more attentive and self-conscious manner than is normally the case. So it is useful to supplement the evidence of such tests with two other sources of information, both of which are indirect but have greater ecological validity.

One of these sources of information is the way in which composers structure certain of their compositions. When a classical composer wrote a sonata or a symphony, he was working within a traditional genre which to a considerable degree dictated both the kind of expressive effect which the music would aim to create, and the technical means by which this would be achieved. Even the first movement of as quintessentially romantic a symphony as Berlioz's *Symphonie fantastique* has a large-scale symmetry of tonal and thematic organization which, though traditional in symphonic terms, is in a sense quite inappropriate to the evolving monodrama that Berlioz's music is actually designed to project, illustrating as it does 'the passage from [a] state of melancholy reverie, interrupted by a few fits of groundless joy, to one of frenzied passion, with its movements of fury, of jealousy, its return of tenderness, its tears, its religious consolations' (Cone 1971: 23). At the same time, if one looks upon it as a symphony in the classical mould, it is hard to avoid the conclusion that Berlioz's work is strangely misproportioned and even badly constructed. And this tension, or even contradiction, between the *Symphonie fantastique* and the genre which it exemplifies highlights the distinction between those aspects of a musical composition that are designed in terms of acoustic and expressive effect on the one hand, and those aspects that are the result of historical and stylistic sedimentation on the other: a distinction which is quite general, at least in Western art music.

But while this means that the structure of compositions cast into such traditional forms as symphony and sonata reflects historical as much as phenomenological factors, there are other genres of classical music in which the influence of these historical factors is very much smaller. For instance, though the variation set is well enough established as a musical form, it is one which imposes little in the way of presupposed structure beyond the requirement that the variations will relate to one another in some way, and the likelihood that the variation set as a whole will begin and end in the same key and move towards a climax of tension or virtuosity at the end. Beyond that, virtually nothing is taken for granted in composing a variation set. And for this reason, it is probable that much, if not all, of whatever more complex structural organization is found in the set is there for a directly phenomenological purpose—that is to say, that it has been written to be heard, rather than simply because things are conventionally done that way. A variation set, in other words, is likely to be a more direct reflection of its composer's beliefs about how listeners experience structure than a piece belonging to a genre such as symphony or sonata.

To take a specific example, what do Brahms' Handel Variations reveal when considered in this light? The Handel Variations consist of a theme and twenty-five variations, each of equal length,[28] plus a much longer fugue at the end which provides the climax of the movement in terms of duration, dynamics, and contrapuntal complexity. The individual variations are grouped in such a way as to create a series of waves, both in terms of tempo and dynamics, leading to the final fugue, and superimposed upon this overall organization are a number of subordinate patterns. Variations in tonic major and minor more or less alternate with

[28] Some variations look longer than others in the score, but this is merely because passages which were marked with repeats in the theme have been written out in full. All the variations correspond to the theme bar for bar.

each other; only once is there a variation in another key (the twenty-first, which is in the relative minor). Legato variations are usually succeeded by staccato ones; variations whose texture is fragmentary are in general followed by more homophonic ones. And there are also groups of variations defined by the way in which they relate to the theme; Ex. 17 illustrates some of these relationships in the first two bars of each variation.

In Ex. 17, (a) and (b) show the theme and its principal melodic notes. In many cases these appear in the melody of the variation, as in (c), though sometimes they are surrounded with neighbour-notes (d), hidden in figuration (e), or dislocated in time (f); the subject of the fugue (g) is also an example of this. In other variations the same notes appear, again at the top of the texture, but with registral changes: (h) provides an illustration. Or the same notes may appear, but shared between two different parts in one hand, as in (i), or between the hands (j). The first few notes of this last-mentioned variation suggest the traditional two-part figure known as the 'horn-call', which duly reappears in the twelfth variation and then again from the fifteenth to the eighteenth, as in (k). Sometimes, on the other hand, the melodic notes of the theme are so fragmented that there is no discernable connection between a variation and the theme in a melodic sense: in (l) the connection is really no more than a harmonic one. And in the twenty-third variation (m) there is neither a discernable melodic connection with the theme, nor a close harmonic one either; the tonic chords appear in the same places, but everything else is different.

In what sense, then, is Variation 23 a variation on the theme at all? In the first place, it does embody an important aspect of the theme that I have not as yet mentioned: its third bar is a repeat of the first bar a third higher (and, like the theme, this variation retains the tonic harmony of the third bar, in contrast with a number of the other variations which substitute mediant harmony for it). In the second place, the subdominant minor harmony of the second beat in Variation 23 does have some connection with the variations preceding and following it (n, o), in each of which the harmony and at least some of the melody of the theme can be discerned; in both cases a seventh, E♮, is added to the second chord (hence the use of the subdominant in Variation 23) over a tonic pedal (hence its low B♭), while Variation 24 also provides a link with the minor inflection of the subdominant through the

Ex. 17

flattening of the G. In this way the melody and harmony of Variation 23 do not relate directly to that of the theme at all: rather, they relate to that of Variations 22 and 24, which in turn relate to the theme. In other words, Variation 23 is intelligible as a variation on the theme only because it appears between Variations 22 and 24; had Brahms used it as the first variation—that is, had Variation 23 followed directly on the theme—then it might well not have been heard as a variation at all.

If this is correct, then it confirms the existence of large-scale form (in the sense that I have defined) in Brahms's Handel Variations, because the context within which Variation 23 is heard determines whether or not it is heard as a coherent part of the whole. But it also shows that this coherence arises not from the relationship of Variation 23 to the theme, but rather from its relationship to its neighbours. And this means that the organization of the variation set is not so much concentric—with each variation deriving coherence from its relationship to the theme— as edge-related, with each variation being lent significance by its relationship to what comes before and after it, or by the group of variations within which it is located. In other words, what gives unity to the variation set—and this is a quite general principle rather than something specific to the Handel Variations—is not the theme as such, but rather a network of 'family resemblances', to use Wittgenstein's term, between the different variations.[29] Indeed, one might say that in many variation sets the theme is not really a theme at all, but simply the variation that comes before Variation 1. A particularly clear example of this is supplied by one of Handel's own variation sets, the Chaconne and Sixty-two Variations; the chaconne with which the set begins (Ex. 18a) is obviously an elaboration of the much more basic linear and harmonic pattern that appears as Variation 8 (Ex. 18b), which is in fact almost identical to the left-hand part of the chaconne.

Ex. 18

[29] See Stephen Davies's discussion of this concept as applied to the analysis of music (1983: 205). Cone (1987: 242) has described the thematic unity of Schubert's music in similar terms.

In the case of Handel's Chaconne and Sixty-two Variations it would be appropriate to think of Variation 8 as being the real theme of the entire variation set, because its harmonic pattern (and to a large extent its melodic pattern too) does form the basis of all the other variations. But there are plenty of other works, including Brahms's Handel Variations, in which there is no single harmonic or melodic pattern shared by all the variations. In such cases the work has neither a theme as such, nor overall form in a unitary sense; it is the web of individual connections between its various components that gives it formal coherence. In other words, the form inheres not so much in the influence of the whole over the experiencing of the parts as in the influence of each part over the experiencing of the other parts. And this constitutes a very much more diffuse conception of formal organization than the one that is embodied in most theoretical and analytical approaches to musical structure.

The structure of compositions such as variation sets is one of the sources of indirect, but ecologically valid, information about the organization of listeners' experiences that I have mentioned. The other is people's overt behaviour when responding to music. Actually it is characteristic of Western art music culture that overt responses to music vary greatly from one listening situation to another. In their own homes, people tend to adopt a rather relaxed attitude towards musical listening. Music is used as an acoustic background; one goes to another room to fetch something and comes back without feeling that the musical experience has been seriously impaired by the interruption. People often play a favourite movement by itself, regardless of the context in which it originally belonged; there are widely selling record albums containing arrangements of selected favourite movements, while sophisticated compact disc players are promoted on the basis of their ability to store the user's personal track selection in memory. Such practices reinforce a statement by the composer John White:

As far as I'm concerned many people listen to a lot of classical music just from phrase to phrase, waiting for the really good bit to come up, more or less switching off after the 18th Variation of Rachmaninov's *Paganini Variations*, until the exciting bit towards the end comes up.[30]

Now it might of course be argued that to listen in this way is to

[30] Quoted in Nyman 1976: 237.

miss much of the aesthetic potential of the master-works of the past, and most people can probably recall occasions on which they were so gripped by a piece of music that they listened intently and energetically to the unfolding of the entire work from start to finish. But it is clear from the kind of behaviour I have mentioned that such absorption, while maybe the most rewarding type of engagement with music, is not representative of the enjoyment that is routinely derived from it. Even in the concert-hall, to which people go with the express intention of hearing music (and pay for the privilege), most of them probably listen for most of the time in more or less the way that White describes. It is hard to get more than introspective or anecdotal evidence about this, however, because in contemporary Western and Westernized society there is a very tight code governing what is acceptable behaviour at concerts. As Marcia Herndon and Norma McLeod put it,

Audiences tend to take their cues from particular contexts; their reactions are defined, delimited, and constrained by the nature of the occasion. Those who stray from approved audience behavior in any given context soon learn what behavior is appropriate. This is especially true of more formalized situations. The acute embarrassment of a neophyte concert-goer, applauding vigorously after the first movement of a string quartet and greeted by icy stares from all around the audience, is an intense and immediate learning experience. Anyone with the audacity or the lack of foresight to arrive improperly dressed or to behave incorrectly, will soon receive the negative sanction of other members of the audience and, in some instances, may be forcibly ejected from the premises of a musical event if his or her behavior is too unsuitable. (1982: 56.)

Obviously there is nothing in the phenomenology or psychology of musical listening that makes it impossible to appreciate string quartets while wearing a T-shirt and shorts; this is purely a matter of social convention. And the same is perhaps equally true of the disapproval directed at people who clap between movements. One understands the point: refraining from clapping in the course of an extended work is intended as a recognition of the aesthetic unity of the whole. Someone who claps half-way through a performance of Beethoven's String Quartet Op. 130, for instance, reveals himself as incapable of appreciating this unity and, what is worse, disrupts the enjoyment of other listeners who do have this capacity. Or at least that is the idea; but how far it has a foundation in people's aesthetic experience—rather than in snobbery—is another matter.

Vladimir Konečni (1984) has carried out tests in which subjects heard some of Beethoven's string quartets and piano sonatas with their movements in the wrong order; although such alterations might have been expected to play havoc with the music's formal integrity, the listeners' responses indicated that they in fact had little or no effect on the enjoyment of the music. It is worth recalling in this connection that Beethoven himself originally concluded Op. 130 with the fugal movement now known as the 'Grosse Fuge', later replacing it (at the publisher's instigation) with the present finale. And if it is objected that he must have done this precisely because the original finale was not appropriate in terms of Op. 130's large-scale formal structure, then other instances can be cited of Beethoven sanctioning the reordering of movements within his works, or even their omission. In a frequently quoted letter to his friend Ferdinand Ries,[31] he suggested that in order to ensure the publication of his Sonata Op. 106 in London, Ries could, if he saw fit,

omit the Largo and begin straight away with the Fugue, which is the last movement; or you could use the first movement and then the Adagio, and then for the third movement the Scherzo—and omit entirely no. 4 with the Largo and Allegro risoluto. Or you could take just the first movement and the Scherzo and let them form the whole sonata. I leave it to you to do as you think best.

And this is the 'Hammerklavier'! It is also worth recalling that, though Beethoven presumably did not sanction it, the soloist in the first performance of the Violin Concerto found time between the first two movements to turn his violin upside-down and play a composition of his own—and all on one string (Rosen 1976a: 104).

Imagine what the critics would have to say today if Itzhak Perlman, appearing at Carnegie Hall or on the South Bank, decided to play a selection of his favourite tunes for one-string upside-down fiddle half-way through a performance of Beethoven's Violin Concerto! What was quite normal in Beethoven's

---

[31] See Anderson 1961: ii, 804–5.

day[32] is nowadays absolutely unthinkable. But what has changed is, presumably, the code governing what is socially acceptable behaviour in the concert-hall, not the capacity of audiences for perceiving large-scale compositional structure.

IV

It does seem, then, as if there is a rather glaring disparity between the way in which the arbiters of musical taste approach musical structure and the way in which listeners generally respond to it.[33] For the theorist—and this idea is obviously very influential in critical circles too—musical forms are to be understood in terms of unitary, integrated structure, whether this unity is realized through tonal closure, serialism, or some other type of hierarchical organization. But it appears that such integrated structure passes over the heads of most listeners most of the time, so that West, Howell, and Cross are perhaps rather understating the case when they say that 'Listeners do not necessarily perceive music in terms of a fully coordinated structure. . . . A listener unfamiliar with a Chopin sonata or a Mozart symphony may not perceive fully articulated phrases—let alone how these combine to produce larger structures.' (1985: 46.) Indeed, one might reasonably maintain that few people actually experience musical compositions as such, in the sense of constituting them as fully co-ordinated, objective structures. Unless they have both the training and the inclination to track the form of a piece of music in theoretical terms as they listen, people experience recurrence without actually observing what it is that recurs; they experience coherence but not the unitary organization in terms of which a theorist or analyst would explain that coherence. People enjoy musical compositions, in other words, without really perceiving them at all; rather than listening *to* them in Collingwood's sense, they 'just listen'.

---

[32] Right through the 19th cent. it was common practice to perform the movements of symphonies or concertos individually (in 1815 a reviewer in the *Allgemeine musikalische Zeitung* remarked that 'it is seldom that one hears a whole concerto or symphony, instead of one or two movements'), or to string together movements taken from separate works into pot-pourris; see J. A. Meyer 1982: 233–4. Clapping between movements was common, too.

[33] The same was true in North America during the 1940s, according to data collated and discussed by J. D. Smith. He concludes: 'the syntactic aesthetic theory written by experts seems to apply only to experts and cannot be extrapolated to lower levels of training. The elite tip has informed us somewhat inaccurately about the aesthetic responses of the rest of the iceberg.' (1987: 388.)

Maybe one should not be too surprised at such a conclusion, for, as Dahlhaus states, though the concept of the musical composition seemed 'self-evident in the nineteenth century according to the letter of the aesthetic law, it was of restricted validity and always in peril from the context of actual musical behaviour' (1987: 221). Or to put it another way, it was an aesthetic ideal and not a perceptual fact. For the listener the distinction between the musical work and its performance on a given occasion remains a parlous one; the musical composition is constantly on the verge of collapsing into a series of more or less fragmented psychological effects. But if this is the case, what is one to make of the divergence that opens up between theoretical accounts of music on the one hand, with their emphasis on the fully co-ordinated structure that defines the composition as such, and the way in which listeners experience music on the other? Konečni's attitude is perfectly straightforward: he deplores the divergence, saying that 'A greater degree of caution, moderation, and humility in the music critics' and theorists' often sweeping claims—mere speculations really —would be a welcome consequence of . . . research in the psychology of music.' (Gotlieb and Konečni 1985: 98.) And he adds sourly that 'The world of music, it has been claimed, is more heavily restricted by authoritarian input than any other artistic realm.'

There is, of course, a measure of truth in this last statement. One might with some justification argue that our present-day concert aesthetic, supported as it is by programme-notes that refer in almost mystical terms to the unity of form possessed by musical master-works, creates a kind of barrier of assumed ignorance between the untutored music-lover and the musical experience itself; and that the music 'Appreciation-racket', as Virgil Thomson contemptuously called it,[34] exists in order to maintain what is really a quite false conception of how music creates pleasure in its listeners. At the same time, however, it is possible to argue that Konečni is actually missing the point of what music critics and theorists are trying to do.

Essentially Konečni regards the music theorist as a would-be social scientist, as someone who observes what people do and attempts to formulate explanations of why they do what they do.

[34] See below, p. 163.

Now it is undeniable that, if music theorists are social scientists, then they are generally very bad ones, in that they produce explanations of people's responses to music without ever properly establishing the facts of the matter. But few music theorists do in fact regard themselves as social scientists, and this is because they do not attempt to stand, as it were, outside the phenomenon of music in order to observe it in a detached and objective manner, as a scientist would aim to do. By and large, music theorists regard themselves not as theorists in a scientific sense, but as musicians: the purpose of their formulations and explanations of musical phenomena is to contribute to the musical culture within which they work. And if one sees the thinking of music theorists—and indeed of musicians in general—as an intrinsic part of a musical culture, then the divergence between the way in which music is thought about and the way in which it is experienced will turn out to be not a failing, but rather a defining attribute of musical culture. Or so I hope to show in the following chapters.

2 Imagining music

2.1 PRODUCTION VERSUS RECEPTION

Analogies have frequently been drawn between the structural organization of music and that of language. Indeed, it was at one time assumed that the two were more or less coextensive; baroque music theory was to a large extent an adaptation of the theory of rhetoric and was centred around the expression of textual meaning, so that, as Dahlhaus puts it (1982: 24), 'Instrumental music, unless provided by a program-note with some intelligible meaning, was regarded not as eloquent but simply as having nothing to say.' Similarly, in his apology for instrumental music published in 1739, the composer and aesthetician Johann Mattheson resorted to the linguistic analogy in order to justify the claim that music without words could have aesthetic validity: it is possible, he wrote, for the composer 'to express truly all the heart's inclinations by means merely of carefully chosen sounds and their skillful combination without words, so that a listener can completely grasp and clearly understand the motive, sense, meaning and force, with all the phrases and sentences pertaining thereto, as if it were a real speech.'[1] And even today the vernacular of the music lesson includes such linguistic borrowings as the 'phrases' and 'sentences' into which musical compositions are divided.

This linguistic analogy has received considerable impetus in recent decades from the dissemination of Schenker's approach to music in terms of structural levels on the one hand, and the development of structural linguistics on the other. Schenker's analytical method is capable of giving a precise meaning to the musical application of terms like 'phrase' and 'sentence' by showing how a piece of music is constructed out of coherently formed units (we can call them phrases), which elaborate certain

---

[1] Trans. from Mattheson's *The Model Capellmeister* (*Der vollkommene Capellmeister*) in Dahlhaus 1982: 25.

structurally important notes, which themselves are organized into coherently formed units (sentences), and so on until the stage is reached at which an entire movement can be seen as a single coherent unit. In other words, Schenker makes it possible to explain surface articulation in terms of background structure; the foreground—the actual notes, tunes, and chords visible in the score—derives its significance and its musical effect from the background which it elaborates (or, to use Schenker's term, prolongs). It is not just the basic idea of surface articulation being given significance by structural context, but the specifically hierarchical manner in which Schenker explained musical organization, that has prompted both musicians (for instance Forte, in Schenker 1979: xx) and psychologists (Sloboda 1985: 11–17) to draw a parallel between his theory of music and transformational linguistics as formulated by Noam Chomksy; indeed, a musician and a linguist have together produced a sophisticated theory of musical perception which is explicitly based on the application of linguistic models (Lerdahl and Jackendoff 1983).

Valuable though the insights gained from this parallel may be for an understanding of structural organization in these two principal branches of auditory communication, there are some important differences in their psychological functioning which need to be appreciated if the comparison of music and language is not to be perilously misleading. One crucial difference relates to the status of the level of organization that Schenker refers to as the background, and Chomsky as deep structure. In the case of language, people normally experience a sentence as a fully co-ordinated structure; if, in reading, one gets to a full stop while the sentence is grammatically incomplete, then one rereads the sentence to see what has gone wrong.[2] The deep structure of a sentence, in other words, has psychological reality for the recipient as well as for the producer of a speech act. But everything that has been said in Chapter 1 tends to the conclusion that people do not in general perceive musical structure as being fully co-ordinated; and this indicates that the Schenkerian background, in which a composition is to be grasped as a single structural unit,

[2] This is not to say that listeners invariably parse sentences down to their deep structure: experiments indicate that they may not do so when semantic factors strongly favour a particular syntactical structure (Herriot 1974: 73). But the deep structure is always available should it be required.

does not have the same kind of psychological reality for the listener as does Chomsky's deep structure. Burton Rosner and Leonard B. Meyer (1986: 37), who bring further empirical evidence to bear upon this issue, explain it like this:

We must point out a fundamental difference between the tree structures used in linguistics and those presented by music theorists like Lerdahl and Jackendoff. The top node of a grammatical tree is an immediately observed datum: a sentence or an utterance. It represents some incident, occurring over time, which can be entered completely and rapidly into memory. The associated tree decomposes that uppermost node into parts at several lower levels of a strict hierarchy. The lowest nodes in music-theoretic tree structures, however, represent a datum: an actual stretch of music. Quite often, only fragments of it are held faithfully in memory. The lower nodes in the tree are not decompositions of higher ones. Instead, higher nodes are *selections* from among lower ones. We therefore cannot believe that the increasingly higher nodes, which represent ever more rarified selections, form the core of musical perception.

A perhaps even more striking difference between music and language concerns the relationship between reception and production. Chomsky coined the terms 'competence' and 'performance' to refer respectively to the repertoire of linguistic devices that a language user is familiar with and can respond correctly to, and those that he actually uses himself while speaking or writing. The distinction is, of course, a valid one in the case of language: most people know more words than they actually use, and can cope with sentences of greater syntactical complexity than anything they would themselves say or write. But this distinction is of a quite different order of significance from the parallel distinction in the case of music. If it were of the same order of significance, we would have to imagine that the average listener to a Beethoven sonata might hear in it certain chords or progressions which he was able to understand, but was not in the habit of using in his own compositions. But this is true of very few listeners! Most people who go to concerts of Beethoven piano sonatas do not compose at all; they may well lack even the most elementary knowledge of harmony in a productional sense. People can enjoy Beethoven's Ninth Symphony and yet be incapable of whistling the 'Ode to Joy' melody in tune. And even someone who is musically experienced in one culture may find himself in a similar situation as regards the music of another culture. To take a personal example, I have attended and enjoyed a number of concerts of Thai music, most of which included singing. Yet I am quite unable to sing what I hear, owing to the unfamiliar intervals of the Thai scale. I can no more sing the music than I can speak the Thai language by imitating the noise it makes; but whereas my productional incapacity in the case of the language extends to reception as well—I simply don't know it—I find that Thai music can sustain my interest for the best part of an evening. This drastic asymmetry between productional and receptive capacity is so familiar a fact of musical life that a statement such as 'generally, most adults retain a severe production deficiency in music' (Sloboda 1985: 19) may at first sight seem positively simple-minded: of course most people can't play music. But the parallel with language in the course of which Sloboda makes this comment does indeed show how remarkable it is, if most people cannot play music, that they can nevertheless derive the most profound satisfaction from listening to it.

What exactly is the nature of these productional difficulties? Consider the problems that would be encountered by someone who had never played the piano and wanted to learn how to play No. 3 of Liszt's *Fünf kleine Klavierstücke* (Ex. 14 above). This piece is so slow—Liszt has marked it 'sehr langsam'—that performing it is not really problematic in a physical sense: every motion of the hand or finger that is required is, in itself, easy enough to make. (It is the sort of piece that a pianist who had been in gaol for ten years could play as soon as he was released, without needing to work up his technique again.) The fingering that is marked in Ex. 14[3] does admittedly include some rather awkward hand-positions; the beginner might have some difficulty with the thumb-under motions (indicated in bars 1, 5, etc.), and bars 18–19 might, in particular, present problems. The purpose of these slightly awkward fingerings—not that they present any problem to a proficient player—is to ensure legato playing even without the use of the pedal, rather in the manner of organ technique. At the slow tempo of this music, however, it would be perfectly possible to adopt a simpler fingering and fake the legato by pedalling; and in any case a good deal of the piece (bars 8–14) can be played perfectly

---

[3] This fingering is as given in *Franz Liszt: Neue Ausgabe sämtlicher Werke*, ser. I, 10 (Kassel and Budapest, 1980).

satisfactorily using nothing but five-finger positions. So the difficulties a novice would face in trying to play this piece would not be primarily physical ones.

Being able to play the piano is a matter not so much of mastering the actions required in performance as of knowing how to organize them into a coherent motor sequence. Because *Kleines Klavierstück* No. 3 is not only slow but also very short and simple, it is possible to imagine that someone could learn how to perform it simply as a stereotyped sequence of physical motions (though whether this could in practice be achieved is something that could only be determined experimentally). But if someone were to accomplish this feat, one would still hardly want to say that he could 'play the piano' in any normal sense, because his skill would not be transferable to any other piece. If he wanted to learn another piece, he would have to start again at the beginning, and learn it simply as another, essentially unrelated, stereotyped sequence. But that is not how people learn the piano in the real world. They are able to play one piece because they have acquired a set of skills that equally enable them (maybe after a little practice) to play an indefinite number of other pieces as well;[4] and it is primarily at the organizational level that knowledge appropriate to the perform-ance of one piece can be applied to another. Indeed, the fact that a pianist who knows how to play a given piece can play it faster or slower on request, play it in a smoother or more dramatic style, play it on a harpischord instead of a piano, or even (if it is not too technically demanding) play it in another key, makes it clear that his knowledge of the music is at least partly at an organizational level, because otherwise it would not be transferable from one performance situation to another; hence, as John Sloboda puts it, 'The performance plans that most people formulate must be couched, at least in part, in abstract tonal and rhythmic form rather than in terms of specific motor sequences or even sequences of items related by relative pitch and duration.' (1982: 494.)

Basic to this grasp of the music's abstract structure is an understanding of how it breaks into more or less coherent segments. In the case of *Kleines Klavierstück* No. 3, for instance, a competent pianist will grasp the opening phrase (up to bar 3) as a coherent unit even while sight-reading; equally, he will recognize

[4] Cf. Sloboda 1985: 94.

the following phrase (bars 4–7) as a balancing unit which opens up the tonality of the piece (because it moves towards the dominant) and which leads to a series of shorter phrases alternating between the hands (bars 8–14), ending with the climax that dies quickly away (bars 14–15). Looking in a little more detail at the first phrase, he is likely to have some awareness of the falling thirds of the initial one and a half bars, and of the falling sixths that underlie the harmony of bars 2–3 (Ex. 19); these have an immediate physical correlate for the pianist, because the sequence of structurally significant notes forms the framework for his hand motions, the intervening notes being accommodated within it through the action of the individual fingers.

Ex. 19

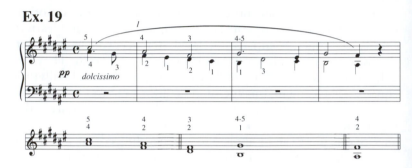

What I have described is a hierarchical organization in which the first three bars constitute a structural unit that is in turn subdivided into the five segments shown in Ex. 19. Now it would be foolhardy to claim that this corresponds directly to the structure of the motor actions involved in performance; the most one could reasonably say is that it would be consistent with the results of experimental studies of motor programming in piano perform-ance, which do indicate some degree of hierarchical organization (Shaffer 1981). But it is evident that some kind of analytical grasp of the musical structure such as I have described is involved in performance, because expressive control of timing and dynamics is clearly organized on the basis of it (Clarke 1985). Indeed, Sloboda (1983) has shown by means of experiments that one of the principal features of expert performance is the use of timing and dynamics to express fully co-ordinated structure on a comparatively large musical scale (in Schenkerian terms, at a middleground or even background level),[5] as compared to the less expert player who organizes what he does primarily in terms of surface grouping. There are, then, distinctions between the degrees to which the beginner, intermediate, and professional pianist embody a structural understanding of music in their performances; but in so far as one can draw a distinction between people who can play the piano (professionally, a little, well, badly) and people who cannot, it is probably true to say that this lies primarily in their capacity to grasp musical structure in an abstract manner.

This means that learning how to play a piece on the piano, and even sight-reading it (Sloboda 1984), is in the first place an analytical activity: the pianist has to 'deconstruct' the musical text into its essential components so that he can then organize his motor actions round the resulting abstract scheme. And it is this analytical capacity, as much as the repertoire of motor sequences with which it has to be co-ordinated, that the novice pianist lacks; it is in this sense that a complete beginner who longs to play some particular piece has first to learn the piano, or to learn music, rather than simply trying to learn that piece as such. A great deal of what goes on in piano lessons is actually directed to enhancing this analytical capacity, rather than to the acquisition of piano technique *per se*. On the whole, however, piano teachers do not present the analytical issues that are involved in learning a piece in a directly abstract manner; rather, these issues are embodied in various technical aspects of piano performance, and most notably in fingering.

In a way, the emphasis that teachers place on fingering may seem strange. In technically demanding music, of course, it can be essential for a performer to work out a fingering in advance: this is because in performance there may be insufficient time to make the necessary decisions, so that there is a danger of 'running out' of fingers or in some other way finding oneself in an impossible situation and so breaking down. But piano teachers (and the same goes for music editors and some composers too) tend to be equally concerned about fingering in the case of pieces that go so slowly that it can simply be made up as one goes along. The reason for this is that pianists adopt fingerings not just as a practical expedient—a

For some additional data on this see Cook 1987c.

way of averting potential problems in performance—but as an integral part of their musical knowledge of a piece.

In part this is simply a matter of memorization: according to Ralph Kirkpatrick,

careful and consistent fingerings are . . . an enormous help to the memory. The careless and inefficient fingerings of many organists originate in their habit of playing from music and thereby escaping some of the direct consequences of those awkward shifts of hand position and of unnecessary substitution of fingers that can trip up a performer who is playing from memory. (1984: 112.)

However, avoiding awkward hand-positions is only one of the purposes of working out fingerings, and not always the most important one. Sometimes a hand-position that is physically awkward may actually be better than a more immediately convenient one in the sense that it reinforces a point regarding the music's structure. A good illustration of this is provided by the fingerings Beethoven notated in his piano compositions, which are the subject of a detailed study by Jeanne Bamberger (1976).

Beethoven did not generally mark fingerings: therefore on the occasions when they do occur, his fingerings indicate some special purpose. This purpose is almost always a musical rather than a technical one. A very simple instance may be found in bars 107–8 of the fugue from the Sonata Op. 110, shown in Ex. 20a, on which Bamberger comments:

Ex. 20

The remarkable fact about the fingering . . . is that no other fingering is possible. What then is its purpose? Evidently Beethoven is trying to draw attention to the inner voice: at the moment when the fugal subject breaks up into a more rapidly rising series of ascending fourths, Beethoven asks the performer to clearly articulate this inner voice (all of the eighth-notes), thus reinforcing the sense of greater activity by giving an impression of increase in the rate of attacks. (1976: 265.)

Actually it is hard to understand the remark about no other fingering being possible: the fingering given in Ex. 20*b* is a perfectly viable alternative for all players except those with the smallest hands, and it eliminates the essential feature of Beethoven's fingering, namely the successive thumb-strokes in bar 107 (those in bar 108 are of less consequence, since the slide from the black note to the white can be accomplished smoothly and without undue emphasis). But this does not detract from Bamberger's main contention, which is that Beethoven is using fingering to make a musical rather than a technical point.

Whereas the example just given relates purely to surface articulation, there are instances in which Beethoven's fingerings are clearly intended to project larger-scale grouping. An example of this, which Bamberger discusses in some detail, is bars 96–7 of the first movement of the 'Hammerklavier' Sonata, Op. 106. Ex. 21*a* shows what Beethoven wrote, whereas Ex. 21*b* shows the fingering given by Hans von Bülow. Bülow, who was one of Liszt's pupils, edited the most popular nineteenth-century edition of the Beethoven piano sonatas,[6] and was one of the principal figures in the development of modern fingering, which Robert Donington has described as 'minimizing the irregularities imposed by nature and by the technique of keyboard instruments in order to increase facility, leaving the desired phrasing to be consciously superimposed' (Bamberger 1976: 250). The educational implications of this are easy to see: technical considerations are separated from matters of interpretation.[7] What this means as applied to the

---

[6] The edition was edited jointly with Lebert, but Op. 106 is Bülow's work alone.

[7] Cf. Kirkpatrick (1984: 128): 'My conception of expression varies from that of my first piano teachers. Their admonition was, Learn the notes and then put in the expression. . . . My admonition is to learn the notes and understand their relationships, and then to draw the expression out.' In fairness to Bülow it should be said that his fingerings do not always separate technique from interpretation: with this passage from Op. 106 compare his fingering of a similar left-hand pattern in Bach's Italian Concerto, I, bars 142-3. I owe this observation to Susan Chan Siu Ying.

Ex. 21

passage from Op. 106 is that Bülow's fingering is based on the repetition of a single left-hand pattern taken within one hand-position and reduplicated in successively higher octaves, as follows:

$$
\begin{array}{ccccc|cccc|ccc}
5 & 4 & 3 & 2 & 1 & 4 & 3 & 2 & 1 & 4 & 3 & 2 \\
D & F\sharp & G & B & D & F\sharp & G & B & D & F\sharp & G & B
\end{array}
$$

This is an easy fingering to learn because it is organized round the surface grouping of the music. Beethoven's fingering, on the other hand, is irregular and for this reason harder to learn:

$$
\begin{array}{ccccc|cccc|cccc}
5 & 4 & 3 & 2 & 1 & 3 & 2 & 1 & & 5 & 3 & 2 & 1 \\
D & F\sharp & G & B & D & F\sharp & G & B & & D & F\sharp & G & B
\end{array}
$$

What then is the point of Beethoven's fingering? Its effect is to create some kind of emphasis at the beginning of bar 97 (because of the major shift of the hand involved in going from the 1 at the end of bar 96 to the 5 at the beginning of the following bar), and so to keep up the momentum of the entire passage based on the eighth-note figure. Bülow's fingering, by contrast, creates a tendency for the passage to sag in the middle—as is suggested by his dynamic markings, which contradict Beethoven's and weaken the effect of the closing section to which the passage leads.

The rationale for Bülow's fingering lies in the patterning of the musical foreground; Beethoven's, on the other hand, is organized around the structural properties of the entire phrase containing these patterns. To use Schenkerian terminology, Bülow's fingering is all on the surface, while Beethoven's derives from the middleground. And the reference to Schenker is apt, for Schenker was himself responsible for one of the principal twentieth-century editions of Beethoven's sonatas, and his belief in the musical rather than merely technical significance of fingering is epitomized in his statement that 'Fingering must . . . be true; the hand—like the mouth—must speak the truth.' (Rothstein 1984: 21.) Indeed, the whole of Schenker's highly abstract and sophisticated analytical theory may be seen as being intended primarily to serve the purposes of better musical performance through enhancing the player's awareness of middleground structure.

A fingering, then, embodies an interpretation of musical structure: to adopt a fingering is to take up an interpretative stance in relation to the music in question, whether or not it is one that the performer can rationalize in analytical terms. In fact it is quite possible for a fingering to be more valuable for communicating an interpretation than for providing the best means to realize that interpretation; a performer might perfectly reasonably take note of Beethoven's fingerings, but then substitute his own, while still bearing Beethoven's suggested interpretation in mind. (One might say that the performer who understands Beethoven's fingerings has no need to adopt them, while for the performer who does not understand them, there is no point in adopting them.) In this way such fingerings are best seen as an appeal to the performer's imaginative understanding of the intended effect, and not as a series of instructions which, if followed to the letter, will infallibly result in good performance. After all, the essence of the modern style of fingering, of which Bülow was an early exponent, is that physical solutions should be found which are sufficiently flexible to allow any desired interpretation to be superimposed: in this sense, what Kirkpatrick (1984: 111) refers to as 'a frankly modern technique designed for all purposes' renders unnecessary the kind of fingerings given by Beethoven and Schenker.[8]

The emphasis that teachers, and indeed musicians in general, place on fingering is therefore not to be understood simply in terms of pragmatic considerations of performance: rather, it is a means by which abstract interpretations of musical structure can be evaluated, remembered, and communicated in terms of concrete musical contexts. And the ability to interpret music in this abstract manner is the foundation of any musical training; in her more psychologically orientated writings, Bamberger herself describes the ability to perceive a musical event in terms of structurally relevant categories as constituting the main difference between how trained and untrained people apprehend music. Bamberger has carried out a number of experiments that bear upon this, and Melissa Howe (1984: 14) summarizes the results of these by saying that 'musically naive listeners often construct groups on the basis of meaningful musical material found in the immediate features presented, whereas trained musicians tend to classify, using formal networks into which they place the immediate features.' In other words, non-musicians' perceptions are less influenced by the structural context than musicians'.[9] Moreover, the distinction between an essentially surface-orientated grasp of music, and one in which surface features are interpreted in relation to their structural context, is clearly implicated in the reading of music, which it is probably fair to regard as the foundational skill of our contemporary musical culture; as Sloboda says, 'good sight readers are particularly attuned to important superordinate structures within a score, structures that link notes together in musical groups. They organize their perception and performance in terms of discovering these higher order groupings, with consequential economy of coding.' (1984: 231.) Indeed, he goes as far as to

---

[8] Bamberger's experiments (1976: 238), in which listeners proved able to distinguish performances that used Beethoven's fingerings from others, might appear to contradict this. But this would not in fact be the case unless the performances using modern fingerings were specifically intended to reduplicate the interpretation suggested by Beethoven's fingerings.

[9] Deliège (1987: 338–9) presents further empirical evidence that supports this; see also Pollard-Gott 1983: 73.

comment in another context (1982: 482) that 'In general, what we would call "musicianship" seems to entail the ability to mobilize the higher, more abstract levels in a wide variety of circumstances.'

I have discussed the issue of piano fingering at some length because it is a representative example of the type of knowledge that is embodied in the production of music but hardly, if at all, implicated in its reception, at least in the case of the untrained listener. Obviously, one need know nothing about fingering in order to derive aesthetic interest and enjoyment from listening to Beethoven's piano sonatas. In the same way, it is not necessary to have a reflective (that is, 'theoretical') knowledge of the patterns of grouping and hierarchical organization that are appropriate to a given musical style, essential though an understanding of these may be in terms of production. Now this is of course equally true in the case of language. Natural language users may have no reflective awareness of the syntactical organization of their language. Nevertheless they have an internalized knowledge of this organization; the structural units of syntactical theory are, to some degree at least, psychologically real in the sense of corresponding to the perceptual processes involved in speech perception (Swain 1986: 126).

This has been verified by a number of experimental methods, among which are the so-called 'click tests'. In these tests, subjects listen to recordings of speech, on each of which an audible click has been superimposed at some point; the subjects are asked to say at which point they have heard each click. When clicks occur at the boundaries between coherent syntactical or semantic units—such as phrases of four or five words—subjects generally locate them correctly. But when they occur in the course of a unit, the clicks appear to migrate perceptually to boundary points between units, and this is clear evidence for the psychological reality of the units. Now similar click tests have been carried out with regard to musical perception (Sloboda and Gregory 1980; Stoffer 1985), and the results again indicate the psychological reality of short phrases, based for instance on a single chord or a simple cadential progression. Other experiments (see Sloboda 1985: 189–90 and Hantz 1982: 64–7) suggest that such phrases also play a role in memory organization, and Deutsch (1982b: 304–11) has outlined a hierarchical model of how this may work.[10] Furthermore, Irène Deliège (1987) has carried out a series of tests showing that the manner in which listeners hear music as being divided into small-scale segments corresponds quite well to the music-theoretical predictions of Lerdahl and Jackendoff.

At first sight all these results might seem to demonstrate a general correspondence between the perceptual processes that take place when people listen to music and the manner in which music theorists rationalize the structure of music. But there are two points that need to be made. The first is that in all these experiments except Deliège's, the subjects were musically trained; in fact notational skills were directly involved in the subjects' reponses to Sloboda's and Gregory's, Stoffer's, and Deutsch's tests. In other words, these were people who had acquired a knowledge of the patterns of grouping appropriate to Western music, and the ability to co-ordinate this knowledge with what they heard, through precisely the kind of instrumental training I have described; therefore what these experiments revealed is not necessarily representative of what happens in the ordinary way when people listen to music. Indeed, a similar test of the memorization of rhythmic groups showed striking differences between the responses of trained and untrained listeners. Sloboda (1985: 188) comments that this study shows

not only the importance of relatively abstract underlying patterning in determining memory for rhythm, but also the fact that the use made of such patterning depends upon musical experience. This reminds us of the generally applicable, but sometimes overlooked, fact that many aspects of the ability to deal with music are crucially dependent on musical experience.

Deliège, however, did test musically untrained listeners, as well as trained ones; she found that in general both groups performed in accordance with music-theoretical predictions, though trained listeners were considerably more reliable in this regard. But (and this is the second of the points I referred to) Deliège's tests may not have been ecologically valid as a means of obtaining information about how people listen to music in the ordinary way. Her subjects were given sheets on which each note of the music they heard was

[10] For a critique of Deutsch's hierarchical model see West, Howell, and Cross (1985: 26–8).

shown by a dot; they had to indicate the segments into which the music fell. But of course this meant that they were listening to the music in something very different from a normal manner. Deliège's results indicate that Lerdahl's and Jackendoff's theoretical model has some psychological reality as regards the manner in which listeners divide a visual representation of music into segments when asked to do so; how far it has psychological reality as regards ordinary musical listening is another matter.

It would be surprising if there were not some degree of correspondence between the perceptual processes involved in normal musical listening and the productional categories that form the basis of most theorizing about music. But the extent of the correspondence is clearly limited. Even if the small-scale segments on which the click tests are based do have some degree of psychological reality for the listener under normal circumstances, we cannot assume the same of large-scale formal units: I demonstrated this in Chapter 1. And in any case there are other aspects of music's productional structure—such as fingering—that do not correspond in any direct manner to what the listener perceives. To this extent, then, one can speak of a quite drastic asymmetry between production and reception in music. What I want to show next is how this asymmetry is embodied in the very means by which musicians imagine sound as music.

2.2 IMAGINING MUSIC

I

What makes a musician a musician is not that he knows how to play one instrument or another, or that he knows how to read music: it is that he is able to grasp musical structure in a manner appropriate for musical production—the most obvious (though of course by no means the only) example of such production being performance. As I explained in the preceding section, the educational importance of fingering derives from the fact that it is one of the strategies pianists have at their disposal for knowing a piece of music in a productional sense: that is, it is one of the ways in which they formulate productionally adequate cognitive representations of musical structure, or—to use a philosophical rather than a psychological term—it is one of the means by which they imagine the music that they play. My purpose in this section is to clarify the nature of the specifically musicianly ways of grasping music of which fingering is an example, and a convenient way to do this is to trace their emergence in the individual as he attempts to imagine (or represent) musical sounds in an increasingly production-orientated manner. Though there is a certain amount of empirical material that can be brought to bear upon this, much of what follows is introspective or even anecdotal in nature; but the reader is invited to validate, or refute, what is said by checking it against his own experience.

It is a common enough experience among musicians and non-musicians alike to get a familiar tune 'on the brain'. This just happens: it is not a matter of voluntary recollection, and indeed it can be annoyingly difficult to get the tune 'off the brain' again. How does a tune present itself to someone under these circumstances? Here is an example: I am reading a novel when I realize that for some time I have been 'hearing'[11] a passage from Allegri's *Miserere* (Ex. 22).[12] But this 'hearing' is very different from what it would be like to hear the music in real life, for instance if someone suddenly switched on a radio in the next room. In particular its temporal aspect is different, for there is a kind of static quality in the image that is quite alien to the world of real, audible music. The music does not seem to progress from bar to bar in strict tempo: rather, it is focused on a single point in time, namely the high note sung by the boy soprano just before the melody falls to its melismatic cadence (bars 3–4 in Ex. 22). But it is hard to describe this experience adequately in terms of our ordinary, perceptually orientated vocabulary for music. It is not as if the phrase were repeating itself over and over again like a record player with a stuck needle, or as if the boy's high note were being sustained indefinitely like the sound of an organ with a jammed key: for though my image of the music is centred upon that note, I grasp it as being already imbued with the melodic descent that follows it in the score. That is to say, the temporal evolution of the phrase as a whole forms an essential part of my imaginative experience of the

[11] By the inverted commas I mean that this is an imaginative perception, not a real one; this usage, discussed e.g. by Ryle (1973: 233), is widespread in common language as well as in professional discourse.

[12] Ex. 22 shows the passsage as it is generally performed, incorporating Alfieri's and Rockstro's *abbellimenti* (melodic elaborations).

Ex. 22

boy's high note, even though the experience itself does not seem to change from one moment to the next, or at least not in the same manner as the real, audible music does.

The difficulties that emerge as one attempts to frame these imaginative experiences in terms of a perceptually orientated vocabulary arise from the discrepancies between the ways in which music presents itself to the inner and, so to speak, the outer ear. Consider, as a further illustration of this, what it would be like to have the passage from the first movement of Bruckner's Ninth Symphony shown in Ex. 23 on the brain. Speaking personally, I find that my image of the music is centred round two main points: the C♯s of the main melodic line in the first two bars of the passage, which are coloured by the supporting motion from tonic to mediant major harmony; and the strangely unstable E major chord in the fourth bar of this passage, which forms the summit of the

Ex. 23

arch-shaped contour of the melody, and which I 'hear' both in relation to the A major region in which the passage begins (with its implied D♮s) and the E major–B major region in which it ends (with its D♯s). For me these two characteristic points in the music embody the motion of the passage as a whole in much the same sense as the focal point of a landscape painting subsumes its overall composition, and if I wish I can focus my attention on one or the other of these points, just as I can look at one place in the painting or another; but in the passive state of awareness that constitutes having the music on the brain, it is as if I am aware of both these points at once; or perhaps it would be more accurate to say that the passage as a whole presents itself to me from the perspectives of both these points at the same time.

This makes no more sense in real-life terms than it does to see a physical object from different perspectives at the same time. In imagination, however, as in Cubist paintings, such things can be readily accomplished. Jean-Paul Sartre, whose book *The Psychology of the Imagination* is the classic study of imagination as a mode of consciousness, offers an example that bears upon this. Imagine, he says (1972: 105), a thimble. Your image will probably incorporate a visual awareness of the back of the thimble as well as its front, its inside as well as its outside. In the imagination these different aspects coincide with each other, whereas in real life it is necessary to alternate between different viewpoints. In other words, the imagination synthesizes within a single awareness contents which in the real world are incompatible with each other; it presents not simply a series of visual aspects of the thimble, but rather the integration of these into an experienced whole.[13] And

[13] 'What is successive in perception is simultaneous in the image: and this could not be otherwise, since the object as an image is given at once by all our intellectual and affective experience.' (Sartre 1972: 106.)

this explains the sense in which an object can appear to the imagination with a kind of fullness and completeness—one almost wants to say, a kind of reality—that it lacks in ordinary perception. Iser comments on something like this in reading:

When we imagine Tom Jones, during our reading of the novel, we have to put together various facets that have been revealed to us at different times—in contrast to the film, where we always see him as a whole in every situation. . . . In imagining the character, we do not try to seize upon one particular aspect, but we are made to view him as a synthesis of all aspects. The image produced is therefore always more than the facet given in one particular reading moment. (1978: 138.)

Hence the sense in which the character in the book seems more convincing, more vividly real, than the one in the film.

Much the same applies to music. There can be something peculiarly compelling about the kind of musical images I have described; it is as if what is heard sequentially in the concert-hall were distilled into a single, heightened experience that embodies everything that is characteristic of the music, and this is an experience which is available to anybody, regardless of their level of musical training. At the same time, there is something illusory about this sort of musical experience, and in general about music as it presents itself to the imagination. This becomes evident if one considers what can happen when someone who lacks any musical skills has an image of full, complete music which he wants to realize in actual sound. He tries to pick out the notes on a piano: but either he cannot find the notes at all, or when he has found them, they appear awkward, abrupt, and impersonal. Actually something of the sort can on occasion happen even to the trained musician: one thinks up a tune and begins to write it down, only to find that there are impossible transitions between notes, or that basic compositional decisions have not been made and are required in the course of getting the music down on paper. Or a performer may start to write out the score of a familiar piece for a pupil, only to discover that in fact he does not know how it goes: as Kirkpatrick comments,

How easy it is for us in a dreamlike state to think that we can remember a piece or a set of ideas. How embarrassing it is in full consciousness to discover that we have only the haziest vague outline instead of what we thought was a precise and fully worked-out conception. (1984: 109.)

In all these cases the image seems to embody a full and complete musical awareness; it seems as if all one has to do in order to bring the music into reality is to attend closely to one's image of it, that the details of the music will emerge under inspection in the same way that the details of an Elizabethan miniature emerge as one examines it under a magnifying glass. But when it comes to testing that awareness against reality, whether by playing it or writing it down, the musical image turns out to be incompletely formed or even to represent a kind of deception.

In his book, Sartre identifies this phenomenon and calls it the 'illusion of immanence'. He explains it as follows. Imagine, he says (1972: 100–1), the Pantheon. You may have a clear visual image of it, including its columned portico; but can you count the columns? You can choose to 'see' it as having three columns, or five or six, but how many columns were there in your original image? The question is, of course, unanswerable, because the image did not contain a set number of columns as such at all: rather, it embodied a generic property—we might call it 'many-columnedness'—which constituted one of the aspects in which the Pantheon presented itself to you. Again, Sartre's argument, while expressed in terms of visual imagery, applies equally well to images of music. Imagine the sound of Dietrich Fischer-Dieskau's voice. And now try to answer the following questions: were you imagining him singing piano or forte? What syllable was he singing? Was he singing the beginning of a note, the middle, or the end? It is, of course, possible to imagine Fischer-Dieskau singing something that has all these attributes—maybe bar 12 of a particular Schubert song—and yet it is equally possible (and perhaps more natural) to imagine simply Fischer-Dieskau's singing. In such a case one is imagining the mellowness of his voice, the particular emphasis of his articulation, and so forth, but not specific, perceptible sounds that embody these qualities. In other words, the image is at least in part a generic one.

Normally the generic properties of musical images do not reveal themselves as such: they are, so to speak, subsumed within the specific music that is being imagined. There is, however, a situation in which these generic properties are thrown into relief, and this is the musical equivalent of having a word 'on the tip of the tongue': that is, when one has a clear sense of a particular tune one is trying to recollect—one is specifically aware, so to speak, of its absence—but cannot for the time being bring it into consciousness as a series of notes. In what, then, does this specific sense of the tune lie? To take an example from personal experience, I remember trying to recall the Dance of the Reed Flutes from Tchaikovsky's 'Nutcracker' Suite (Ex. 24). Though I could not at first remember a single note of the tune, I had a vivid sense of its luxuriant but light orchestration, of its graceful harmony, of the airy kinaesthetic quality of its rhythm, even of the pirouette-like figure at the end of the first melodic phrase. All these, then, presented themselves to me not as being subsumed within the specific music of the Dance of the Reed Flutes, but as fragmented aspects of my image of the music. They were not sound-images possessing certain generic properties, but rather generic images which for the time being had become divorced from the specific sounds with which they were associated in my mind and which provided their common focus.

But when a few moments later the tune came back to me, these fragmented images disappeared, and I was no longer aware of the music's generic properties of luxuriance, grace, and so on; the music simply presented itself to me as the particularly experienced sequence of sounds that I know as the Dance of the Reed Flutes. And as such I experienced it as possessing all those specifics, not only of melody but also of harmony and orchestration, that give

Ex. 24

rise to the qualities of luxuriance and grace. Yet though I know the tune well enough to be able to whistle it, in reality I only have a vague and hazy knowledge of the harmony and orchestration; I can sit down at the piano and play something that is recognizable as the Dance of the Reed Flutes, to be sure, but the chords I play are not quite what Tchaikovsky wrote, and indeed I may have to play it through two or three times before settling on a harmonization that seems adequate to me. But in that case what were those graceful harmonies that I was 'hearing' as I imagined the music? And what were those luxuriant orchestral sounds? The answer, of course, is that, to some extent at least, I was not actually imagining graceful harmonies at all, or luxuriant orchestral sounds; what I was imagining was the harmonic gracefulness and orchestral luxuriance of the music Tchaikovsky wrote. In other words, I had settled comfortably back into the illusion of immanence.

The inadequacies of the generic images of music that I have described emerge as they are pressed into service for productional purposes; at the keyboard the illusion of immanence is revealed in the incoherence of what is played, while at the desk it is revealed in the composer's indecision as he tries to figure out just what it was that he imagined. Indeed, the productional inadequacy of this kind of imagery is perhaps revealed in the way people sing or whistle as they work, or in the bath; inane repetitions, absurdly exaggerated vibrato and rubato, abrupt changes of key, odd swoops and glides, and a general lack of clear articulation all become audible under such circumstances to anyone who happens to overhear them. Such music, if it can be so called, is not intended for listening to: people characteristically sing like this only when they think they are not being observed, or when they are absorbed in what they are doing.[14] What is heard by someone who overhears such singing possibly corresponds to the specifically auditory component of the kind of musical imagery I have described: what he cannot hear are the generic, subjective qualities of the sound as it presents itself to the singer's imagination. And unfit for the listener's ear as this kind of music-making may be, it does represent one of the principal modes of musical consciousness, in that people spend a lot of time singing or whistling in this manner, or simply imagining music in

---

[14] Dowling (1984: 161–2) observed that his children generally sang like this only when they thought they were alone.

silence—more time, perhaps, than they spend in actually listening to it. (Or have ghetto-blasters and Walkmans changed all this?)

In a way it would be better to describe such activity as fantasizing or day-dreaming than as imagining, because it lacks the creative quality that has generally been associated with imagination since the time of Coleridge's writings on the subject. Musical imagery such as I have described is uncreative to the extent that it does not distinguish between what is possible in the real world of intersubjectively perceived sound and what is not. For example, I can imagine a piece of four-part harmony in which the top two parts cadence in C major, and the bottom two in G major, but in which the overall effect is perfectly harmonious in a traditional tonal sense. But I cannot play such a passage! In real life the tonal conflict between the upper and lower parts destroys any harmonious quality that the passage might otherwise have as a whole; whereas when I imagined the passage, I grasped the lines in terms of a generic quality, that of harmoniousness, which I simply imposed upon them.[15] My freedom to 'hear' the passage as being harmonious or not is the freedom of uncontrolled subjectivity, a freedom to impose or combine any experienced musical effects regardless of the possibility of their intersubjective realization.

But the creative imagination in music—that is to say, imagination as part of the music-productional enterprise—is directed towards what can be realized in perceptible sound; and so it embodies types of imagery which fulfil specifically productional roles, and which require of the individual some degree of specifically musical training.

II

When musicians imagine musical sounds they make use of images that derive from sensory modes other than the auditory, but which are co-ordinated with auditory effects in a more or less predictable

---

[15] 'Two colours . . . which in reality possess a certain discordant relationship, can exist together in imagery without any sort of relationship between them. Objects exist only in so far as they are thought of. This is what all those who consider the image to be a reborn perception fail to understand. The difference is not that of vividness but rather that the objects of the world of images can in no way exist in the world of perception: they do not meet the necessary conditions.' (Sartre 1972: 8.) Sartre called this the phenomenon of quasi-observation.

manner. These images have specific production-orientated content, but they never embody more than some partial aspect of the intended musical experience.

As in the case of having the Dance of the Reed Flutes 'on the tip of the tongue', such imagery is in general not directly experienced as such, because it is subsumed within the experience of the imagined music. But again there are situations where this integration of image and intended experience is disrupted, so that the imagery is thrown into relief. An example of such a situation is when one tries to imagine one piece of music while hearing another. To take a concrete example, suppose that someone who knows the piece is asked to recall the opening of Debussy's *Danseuses de Delphes* (from Book 1 of the *Préludes*; Ex. 25) while

Ex. 25

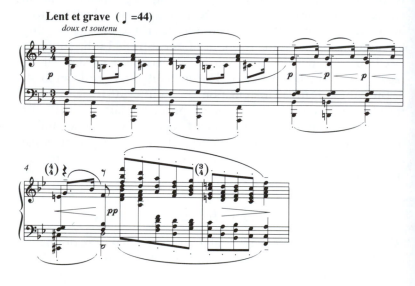

Liszt's B minor Sonata is being played on the radio. There is a problem of interference here: as every musician knows, and as experimental studies have confirmed (Sloboda 1982: 488–9), auditory recall of a given music stimulus is inhibited in the presence of a second stimulus whose structure is incompatible with that of the first. As a result of this interference effect, a listener who has no musical training is likely to find the request to recall one piece while listening to another more or less unintelligible: he may be able to visualize Michelangeli playing it, or recall such generic features as whether it was fast or slow, lyrical or dramatic, but that is not the same as being able to recall the music as such. But for a trained keyboard player who knows how to play *Danseuses de Delphes*, the request is by no means unintelligible; in the course of informal experiments I have found it quite possible to recall the Debussy piece while listening to Liszt, or even to play it on a silent keyboard. To be sure, this involves a certain effort of will, and in my silent performances I find a tendency to lose the thread of the music between phrases; but it can be done.

In what does this recollection consist, if the actual sound of the Liszt is inhibiting my auditory awareness of the Debussy? It may be in some degree visual; but mainly it is kinaesthetic, for even if I have no keyboard at hand it is through consciously focusing on the fingers and hands and arms that I recapture Debussy's music—through focusing on the second finger of the right hand straining to bring out the melody, on the spread of the hands to take the octaves, on the outward movement of the arms through the first bar and their lift-off before the second. And with this kinaesthetic image of the music comes something of the tensional quality, the dynamic ebb-and-flow of the original, so that what is evoked is at least to some minimal degree a musical experience rather than simply a sequence of stereotyped action schemes.

A great deal of the productional imagery employed by musicians is kinaesthetic in origin. Some has its source in the synaesthetic connectedness of music and dance or—if this means something different—in the complementary ways in which common patterns of tension and release can be expressed in the modalities of sound and bodily motion; the overt dance that the conductor performs in front of the orchestra has its invisible analogue in the imagined dance of the keyboard player for whom, in Kirkpatrick's words (1984: 86), 'rhythm only comes to life through transmutation into imaginary movement.' Though such imagery represents only a single aspect of the musical experience (a clear recollection of the kinaesthetic quality of a piece may not help the concert pianist who has suddenly forgotten its first few notes), it can do so with a kind of focused precision that is otherwise hard to achieve; one of Kirkpatrick's basic teaching principles can be summarized in the injuction, 'If you don't know how to play a piece, then dance it.' But the most important source of the musician's kinaesthetic imagery is vocal or instrumental performance. And because the voice and the various instruments give rise to very different manners of representing music imaginatively, it is worth considering a few of these in some detail.

Don Ihde has decribed the role of what he calls 'inner speech' as the constant companion to human consciousness, appearing, for instance, in the 'voice of conscience', and the more noticeable in its silence when some shock or novel experience leaves one 'speechless' (1976: 144). Sometimes this inner speech forms itself into actual words that can readily be spoken aloud or written down; at other times it creates the impression of being verbally constituted, but when one tries to frame what one is thinking in actual words one finds that the words are not yet formed. That is to say, inner speech can range from the perceptual condition of real words to the purely imaginative condition in which it presents itself not as words but in terms of a generic quality of verbosity. Now what one might call 'inner singing' plays an equally foundational role for the musician, who almost inevitably grasps any kind of melodic formation, at least if it is of a lyrical nature, as being to some degree framed in terms of the imagery of song. Like the inner voice of speech, such imagery may vary from the essentially perceptual to the purely imaginative. Reading the score in a library, without a piano at hand and unable to sing out loud without drawing unfavourable attention upon myself, I strain to grasp the sound of Schoenberg's Four Orchestral Songs: I can sense the virtual (or even, on occasion, actual) tensing and relaxing of my throat muscles as the vocal line soars to a high note or plunges to a low one, and though to read the music in this manner is not to hear it as it would sound in real life, it does allow me to capture something of the melody's expresssive character. Here my 'inner singing' approaches the condition of the real singing voice, as it does also when I effortlessly 'think' a folksong through to myself in no particular key. When, by contrast, I think through a fugue, I necessarily have a sense of its being in a particular key; and this is not something that is given in the imagery of the voice, but something whose basis lies in the kinaesthetic or visual imagery— the imagery of the keyboard or score—without which I would be unable to grasp the specific nature of the music's multiple lines.

Nevertheless I still grasp these lines in terms of the vocal quality of their melodic shaping; vocal imagery, in other words, is still present but it is now more distantly removed from the conditions of the physical voice.

This imaginative vocalization is a deeply entrenched element in musicians' productional engagement with sound. In the eighteenth century C. P. E. Bach spoke of the need for all musicians 'to hear truly skilled singers; in doing so, one learns to think singingly, and one would do well thereafter to sing a phrase himself in order to come upon the proper performance of the same'.[16] This advice remains as pertinent now as it was when it was written. Kirkpatrick (1984: 49) begins his discussion of melody in J. S. Bach's *Well-Tempered Clavier* with, as he expresses it, a 'eulogy of the human voice', in the course of which he states:

If there is any shortcut for achieving a feeling for every aspect of harmony and tonality, as well as for melody, it is the ability to sing every note of a piece. . . . Not only does the vocal approach, the ability to sing every note, furnish an inside track into the very essence of any music with which one is dealing, but it provides a tremendous aid to the musical memory. . . . If anything on an off night can bring one back when one has had lapses of concentration, it is that blind animal homing sense that dogs have, and birds, and people who sing the notes of pieces they play.

David Sudnow (1978: 149–50), in his extraordinary phenomenological study of jazz piano improvisation, speaks in similar terms of the security that comes from a vocal awareness of what one is playing, as well as of its indispensability in eliciting and reinforcing the same kind of improvisational fluency at the keyboard that the accomplished speaker displays in the lecture theatre:

How am I taking my fingers to places, for it makes good sense for this I to speak that way (I reach for a cup just there, ready-set-go, now I move my arm there), and singing in perfect concert? How do I know what the next notes will sound like as a joint knowing of voice and fingers, going there together, not singing along with the fingers, but singing with the fingers? A speaking I is struck by the awesomeness of an altogether new coupling, a new hookup, a new organization between my vocalizations and my fingerings. . . . I take my fingers to places so deeply 'mindful' of what they will sound like that I can sing *at the same time.*

---

[16] See Bach trans. 1949: 151. This trans., however, is taken from Kalib 1973: ii, 57. Cone (1974: 121) quotes and discusses a similar remark by Schumann; see also his comments on the 'inner voice' (p. 157).

One can sometimes actually hear a similar kind of *sotto voce* singing in the playing of jazz musicians, and in other types of music too. The *kora* players of The Gambia, for instance, such as Amadu Bansang Jobarteh, can be heard to sing a kind of essentialized melodic version of what they are playing. It was also one of Glenn Gould's eccentricities to sing quite audibly while he played, as his recordings testify.[17]

But of course no jazz musician (or *kora* player, or Glenn Gould) can literally sing everything he plays: what is sung, or what is imagined to be sung, is a vocal metaphor for what is played, its accompaniment in the same sense that inner speech is the accompaniment of everyday actions. And so this musicianly singing in the imagination may be at some considerable remove from the music that is actually sounded: an especially clear example of this is the so-called 'inner melody', or *lagu*, of Javanese music, which is 'a continuous, smoothly flowing, multi-octave melody a Javanese musician hears in a piece, but which no one instrumentalist or vocalist renders. Rather . . . [the musicians] fashion or realize the melody of their part by co-ordinating their inner melody with stereotyped patterns associated with each particular instrument.'[18] And it is perhaps not going too far to see in the products of Schenkerian analysis the revelation of a vocal sensibility in Western tonal composers—that is to say, an approach to sound in terms of conjunct, directed melodic motion within a relatively narrow tessitura—that has been transferred from the perceptual level of the musical surface to the imaginative level of large-scale musical organization.[19]

What are the structural characteristics of the voice as a means of representing music imaginatively? To grasp a passage of music in vocal terms is to have a fine awareness of its tensional morphology as arrayed in a continuum from low to high. But the fact that it presents the dimension of pitch as a continuum means that the vocal awareness is far from complete as a representation of music's tensional morphology. For instance, in the world of audible

---

[17] Gould said about this, 'I don't know how anyone puts up with my singing, but I do know that I play less well without it.' (ed. 1987: xiii.)

[18] Vetter 1981: 206. Much the same applies to the *shōga* of Japanese *gagaku* music (Shono 1987: 20–3) and to the 'reference melody' of Central African pygmy music (Arom 1976: 491).

[19] See below, pp. 194–5. Schenker himself hinted at this (trans. 1979: 98–9).

sounds a melody that cadences on the tonic may create an experience of resolution, even though this tonic is an octave higher than the one with which the melody began. That is, the resolving of tension may be accomplished through harmonic means, and in terms of harmonic structure two pitches an octave apart are equivalent to each other. But in itself the vocal sense knows nothing of the octave: octave equivalence is not given in the physiological constitution of the voice, but is rather a psycho-acoustical attribute imposed upon the voice in the course of singing. Again, the structure of a vocal awareness of music is only to some limited degree operational (in Piaget's sense). In other words, while vocal imagery presents successive movements of pitch with great accuracy—from C to C♯ is one thing, from C to D is something quite different—it does not reinforce such relationships at a structural level. Purely in terms of vocal imagery, a tune that moves from C through ten successive intervals back to C will be hardly distinguishable from one that moves from C to D♭; the vocal awareness of absolute pitch values, though it exists (clearly, notes can be sensed vocally as being in a high or low register), is by no means fine enough to permit distinctions of a semitone. In consequence, the distinction between a melody that remains centred on C and a melody that moves from a C centricity to a D♭ one—which is a crucial distinction in musical terms—is not one that is reinforced by vocal imagery.

Imagery derived from woodwind instruments, on the other hand, makes good both these deficiencies in the vocal awareness of music—that is, as regards the equivalence in certain respects of notes an octave apart, and the conservation of pitch identity. With the exception of the clarinet (which overblows at the twelfth), the fingering for, say, a C in the middle of a woodwind instrument's range is much the same as the fingering for the C an octave above (typically the higher note will require the additional depressing of an octave key, or may simply need blowing harder). If then as an oboist I employ oboe-based imagery in 'thinking' a melody—which simply means that I imagine playing it on an oboe—my imagery represents the two Cs as being related to one another: I experience the melody's upward motion away from the lower C as being also, in another sense, a return when the melody cadences on the higher C. Moreover, when I play a phrase that begins and ends on the same note, my imagery reinforces the identity of starting-

and finishing-point, even in the case of a very extended musical passage in which the identity of the first and last notes may have no perceptual reality for the listener. In such an instance—and music is full of such instances—the means of representing musical structure is giving rise to a coherence whose existence is not perceptual, in the sense of what the listener hears, but imaginary: it is a productional coherence and not (if the word can be tolerated) a receptional one.

The essence of the instrumental (as opposed to vocal) awareness of musical sound is that the dimension of pitch height is presented not as a continuum but as a series of discrete values, each of which corresponds to a distinct position or motion of the hand. This is why patterns such as scales or arpeggios, which are permutations of discrete pitches, are represented much more readily through instrumental than through vocal imagery; though it is of course possible to sing such patterns, they tend to create the slightly disagreeable impression that the voice has been forced into an instrumental mould, especially at fast tempos. In this way different media of musical performance—the voice, the various instruments—favour different types of musical organization. The guitar, for instance, is perfectly capable of accommodating quite intricate contrapuntal textures, as Segovia's Bach transcriptions demonstrate; nevertheless the basic manner in which the player engages physically with the instrument, and in particular the division of the hands into the distinct functions of pitch specification (left hand) and rhythmic articulation (right hand), is such as to favour an essentially homophonic approach to musical texture. The prevailingly homophonic construction of pop music, which was dominated by the guitar until quite recently, thus reflects a basic imaginative orientation among its players rather than the literal constraints of what can be achieved in guitar technique.[20]

If the physical engagement between the guitar and its player constitutes one of the basic structural determinants of pop music, then keyboard instruments (first the harpsichord, then the piano) have fulfilled a similar role in relation to the art music of the last three hundred years or more; and the reason for this is to be found not so much in the particular acoustic properties of these

---

[20] A detailed discussion of the imaginative orientation that arises from playing the guitar, and its possible influence on Berlioz's musical style, may be found in Rushton 1983: 56–60.

instruments as in their fecundity as a source of compositionally useful kinaesthetic imagery. For instance, when someone plays a keyboard instrument, each of his hands is a self-sufficient sound-producing agent, which is not the case in playing the guitar; this reinforces and facilitates the playing of both textures based on two equal and similar musical elements (such as two–part linear counterpoint) and those made up of unlike components such as the passage shown in Ex. 26,[21] with its lyrical melody in 3/4 set against

Ex. 26

a homophonic, repeated–chord accompaniment in 9/8. Again, there is a distinction in keyboard playing between the motions of the hand and those of the fingers, which is of considerable significance for the imaginative representation of music. To play an arpeggio on the oboe, on which the hands have no function as distinct from the fingers, is simply to play a sequence of notes; there is no sense in which the chord that is being arpeggiated is presented as an immediate Gestalt. (Ex. 27 indicates this by means

Ex. 27

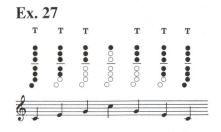

[21] From Mendelssohn's *Song without Words* Op. 53 No. 2.

of a notation in which filled-in circles denote holes that are covered by the fingers, while unfilled circles show holes that are not covered; 'T' indicates the thumb-plate.) But on the piano this arpeggio is played by means of moving the fingers within a single, sustained hand-position; the hand-position forms a physical analogue to the chord as a Gestalt, which is thereby distinguished from the arpeggiation constituted by the finger motions. In other words, the manner of the player's physical engagement with the keyboard is such as to present in kinaesthetic terms the distinction of harmonic structure from elaboratory figuration, which is a distinction of considerable importance for any kind of abstract understanding of music.

It is perhaps in the area of tonal structure that the keyboard is most outstandingly well adapted to function as, so to speak, a representational calculus of musical sounds. It is more or less equally easy to play in any key on keyboard instruments (some keyboard players will no doubt disagree with this statement, but the differences in difficulty between the various keys on keyboard instruments are negligible in comparison with those encountered on the woodwinds). But every key has its own 'feel'; the distinct location of each tonic on the keyboard in relation to the two-plus-three pattern of the black notes reinforces the identity of each key. At the same time, some keys are more closely associated with each other than others: in general, keys that are closely related in terms of the cycle of fifths have similar 'feels' to the player, which means principally that they share common fingering patterns through the relationship of their diatonic notes to the black-versus-white layout of the keyboard. This is a valuable reinforcement, musically speaking, because the relationship of keys according to the cycle of fifths is acoustically salient and, indeed, constitutes one of the fundamental principles of compositional structure in Western tonal music. Moreover, the exceptionally rich kinaesthetic imagery that keyboard instruments provide for representing musical structure is supplemented by the visual availability of the keyboard to the performer as he plays; whereas neither the woodwind player nor the guitarist can easily see what he is doing, the keyboard player has his entire scene of operations laid out before him, so that he can literally see where he is going in planning or executing some tonal manoeuvre. Even while working at his desk, then, the composer who has internalized the structure of the keyboard has access to a whole repertoire of kinaesthetic and visual representations for music—representations which are equally capable of reinforcing what is audible and of proposing structural relationships that in fact have no perceptual reality for the listener.

III

The productional imagery that musicians use is by no means restricted to the internalized performance actions which I have described. Another important source of imagery is notation and, more generally, the appearance of music on the printed page. For instance, when a pianist plays from memory, his knowledge of which section of an episodic piece comes next may be reinforced by his 'seeing' it as being half-way down the right-hand page; in the early stages of learning a piece it can be quite annoying to change editions and find that everything is in a different place from where one remembered it. Visual imagery is important at a more detailed level of musical organization, too. When a violinist plays a very rapid scale, for instance, an untrained listener may hear little more than a generalized rising or falling smear of sound, and indeed if the pitches that the violinist played were plotted by mechanical means it would very likely be found that the individual notes were not all cleanly articulated. But a trained musician will still hear the sound as a scale. In other words, he will have an imaginative awareness of it as a series of discrete pitches, and this is as likely to be constituted in visual terms (through the familiar look of a rapid scale on the page) as kinaesthetically. However, visual and kinaesthetic imagery may reinforce each other to such a degree—as in this case—that it becomes hard to disentangle the one from the other; each is deeply embedded in the musician's productional awareness of sound. In any case, my purpose in this section is not so much to provide an exhaustive account of the sources of this imagery as to analyse the structural means by which it gives rise to productionally adequate representations of music.

The account I have given of kinaesthetic imagery may prompt the following question: how can it be that the singer represents music one way, the pianist differently, and the woodwind player in yet another way, given that each is a participant in a more or less integrated musical culture—the culture, that is to say, of contemporary Western art music? It is of course true that a musician's practical experience does tend to influence his attitude to musical sound. Singers, for instance, tend to have a rather poorly developed harmonic sense; this can be seen in their habit of sight-singing by means of relative pitch rather than through grasping the music in terms of its harmonic structure, and the source of this lies very possibly in the lack of positive reinforcement of harmonic relations that the physiognomy of the voice supplies. (Some people would say it has to do with the general level of singers' musical education, too.) By contrast, pianists tend to have a better developed harmonic sense, but their awareness of melodic contour can be less refined, because the keyboard presents contour only in the gross motions of the hand as a whole; it is for this reason that piano teachers sometimes advise their students to practise playing a melody with one finger, in order to draw out its full expressive potential.[22] Pianists also tend to be insensitive to the dynamic moulding of individual notes that is second nature to wind players; this can become very obvious if, for example, an accomplished pianist starts to learn the recorder. On the other hand, people who play flutes and oboes tend to be 'treble-dominated'; they may encounter difficulties in moulding harmonically supportive bass-lines if they start to write music. And so on. But all of these are merely tendencies, which in any case the good vocal or instrumental teacher will strive to overcome: music teachers can frequently be heard to say that the aim of learning the clarinet (or piano, or trumpet) should not be simply to acquire facility on that instrument, but to acquire musicianship *through* it.[23] A singer who does not understand harmony is for that reason not only a poor musician, but also a less than accomplished singer; it is precisely in the existence of a common core of musicianship shared by singers, players of different instruments, and indeed composers and teachers, that contemporary Western art music finds its definition

[22] See e.g. Kirkpatrick 1984: 59.

[23] Much the same applies to the various techniques by which musical educators try to stimulate the development of productionally adequate representations for pitch structures in their students: movable-doh sol-fa, fixed-doh sol-fa, roman-numeral chord symbols, and figured bass are all employed for this purpose, and each gives rise to a different pattern of strengths and weaknesses. The weaknesses—the insensitivity to harmonic function of people trained in fixed-doh sol-fa, the insensitivity to counterpoint of people who think in terms of roman numerals, and so on—have to be overcome if this education is to be wholly successful, for in each case the aim is the same, i.e. the development of a general musicianship.

as a more or less integrated culture. And it is in being based on an essentially different type of musicianship—which means, more than anything else, a different repertoire of productional images for music—that jazz finds its cultural distinctness from Western art music, despite the fact that both use more or less the same instruments. More will be said on these matters in the final chapter of this book.

The reason why singers do not simply approach music as singers, pianists as pianists, and so on—the reason why singers and instrumentalists are able to approach music as musicians—is that their imaginative representations of musical structure are not monolithic. A pianist does not know a piece that he plays simply as a single, stereotyped sequence of action schemes; rather, he represents it through a multiplicity of images, each of which embodies some aspect of the intended whole, and which together converge in a productionally adequate manner upon the music that is to be played. In other words, a musician's knowledge of a piece of music is based upon a kind of analytical, or deconstructive, apprehension of it: to know a piece is in the first place to have grasped it as a multitude of separate aspects, and in the second place to be able to reconstruct it from these aspects in a manner that is adequate for the particular kind of production required; for in this sense it can be something quite different for a pianist to know a piece—he must be able to recall every note at the keyboard—from what it is for a conductor or a music analyst to know it.

In saying this I am following the general theory of memory coding set out by such psychologists as Peter Herriot, according to whom memory is best seen as a process consisting of initial deconstruction followed by subsequent reconstruction. Items to be remembered are grasped only to the extent that they have been analysed into a set of experienced aspects, or, as Herriot calls them, attributes: 'one cannot conceive of the item as presented being stored with a set of attributes or tags; rather, what is stored is a set of attributes from which the item may be reconstructed when required.' (1974: 46.) Under normal circumstances, that is to say when recall is successful, it is hard to discern the various stored attributes, or images, from which the item has been reconstructed. But the nature of the process that is involved may come to light when the attempt at recall is only partially successful. Some empirical data which have a bearing on memory coding for music, at least in a short-term context, are provided by Sloboda's and Parker's tests (1985) of immediate recall of melodies.

Sloboda and Parker played the Russian folksong shown in Ex. 28 to a number of subjects, of whom some were musically

Ex. 28

trained while others were not. The subjects were asked to sing back the tune as soon as it had finished; they were given six chances to hear the tune and sing it back. Ex. 29 shows one subject's six

Ex. 29

attempts to recall the song. The metrical framework of the song (that is, the four beats per bar) is present from the start; this was true with all the subjects, and so Sloboda and Parker conclude that 'metre is a primary structural frame for melodic comprehension and recall.' (p. 159.) Recall of some of the other important structural features of the song can be seen to improve over the first two or three attempts shown in Ex. 29: for instance, the diatonic scale within which the tune falls is hardly grasped at all in the first attempt, and only imperfectly in the second (observe in both of these the faulty intonation marked by small circles above the notes),[24] but it is recalled perfectly in the third attempt and maintained thereafter. Much the same applies to the song's formal organization. Essentially it consists of three phrases, each of two bars; the second phrase is a variant of the first one, while the final phrase is different, giving rise to a plan that may be represented as AA′B. Each of these phrases may in turn be divided into two more or less distinct sub-phrases, each about a bar long. The first attempt at recall shown in Ex. 29 embodies an awareness of the repetition of the first main phrase, and of its internal organization into two sub-phrases; but the tripartite organization of the song as a whole has not been grasped at all. In the second attempt, however, the overall organization is correct, except that the last sub-phrase has been abbreviated; by the third attempt this, too, has been rectified, and it remains correct in all the subsequent versions.

But there is one respect in which there is no improvement—indeed, rather the reverse—and this concerns the opening of the tune. In the original folksong the first main phrase essentially consists of a fall from A through G, F, and E to D, which is elaborated with notes of lesser structural importance so as to create a wave-like contour. All the attempts at recall shown in Ex. 29 retain the essentials of this contour, but in no case are its structural notes correctly represented. The initial attempt begins correctly, with an A, but loses direction thereafter. Subsequent attempts are correct as regards the motion of the phrase to D (at least, this is true from the third attempt onwards), but the first note is wrong: it is in each case not A but C, and the last four attempts show that this error is associated with the rising octave C–C, which in the original song comes only at the beginning of the third main phrase.

---

[24] The crosses indicate rhythmic approximations.

In this subject's recollection the first phrase also begins with the rising octave, with the result that the first and third phrases are identical to one another—which they were not in the original song. The rising octave, in other words, appears to have been coded individually rather than in its structural context; and the same is perhaps true of the repetition of the E, which in the original song appears at the beginning of bar 2, and which reappears in all this subject's versions from the second one on, but in very much altered rhythmic and melodic contexts.

Recall data such as these can at first sight be puzzling, suggesting as they do that when people listen to music they may not 'retain the contour, pitch ratios, or tonality of the original in any simple way. Rather, fragments of a melody are distorted and recombined in complex ways to make up a response that is often, on any simple analysis, quite unlike the original.' (Sloboda 1982: 485.) But as is frequently the case with musical phenomena, what appears incomprehensible when viewed simply as a surface configuration becomes more intelligible when seen in terms of some kind of distinction between underlying structure and elaboratory detail. Essentially, what appears to have happened during the sequence of recalls shown in Ex. 29 is that certain structural features of the original tune have been grasped by the listener and used as a framework within which to accommodate a number of more fragmentary details. In this instance the structural framework is more or less correct (though with some other subjects it was less so), but even so it manifests a characteristic on which Sloboda and Parker comment (1985: 156–7): the recalled structure tends to be simpler and more consistent than that of the original, as for example in the alteration of the final phrase so that it matches the first. All this means that the process of recall has involved an initial stage of deconstruction, in which various attributes of the original tune—some structural, others incidental—are extrapolated and stored; and a subsequent process of reconstruction, in which the stored aspects of the original are put together into some stylistically plausible whole. As Sloboda and Parker put it (p. 160), 'Recall involves processes akin to improvisation, which fill in structurally marked slots according to general constraints about what is appropriate to the piece or genre.'

It seems likely that the kind of memory processes that operate in immediate recall also operate in the longer-term memory that is

implicated in a pianist's 'knowing' a piece, though here it is harder
to come by adequate empirical data. As usual, the network of
complementary and inter-crossing imagery through which the
music presents itself to the musician is concealed in the seamless
continuity of successful performance; but as a piece begins to be
forgotten and its performance breaks up into relationally dislocated fragments, the structure of the performer's internal representation of the music will be revealed. There is in principle no reason
why an experimental investigation under controlled conditions
could not be made of the process by which performers forget
pieces; but in the current absence of such data I shall present some
informal observations that are at least indicative of what happens.

At one time I learned Debussy's *Danseuses de Delphes* so that I
could play it by heart; but after that some years passed during
which I neither played nor heard the piece. Deciding one day to try
and play it from memory, I sat at the piano and played what is
shown in Ex. 30.[25] The tonality, the phrase structure, and the entire

Ex. 30

left-hand part of the original have all been reproduced without
error. And in the first two bars the harmony is correct, too. What
has gone wrong is that the tune—which in Debussy's version is in
the inner line of the right-hand part—has migrated to a more
conventional place at the top of the musical texture, and has been
doubled in octaves. This has necessitated some adjustment to the
intervallic structure of the tune. In the original it is a series of
semitones rising through a minor third, from B♭ (part of the B flat
major harmony of the first beat) to C♯ (part of the augmented

---

[25] For Debussy's original see Ex. 25, p. 94 above.

harmony of the third beat); but in my version (which is rather crude and obvious in comparison with Debussy's) it has to rise through a major third, from F to A, in order to be consistent with the harmony. From this it is evident that I had coded these bars in terms of harmonic structure, and in terms of there being a chromatically rising dotted-note melody, but not in terms of the melody's precise intervallic values. A similar situation can be seen in bars 3–4. Here the problem is that the inner line of the right-hand part (D–E♭–E♮–F) has got out of kilter with the motion of the bass, producing harmonies that are, if not impossible in Debussian style, then at least a little unlikely, and—what is worse—resulting in a decidedly inelegant compositional situation on the second beat of bar 4, where the F of the B flat major harmony has been anticipated a beat earlier. In this case it appears that the specific harmonies were not coded (which is hardly suprising, since they have little coherence *qua* harmonies); instead what has been coded is the semitonal rise of the inner line, and the fact that it moves in tenths with the bass. What sort of tenths, however, has not been specified; I went wrong because I seized on the first opportunity to introduce them, so beginning the inner-line motion one beat too early.

Though clearly unsatisfactory, my version of these bars was viable; I was able to continue playing, and in due course arrived at bar 11. In Ex. 31, (*a*) shows what I played and (*b*) what Debussy wrote. Here my version retains the principal melodic line, at the top of the texture; but whereas Debussy is content to let the motion in the upper parts unfold over a sustained pedal-note in the bass, my version attempts to gild the lily, so to speak, by reflecting the upper line through contrary motion in the bass. It may be that I had specifically coded the C–D–E♭ motif of the parallel triads in the middle of the texture in Debussy's version, for it is this same motif that appears in transposition as my bass-line (F–G–A♭); but the result is that the harmonic pattern of the original is altogether lost, the harmonies of my version simply being a consequence of my bass-line. This time the error was fatal; though it would have been possible to find a viable musical continuation to what I played, the music ceased to be even an incorrect version of the original, and so the attempt at recollection failed.

Turning to my copy of the *Préludes*, I refreshed my memory of this bar and continued playing, only to break down again two bars

Ex. 31

later. Ex. 32 compares what I played (*a*) with what Debussy wrote (*b*). Again the top line has been recalled without error; and the rising stepwise parallel harmony has also been reproduced correctly, except that it has all been transposed up a fourth as against what Debussy wrote. The reason for this is that the bass has also been shifted up a fourth, from Debussy's F pedal to a B♮; but why should this have happened? The explanation lies in Sloboda's and Parker's observation that the structure of recall tends to be more consistent than that of the original music. Being aware of the fact that the melody of bar 13 is a transposition of that of bar 11, I quite logically (but, as it happens, wrongly) transposed the bass and the chord sequence along with it. And again no plausible continuation was possible; this time I gave up trying to remember the piece and played the rest of it from the music.

As Sloboda remarks, it is generally agreed by piano teachers that 'secure knowledge of a piece of music involves forming multiple representations of it'. (1985: 91.) That is to say, it is not enough simply to know a piece as a stereotyped action sequence, or as a series of individually known sections, or as a tune supported by harmony, or in terms of how it looks on the page. What is required is a tissue of intertwined, mutually reinforcing imagery; the

Ex. 32

security such a complex representation gives the performer is comparable to the strength of a length of rope made up of a large number of individually short and insubstantial fibres. My attempt at recalling *Danseuses de Delphes* indicates something of the nature of such images and the way in which they interact with each other, though of course it failed because too little of my original coding of the piece had survived the passage of the years; and it also makes clear the thin line that exists between recall as such and the kind of improvisation I was forced to indulge in as gaps appeared in my representation of the original music.

The distinction between recollection and improvisation is one of degree rather than one of kind; at any rate, it is evident that such aspects of recall at the keyboard as fingering (Sloboda 1985: 97) and expressive timing are in fact largely constructed in the real time of performance. As Clarke explains (1985: 233), speaking of performance from written music,

The expressive system must take a large number of varied factors into account when constructing an appropriate performance strategy. The system is undoubtedly generative, in the sense that an expressive profile is generated at the time of performance from stored information about stylistic conventions and particular expressive devices developed during rehearsal (if the performance is not sight-read), as well as from information processed during the performance itself. The non-random variability of performances testifies to the unmemorized nature of expressive strategies.

Precisely the same kind of information regarding what is structurally viable and stylistically probable is required in the process through which the stored attributes of a piece of music are reconstructed when that piece is performed from memory. Indeed, it can be coherently argued that the distinction between performance (in the sense of the authentic recreation of a pre-existing composition) and improvisation is not one that can be made in terms of psychological processes at all, but results purely from social and historical factors.[26] David Sudnow (1978: 53) remarks that the difference between the work of a jazz pianist and that of a classical pianist is that the latter

operates within a social organizaion of professional certification, excellence, and competitiveness differing from that which I was in, as a jazz aspirant, his circumstances placing extraordinary demands upon a faithfulness to the score, where what 'faithfulness' and 'the score' mean is defined by that social organization.

Psychologically speaking, both jazz and classical pianists are improvising, in the sense that they are creatively synthesizing performance schemes in the real time of performance; the difference is merely in the nature of the constraints within which this creativity operates.

I would also argue that there is a similar continuity between what it means to know a pre-existing piece of music, in the sense that I have described, and what it means to compose music. Schenker wrote that 'there is no doubt that the great composers— in contrast to performers and listeners—experienced even their most extended works . . . as entities which could be heard and perceived as a whole.' (trans. 1979: xxiii.) A number of statements by composers can be cited in support of this. Wagner, for instance, wrote in a letter of 1844:

Before I begin to write a single line of verse, or even to outline a scene, I

[26] On this see e.g. Nettl 1983: 27.

am already intoxicated by the musical aroma of my creation, I have all the notes, all the characteristic motives in my head, so that when the lines have been written and the scenes satisfactorily constructed, then so far as I am concerned the opera itself is already finished.[27]

But the most famous of these statements (Schenker quotes it in order to make his point) is the one that Johann Friedrich Rochlitz attributed to Mozart:

When I am, as it were, completely myself . . . my ideas flow best and most abundantly. *Whence* and *how* they come I know not, nor can I force them. Those ideas that please me, I retain in memory, and am accustomed, as I have been told, to hum them to myself. . . . All this fires my soul, and provided I am not disturbed, my subject enlarges itself, becomes methodized and defined, and the whole, though it be long, stands almost finished and complete in my mind, so that I can survey it, like a fine picture or a beautiful statue, at a glance. Nor do I hear in my imagination the parts *successively*, but I hear them, as it were, all at once. . . . When I proceed to write down my ideas, I take out of the bag of my memory, if I may use that phrase, what has previously been collected into it in the way I have mentioned. For this reason, the committing to paper is done quickly enough, for every thing is, as I said before, already finished; and it rarely differs on paper, from what it was in my imagination. (Schulz 1825: 199.)

And according to Louis Schlösser, Beethoven described his own compositional process in almost the same terms:

I carry my thoughts about me for a long time, often a very long time, before I write them down. . . . I change many things, discard and try again until I am satisfied. Then, however, there begins in my head the development in every direction and, in so much as I know exactly what I want, the fundamental idea never deserts me—it arises before me, grows—I see and hear the picture in all its extent and dimensions stand before my mind like a cast and there remains for me nothing but the labor of writing it down, which is quickly accomplished. (Thayer ed. 1921: iii, 126.)

The similarity of these last two accounts is striking. But its significance is undermined by the fact that both of them are

---

[27] Quoted in Westernhagen 1976: 9. According to Lobe (trans. 1897: 307), Gluck used to say much the same about his operas.

probably forgeries.[28] And, in Beethoven's case at least, the evidence of the sketch-books and autograph scores indicates that this is not, in any literal sense, what actually happened. The sketch-books demonstrate that a great deal of the work of elaboration was in fact done on paper, or at least with paper at hand; but it is the autograph scores that are particularly revealing in this regard.

The distinction between sketch-books and autograph scores, as Beethoven scholars draw it, is not one of format, nor is it necessarily based on the degree of detail in which the music is worked out (there are, after all, a few full-score sketches); essentially it is a matter of the purpose for which the manuscript was intended. As Lewis Lockwood puts it (1970a: 36), the autograph is 'designed from the beginning to be read by eyes other than the composer's—a condition that distinguishes it sharply from the sketches' (the eyes in question usually being those of one of Beethoven's copyists). That is, the autograph was a public document, not a private one; its purpose was to convey the finished work to the outside world. Accordingly, autograph scores give full titles of works, list the instruments at the beginning of the staves in an orchestral score and give their transpositions, and where necessary use letter names to clarify smudged or crossed-out notes—all features which were probably redundant from Beethoven's point of view (they rarely if ever appear in the sketch-books) but were required in order to make the score intelligible to anyone else. It is, then, part of the definition of an autograph score that it is intended to represent the final version of a work.

But there were many occasions on which Beethoven began writing an autograph score (so defined) at a stage when the work was still far from its final form, so that major compositional decisions had to be taken as the score progressed. To take one particularly well-documented example, the development section of the first movement of the Cello Sonata Op. 69 underwent massive revisions as Beethoven wrote out its autograph score (Lockwood 1970b); in brief, the roles of the cello and piano were

---

[28] See Solomon 1981. Solomon's main argument against the authenticity of Schlösser's account is that it is so similar to Rochlitz's as to be obviously a paraphrase of it. This argument is not quite conclusive, because Beethoven could himself have read the Rochlitz account; it was published in the *Allgemeine musikalische Zeitung* in 1815 (see Anderson 1961, ii: 517 for evidence that he was following the journal that year)—8 years before the conversation to which Schlösser refers. But it is hard to imagine Beethoven borrowing anybody else's words to describe his own compositional process.

exchanged, which involved almost totally recasting the entire section of nearly sixty bars. Beethoven clearly had no idea that this was going to happen when he began to write out the score; indeed, it appears that when he began to change the music he did not anticipate the extent of the revisions that were entailed, for he ended up writing the second version more or less on top of the first one, creating the most formidable problems of legibility as a result. As Lockwood says,

The manuscript shows that when Beethoven came to the stage of writing down this 'autograph' version of so richly complex a movement, he had not yet finally decided what the functional relationship of the two instruments would be throughout the entire middle section. Another way to put it is to say that it was only when he had written down one version of the development in this autograph that he saw how he really wanted the two instruments to be fitted together. (1970*a*: 38.)

The evidence of such autograph scores as this—and Op. 69 is by no means an isolated case, though it is one of the more extreme ones[29]—would then suggest that Beethoven's (or more probably Schlösser's) account of the work all being done in the head, with only the labour of writing it out remaining, was in fact quite unrealistic.[30]

However, it might be argued that to make such a judgement is to take undue notice of the superficial aspects of what was changed—and the consequent tangle of crossings-out and rewritings that is visible in the score—and too little notice of the underlying coherence that persists throughout such revisions. A

---

[29] Robert Winter comments (1982: 238) on the variations in Op. 101: 'the basic expressive stance of each variation had been achieved by the time the autograph was begun. At the same time, it is astonishing to have to concede that had different decisions been made during the writing down of this document, the resulting movement would—by the sheer cumulative force of the changes—have been quite different.' For other examples of Beethoven's beginning on an autograph score while important compositional decisions still remained to be made, see Lester 1970 and Kramer 1980. Possibly the most extreme example of this is the unfinished piano concerto of 1815, in which the distinction between sketch and autograph effectively breaks down (Lockwood 1971). Nor is it only in the case of Beethoven that such examples are to be found: Daniel Heartz (1980: 252) says of Mozart's autograph revisions in the quartet in Act III of *Idomeneo* that 'clearly, and amazing as it may seem, he was still composing the piece while writing it out in full score.'

[30] It certainly contradicts Beethoven's remark, in a (genuine) letter written in 1821 to A. M. Schlesinger, that 'I merely jot down certain ideas . . . and when I have completed the whole thing in my head everything is written down, but only once' (Anderson 1961: ii, 928). For a discussion of this whole issue see Tyson 1971, esp. p. 15.

specific example that supports this argument comes from the fugue of the Piano Sonata Op. 110, which I mentioned above.[31] Ex. 33 shows the whole of this passage as it appears in the published score; (a), (b), and (c) in Ex. 34 show three successive autograph versions of what in the final version, (c), are bars 107–10, and these are arranged in such a way that equivalent formations are as far as possible aligned vertically with one another.[32] Intuitively one can tell that these three different drafts are all versions of 'the same' music. But in what does their essential identity lie, given the fairly radical differences between them (especially in the earliest version, which has six bars where the later versions have four)?

In the first place—and this is part of the formal function of the passage in respect of the movement's overall structure—each version contains two statements of the fugal subject in stretto (the fugal subject is marked by square brackets in Ex. 33). The difference in this regard between the versions is that, as the vertical alignment of the three versions in Ex. 34 shows, while the first version retains the original note values in the fugal subject, the two later versions present it in diminution; and this is better, musically speaking, because the rhythmic compression enhances the effect of tensional increase as the music builds up to the climax at bar 110.

In the second place, all the versions embody more or less the same voice-leading structure at both the top and the bottom of the texture; but the outer parts of the three versions are aligned and elaborated in different ways. Ex. 34d represents this voice-leading structure as it appears in the final version.[33] In the two later versions, there is a continuous motion in the upper part from the initial E♭ to the highest note of the passage, A♭, whereas in the first version the A♭ appears, so to speak, from nowhere; as Schenker

---

[31] See above, pp. 78–9.

[32] Autograph versions (a) and (b) are transcribed in Schenker's *Erläuterungsausgabe* of Op. 110 (ed. 1972: 94). See also Bamberger's discussion (1976) of the evolution of this passage.

[33] For those not familiar with Schenkerian analytical techniques, it should be explained that the inclusion of a note in the graph indicates that it has a structural importance, and that notes in the graph are, as far as possible, vertically aligned with the original music. Notes joined by a slur constitute a single motion, and several such motions may be grouped together to form a larger one. Brackets indicate that a structural note is implied, but not actually present in the music. The roman numerals pick out the structural harmonies of the passage; everything else is considered as a linear elaboration of these. For further information on Schenkerian analysis see Forte and Gilbert 1982, Cook 1987a, or Dunsby and Whittall 1988.

Ex. 33

Ex. 34

puts it, it is only achieved 'ex machina' (ed. 1972: 94). The reason why the effect is mechanistic is that there is no real motivation for the upward leap from the C to the A♮ in this first version; the C is the end of the fugal subject and therefore does not lead strongly to the A♮ that follows. By contrast, the later versions do not keep literally to the fugal subject, but instead extend its sequential pattern so that it leads right up to the A♮; the result is that the tension keeps on building up, instead of dissipating as in the first version. As for the left-hand part, all three versions embody the same structural motion, from the low C up to A♮; and in the first two versions the elaboration of this is almost identical, despite the fact that the second version is two bars shorter than the first. However, in the final version the line is simplified, and the A♮ is reached sooner; the result of this is that bar 109—the bar before the structural dominant—begins with tonic harmony (the D♮ and F are passing-notes), instead of the passing dominant ninth harmony of the first two versions. This is a substantial improvement: since the whole passage is aiming strongly for the dominant seventh at bar 110, it is highly undesirable that its root be anticipated at the beginning of the previous bar.

Essentially, what is happening is that the two structural features shared by all three versions—the design of the passage as a fugal stretto, and its linear-harmonic formation—are functioning as a basic framework into which the various details are fitted. As will be seen if just the top and bottom lines of the music are played together, the three versions juxtapose in different ways what are in each case basically the same outer parts so as to create different elaborations of the same underlying harmonic progression. And as for the inner line, this is extensively remodelled between versions because it has no real structural significance in its own right; it simply responds to the changes made in the outer parts. The one characteristic feature that this inner part does possess in all three versions is the presence of dissonances over the D♮–B♮–E♮–C of the bass. However, these dissonances take a different form in each version. In the first version, which is the most conventional in this regard, they take the form of suspensions decorated with escape-notes.[34] In the second version, which creates a somewhat Wagnerian effect, they are syncopated chromatic passing-notes. And in the third version, which is also the most characteristic, they take the form of accented passing-notes (a seventh resolving to an octave against the top line—the same notes that Beethoven marked to be played with successive thumb-strokes). One might say that what Beethoven coded in his imaginative representation of the music was the dissonance, but not the specific form that it would take.

Indeed, it can be seen that analysing these successive versions in which Beethoven fashioned his compositional image of the piece is not so different, *mutatis mutandis*, from analysing the successive

---

[34] This idea comes from earlier in the movement, e.g. bars 102–3 (see Ex. 33).

attempts at recall of Sloboda's and Parker's subjects, or my attempts to recollect *Danseuses de Delphes* at the piano. The nature of the enterprise is, of course, quite different, in that it is directed towards the elaboration of a new musical product rather than the recall of a pre-existing one; but the psychological process involved is not so different, involving as it does the creative synthesis of a musical object from a set of attributes, some structural and some incidental. If this is so, it does indicate that Beethoven's (or Schlösser's) description of the way in which he composed was not literally true; certainly he had not made all the necessary compositional decisions when he started to write the autograph of Op. 110. But there is an important sense in which the work of composition probably was complete by then, and this is rather similar to what it might mean for an experienced public speaker to say that he had finished writing a lecture. By this the speaker would not mean that he knew exactly what he was going to say, word for word: part of the skill of public speaking lies in allowing a certain margin for spontaneous elaboration, or for response to the particular audience to which the lecture is given. He would mean that the framework had been fully worked out; that he had at hand a number of particular points or illustrations or jokes that he intended to weave into the lecture; and that he was perfectly confident of being able to elaborate the framework and tie the details together when the time came. It would have been in this sense, if at all, that Beethoven regarded his works as finished and ready to write out before the autograph score had even been begun; and if this is so it would suggest, what one might in any case expect, that Beethoven's way of working was essentially no different from that in which any complex imaginative work is done.

3 Knowing and listening

3.1 THE TWO SIDES OF THE MUSICAL FABRIC

I

Imagine, if you can, that Martian musicologists of ten thousand years hence are attempting to reconstruct an authentic performance of Chopin's E minor Prelude (Ex. 35). We will suppose that a copy of the score and a piano of the period have somehow survived the destruction of human civilization, and that the Martians have also found works of music theory that tell them that the notes of the score correspond to the various keys on the piano, that eighth-notes are all meant to be of a unit duration which is twice that of sixteenth-notes, that a dot prolongs a time value by a half, and so forth. How will this Martian performance sound? The question is unanswerable! But it is possible to imagine a performance being applauded (if Martians applaud) for its meticulous faithfulness to the score, in which the opening note lasted exactly three times as long as the second one, the eighth-notes of the left hand in the first eleven bars were all of precisely the same length, and, in the absence of any indication to the contrary, the dynamic level was exactly the same throughout the first eight bars. (I am not going to speculate as to what the Martians might make of Chopin's 'espressivo' marking.) Such a performance, however, would hardly be likely to attract applause from terrestrial audiences of the present day; indeed, one would be inclined to think of someone who played Chopin's music in this manner, as being not so much unmusical as mentally deranged.

What this shows is the inadequacy of conventional musical notation as a means of specifying the intended musical sound; as Schenker said,[1] the 'notational symbols really hide more than they

---

[1] Trans. 1987: i, xvii. An earth-bound illustration of this is provided by the recordings made in the early 1900s by the last castrato, Alessandro Moreschi. Moreschi sings the notes of familiar scores by Rossini and Gounod, but his voice-production, articulation, and ornamentation—which were highly regarded in his own time—are such that the music sounds quite foreign to today's listener.

Ex. 35

make explicit'. As a means of specifying the actual sound of piano music, a MIDI data file[2] is much more satisfactory, for it is capable in a way that ordinary notation is not of defining the precise rhythmic and dynamic values that are required for adequate performance; a MIDI recording of a performance of the E minor Prelude can incorporate all those subtleties of timing and phrasing that are so crucial for the music's aesthetic effect—the prolongation of the first and sometimes the last beat of each bar, the emphasis through dynamics and rubato of the dominant cadence at bar 12, and so on. Consequently a mechanical performance of this piece, in which a synthesizer executes a MIDI data file, might sound very much more natural and musical—in short, more human—than the Martian performance I have described.

Does this mean that MIDI code is a better way of notating music than the conventional staves, dots, and beams? It depends on the purpose for which the notation is wanted. MIDI code is obviously superior for purposes of mechanical reproduction; but in any other sense it is an extremely inefficient means of communicating one person's musical intentions to another, which is the principal (though by no means the only) function of traditional notation. It is true that, like MIDI code, traditional notation does specify certain perform-ance actions (depress this key now and hold it down for so long); but as the Chopin example shows, it only does so in an approximate or incomplete manner, so that it achieves its intended purpose not when it is executed literally, but when it is interpreted by the performer in accordance with his conception of what the composer wanted and his own musical sensibility.[3] The conductor Wilhelm Furtwängler was making this point when he said that a score 'cannot give any indication as to the really intended volume of a *forte*, the really intended speed of a *tempo*, since every *forte* and every *tempo* has to be modified in practice in accordance with the place of the performance and the setting and the strength of the performing group'.[4] But the point is a more general one, for it extends not just to temporal and dynamic values but to qualities of attack and articulation, to vibrato

[2] MIDI (Musical Instrument Digital Interface) is a code for communications between synthesizers, computers, and related equipment, together with an associated hardware standard. A MIDI data file consists of a series of instructions which, when sent to a MIDI-compatible synthesizer, will cause it to play a predetermined piece of music. It consists of a series of codes signifying key on or off, dynamic value, pitch-bend, etc.

[3] See Stravinsky's discussion of interpretation versus execution (1947: 127 ff.)

[4] Trans. in Schutz ed. 1964: 166. Cf. also Schoenberg ed. 1984: 341.

and tone colour, and in the case of instruments like the violin and the oboe to intonation as well. None of these values is specified in the score to the extent that is required for the achievement of an adequate performance; in each case the notated indications have to be interpreted in terms of the individual musical context.

In fact the general point I am making applies to more than just music. More than 150 years ago, Wilhelm von Humboldt wrote:

Language, grasped in its real essence, is something continual and passing on in every moment. Even its fixing by means of writing always preserves it only incompletely, like a mummy; writing stands in need, again and again, of people's efforts to imagine from writing a living performance.[5]

And Humboldt's words are echoed by Iser when he writes that 'literary texts initiate "performances" of meaning rather than actually formulating meanings themselves.' (1978: 27.) Reading a book, then, is a performance in the sense of being a temporally extended process during which the text yields up its signification through being experienced by the reader; and if this is true of reading books then it is certainly no less true of reading music. For the experience in which the symbols of musical notation yield up their signification to the reader is of necessity one that has temporal extension; it is for this reason that Alfred Schutz, referring to musical recollection in general, says that a composition can only be grasped

by reconstituting the polythetic steps in which it has been built up, by reproducing mentally or actually its development from the first to the last bar as it goes on in time. . . . It will take 'as much time' to reconstitute the work of music in recollection as it will to experience it originally in its unfolding, polythetic constitution while listening to it for the first time.[6]

What Schutz says is not quite literally true. When one recollects

---

[5] Trans. from Humboldt's essay 'On the diversity of human languages' ('Über die Verschiedenheit des menschlichen Sprachbaues') in Dahlhaus 1982: 10.

[6] Schutz ed. 1976: 29. 'Polythetic' is a Husserlian term which may be rendered as 'step-by-step'. Swain (1986: 137) gives a similar account of musical recollection: 'A musician can recall the Fourth Brandenburg Concerto, refer dispassionately to his favorite moments, even whistle the main tune, without feeling anything that approximates the actual listening experience. In order to reproduce this experience, the listener, first of all, must have a very accurate memory trace of it, and then play the piece as a sound image, something like the playback of a tape, in his "mind's ear", taking approximately the same amount of time as a real performance would. In essence, he is reproducing the perceptual processing of the Fourth Brandenburg Concerto.' Sartre and Ryle might have had something to say about such a statement; but this does not affect Swain's point regarding the time of performance.

music—and the same applies to reading it—temporal values are more flexible than they are in real, audible music. One can skim through a passage, or slow down in order to take in the detail of a complex texture, without the authentically musical quality of the experience necessarily being jeopardized as a result. But his basic point is clearly a sound one: a piece of music is grasped not in the instantaneous manner in which one sees the validity of a theorem or the point of a joke, but through an extended process which can appropriately be called inner performance.

Reading music is in essence the same kind of process as those that I described in Chapter 2—recalling a folksong or a piano piece, or composing a piano sonata. In each case the intended music is constructed or reconstructed on the basis of symbols or images which embody certain partial aspects of it; and it is an essential part of this constructive process that it goes beyond what is literally signified by the symbols or images, so embodying the musician's knowledge of what is likely or plausible in a given style. Consider as an example the opening bars of Haydn's String Quartet Op. 33 No. 3 (Ex. 36). It is one thing to read these bars as a series of separate

Ex. 36

symbols (here is an E and there a C; the notes are a minor sixth apart, and suggest a C major or possibly an A minor centricity); but reading them as music is a quite different kind of process in which such observations are synthesized into an imaginative awareness of sound. Doing this means sensing the light, provisional quality of the opening notes in the second violin and viola; it means grasping the contrast between this and the swelling, sustained sonority of the first violin's entry, which breaks in the fourth bar into a cascade of little notes; it means being aware of the cellist's bow digging into the open C string, and the arch-like tensional morphology of the first six bars. And it means experiencing the synthesis of all these things into a continuous, ongoing experience—into the flux of inner time, as Schutz would say.

Such an imaginative synthesis of the score as music exhibits one of the characteristics of specifically musical perception, which is that it becomes hard or impossible to achieve if there is interference from a conflicting musical stimulus. To read a score while people are talking or in the midst of traffic noise presents no particular problem; but to do so within earshot of other music is problematic. It remains easy enough under such conditions to make the kind of fragmented observations of relationships between notes that I mentioned; what becomes parlous is the synthesis of these observations into a musical experience. As Dahlhaus puts it (1982: 12), 'silent reading, insofar as it is not to collapse into thin abstraction, always represents an inner hearing, translating signs into sound,' and it is just this latter process that is inhibited when there is interference from conflicting musical sounds.

This same interference effect can be observed when people play music aloud (whether from a score or from memory). Normally when a pianist plays, he hears what he plays; but experiments using electronic keyboards with speakers that can be switched off have confirmed what every pianist who has used a silent keyboard already knows, namely that it is possible to play music quite adequately in the absence of any immediate auditory feedback (Sloboda 1982: 489). When there is no feedback it is at least possible to imagine the sound of what one is playing; but what these experiments show to be less easy is to play adequately when the music played is audible but delayed by, say, a quarter of a second. It is not that the task is totally impossible: there are occasions when musicians have to cope with situations like this in real life, for instance when monitoring a recording or when playing the organ in a church that has a prolonged echo. But, at least until one has got used to it, playing well under these circumstances is hard: the musical continuity of normal performance is likely to be fragmented into a series of Gestalts that are temporally more or less dislocated. If I play Chopin's E minor Prelude on an electronic keyboard with the speakers switched off, the sound diverted to a tape recorder, and the radio playing some other music at full volume, I find on listening afterwards to the tape that I play either with an exaggerated and uncontrolled rubato, or else stiffly and correctly, with a military precision that results from counting 'one-two, one-two' as I play and slotting in each note at the appropriate point. To play in this mechanical manner is not to interpret the score as it asks to be interpreted in performance, but to execute it in the same way as a regimental sergeant-major expects his orders to be carried out: literally and unthinkingly; in short, without imagination.

Referring to performance from written music, Clarke (1985: 214) says:

The performer's task . . . —far from being a simple translation between a series of discrete, explicit symbols and some internalized analog—is to integrate a variety of types of information over a number of symbols and to incorporate this information into a rather abstract matrix of determining structural forces.

In other words, as the performer reads the music, the discrete significations of the notational symbols give way to a synthetic and contextually dependent interpretation of the information they embody. This kind of interpretation is the basis of all music reading, and it is seen in its most abstract form in the fluent, silent score-reading of which accomplished musicians are capable, at least when the music is not excessively complex or in too unfamiliar a style.[7] Not all musicians can reconstruct the sound of a score in quite such an abstract manner as this, however. As a jazz pianist, David Sudnow (1978: 45, 74) says that his knowledge of

[7] Peter Kivy, adapting Locke's account of language, describes the silent reading of music as follows: 'Concerning scores, they being immediately the signs of men's musical ideas, and by that means the instruments whereby men communicate their musical conceptions, and express to one another those musical thoughts and imaginations they have within their own minds, there comes by continual use such a connection between certain notational devices and the sounds they stand for, that the notational devices almost as readily excite certain "sounds in the mind" as if the sounds themselves did actually affect the senses.' (1984: 105.) But this suggests a direct association between individual notational elements and the

how a passage will sound is an aspect of his physical engagement with his keyboard, which presumably means that he would not be able to envisage exactly how something would sound away from the instrument. The same no doubt applies to many classical pianists, too. But when they play music from a score, such pianists are still interpreting the symbols in the light of the emerging musical context: it is just that, unlike the silent score-readers, they are unable to abstract this musical context from the motor actions of performance and the feedback provided by the keyboard.

This is a situation quite different from that of the beginner who, when he plays from a score, plays first one note, and then another, but has no idea how they are going to sound. The beginner does not interpret the notes in the score: he merely acts upon them. He realizes them in sound. By contrast, fluent performance means that the notational symbols are stripped of their burden of signification and then jettisoned. As Schutz puts it (ed. 1964: 169), such things constitute no more than the prehistory of the performance; they are superseded in the act of making music. This means that, paradoxical though it may appear, the pianist who plays Chopin's E minor Prelude fluently and expressively is in a real sense improvising, even when he is playing from the music; and if this is true in solo performance, it is the more so when players come together to perform chamber music.

How do the members of a string quartet stay together when they play? The obvious answer would be: because they each stay with the beat of the music. Now this could well be the case when the players are sight-reading a new work together: the first violinist will perhaps count 'one, two, three', so that the players begin at the same time, and even though he does not go on counting aloud, the players will remain co-ordinated through their adherence to the regular 'one, two, three' of the musical beat. But

corresponding sounds, whereas empirical studies of music reading show that it involves an abstract representation of the musical structure (for a review of these see Sloboda 1984). It is presumably because of the difficulty of achieving such an abstract representation that music in an unfamiliar style, even if it is not in itself unduly complicated, can prove so baffling to the silent score-reader: Schoenberg (ed. 1984: 42) recounts how when he showed Mahler his 1st String Quartet, Mahler looked at the score and then said, 'I have conducted the most difficult scores of Wagner; I have written complicated music myself in scores of up to thirty staves and more; yet here is a score of not more than four staves, and I am unable to read them.'

string quartet performances are among the most intensively rehearsed of the entire classical repertoire: and in the course of rehearsal, a quite different type of synchronization seems to emerge. A well-established quartet performing a familiar work plays together with a kind of suppleness and mutuality of timing that is altogether different from what happens in the sight-reading session. Rather than abiding by a uniformly agreed beat, the performers keep together because they are, in a quite literal sense, playing by ear.

Experimental investigation has not really established how this works, beyond suggesting that there is a small but general tendency for melodically important instruments to enter slightly before the others;[8] presumably what is involved is an entire network of relational exchanges that depend on the particular organization of the music—though this is not in general something that the players consciously plan out, but rather something that emerges spontaneously in the course of rehearsal. It is perhaps more illuminating to draw a parallel with the rapport and give-and-take of people engaged in conversing together; each speaker listens to the others, accommodating himself to what they are saying and timing his interjections in accordance with the flow of the conversation, so that the conversation as a whole has a kind of rhythmic pacing which is shared by all the participants. And if good conversation can easily be disrupted by the bore who will not listen, will not see anybody else's point of view, but insists on 'saying his piece' as if he were delivering a lecture, then precisely the same applies to chamber music performance: there are musicians, especially those accustomed to solo performance or to playing in orchestras, who play without regard to what everybody else is doing, or who insist upon a rigidly enforced beat—so that the mutuality of performance, which is the distinguishing feature of chamber music, disappears. Perhaps the most damaging

---

[8] See Sloboda 1985: 100. Clayton (1985) has carried out a series of experiments into co-ordination in conducted music, from which he concludes that both the conductor and the instrumentalists are 'engaging in an effectively continuous tracking and monitoring process, that information is being constantly assimilated and that the organising system must be capable of constant and rapid reconfiguration' (p. 325); in other words, there is a mutuality of accord between the conductor and the instrumentalists. He also found that fine co-ordination in performance depends much more upon the players' ability to hear one another than upon the conductor, whose role is normally 'to give general or "ballpark" rather than specific temporal guidance' (p. 107).

criticism that can be made of a chamber player is that he doesn't listen: for this strikes at the heart of an art in which openness to the other is of the very essence. This openness is expressed not only through playing by ear, but through playing by eye too: Schutz (ed. 1964: 176) comments on how important it is for chamber players to be able to see each other as they play, and what this involves is not so much an exchange of specific cues, in the manner of a runner waiting for a starting-pistol, as a kind of shared mutual regard. It might perhaps be likened to the manner in which lovers gaze into each other's eyes.[9]

Schutz describes the mutual interaction between chamber musicians, and between the musicians and their audience, as one in which 'performer and listener are "tuned-in" to one another, are living together through the same flux, are growing older together while the musical process lasts' (ed. 1964: 174–5). Such communal improvisation, which is what true chamber music essentially is,[10] abolishes the notational specifics of the score, with its notional relationships of half as long and twice as long. But not every musical performance abolishes the score in this way. There are performances in which the notational specifics of the score are by no means merely prehistoric, but are actively implicated in the performing process. A simple example of this is when music such as the opening bars of Stockhausen's *Klavierstück IV* (Ex. 37) is sight-read; on first acquaintance most pianists are probably unable to anticipate how this music will sound in anything more than the most rudimentary manner, and in consequence the score has to be executed rather than interpreted, each note being depressed as it comes rather than integrated into a larger abstract structure. This means that the notes will 'speak back' to the performer as he plays, to use Sudnow's term (1978: 64): that is, sounds will be generated which the player has not anticipated in any precise musical sense.

A rather more complex example of notational specifics being implicated in the performing process, also from Stockhausen, is provided by a passage from the orchestral work *Gruppen* (Ex. 38).

---

[9] I have been describing only the way in which players accommodate to one another within the dimension of time; but the same clearly applies to other aspects of performance, and in particular to intonation (see Ward 1970: 417 ff.).

[10] 'There is no difference in principle between the performance of a string quartet and the improvisations at a jam session of accomplished jazz players.' (Schutz ed. 1964: 177.) What there is, of course, is a difference of degree.

Ex. 37

It is hardly possible to envisage music like this being played by ear in the manner of chamber music; indeed, in this sense, it is hardly possible to imagine anything less like chamber music. Consider, for instance, how the musician playing the vibraphone (his entries are circled) knows when to play. Really the only practical way in which he can do this is by following the conductor's beat and slotting in each note at the appropriate point—which is as much as to say that he is not actually playing with the other musicians at all in the sense I have described. In fact none of the instrumentalists in a work like *Gruppen* are really playing together: rather, each of them is playing individually with the conductor. They are not to any significant degree interpreting their parts; they are merely executing them with greater or lesser accuracy. And this means that neither the musical beat nor the symbols of the score are being abolished in the performance; they are being realized.

It also means that the vibraphone player and his colleagues in *Gruppen* are musicians of a very different kind from the chamber player. Essentially they are technicians; there is hardly more a community of experience between them and the audience than there is between the musicians hired to play at a débutante's ball and the guests. The reason for this is the lack of equivalence between the receptional content and the productional means by which this content is realized. The listener, from his vantage-point in the auditorium, hears the total effect that the elaborate

Ex. 38

mechanical construction of the music is designed to create. By contrast, the vibraphone player in *Gruppen* is probably quite unable to grasp the overall effect from his position at the side of the orchestra, and his part, considered in itself, is without aesthetic or (for that matter) any other interest—indeed it is senseless. And though *Gruppen* is admittedly an extreme case, this kind of separation between the individual player's part and the aesthetic coherence of the whole is of the essence of orchestral music; it is hardly less characteristic of Berlioz's *Symphonie fantastique* than it is of *Gruppen*. If a neat historical division were to be made, one might say that Beethoven was the first composer to write truly orchestral music in this sense, and Mozart the last to write chamber music for full orchestra.[11]

Maurice Merleau-Ponty (trans. 1964: 45) coined a metaphor for literary work which is no less applicable to music: 'Like the weaver,' he wrote, 'the writer works on the wrong side of his material. He has to do only with language, and it is thus that he suddenly finds himself surrounded by meaning.' The vibraphone player in *Gruppen* is working on the wrong side of the fabric: he is producing a pattern which is without meaning in itself, and whose purpose is fulfilled only in so far as it is subsumed within the intended experience of the work as a whole. In this he constitutes a paradigm for all the productional imagery and symbology that support the cultural edifice of Western music: for it is in the nature of all images and symbols for music that they have at most a purely localized and provisional significance in themselves, yielding up their full burden of meaning only as they are embodied within the performance of real or imagined music.

II

As I said in the Introduction, my basic argument in this book is that there is always a disparity between the experience of music and the way in which we imagine or think about it. Now this is not a novel observation. In his *Critique of Judgement* Kant speaks—with suspicion, as Dahlhaus comments (1982: 31)—of the way in which, despite its undoubted power to affect people emotionally, music leaves 'no residue for reflection'. The problems inherent in any attempt to grasp music reflectively may arise in part from the extent to which the reflective consciousness is verbally constituted: speaking in the broadest terms of musicology as a discipline based essentially on the word (*logos*), the ethnomusicologist Charles Seeger (1977: 16) states that 'The core of the undertaking is the integration of speech knowledge in general and the speech knowledge of music in particular (which are extrinsic to music and its compositional process) with the music knowledge of music

---

[11] I shall mention, but not enlarge upon, the possibly rather simplistic analogy that can be made between this development and the roughly contemporaneous developments in the division of labour that were consequent upon industrialization.

(which is intrinsic to music and its compositional process).' Such integration, Seeger argues, is never possible beyond a certain limited degree; and some musicologists consider this contradiction lying at the heart of their discipline to be so basic that they have dubbed it 'Seeger's Dilemma' (Herndon 1974: 244). Alfred Schutz, however, locates what is perhaps an even more fundamental problem in the contradiction between the inner and ever-present time within which music is experienced, and the external and retrospective temporality that is imposed in the act of reflection and measured by musical notation. Reflection on music, he argues, is only possible on condition that the listener 'ceases to participate in the ongoing flux, and turns back to his past experiences in an attitude of reflection—making the acts of his listening the object of his reflection' (ed. 1976: 60). It follows from this that any attempt to grasp the musical experience in terms of outer time, for instance through words or diagrammatic representation, poses a variant of the Eleatic paradox, according to which an arrow cannot move because it is impossible to represent the ongoing quality of its motion in such terms. As Schutz puts it, 'you may . . . designate the spot occupied by the arrow at any chosen instant during the flight. But then you have dropped entirely the idea of an ongoing motion.' (p. 30.)

Schutz's point emerges most clearly in music like the saxophone solo from the opening of Ornette Coleman's 'W. R. V.', shown in Ex. 39.[12] Actually the music looks very peculiar when notated like

Ex. 39

[12] From the album *Ornette!* by the Ornette Coleman Quartet (London Atlantic LT2-K 15241).

this, and for readers who do not happen to know this number it may be difficult or even impossible to imagine quite how it sounds. The reason for this is that in Coleman's performance the various notes are so linked together through pitch-bending and slurred articulation, and the speed is in any case so fast, that it is hard or even impossible to distinguish the individual notes (I had to play the disc at half-speed in order to make this transcription). Indeed, it could reasonably be said that some of these notes are not really there at all, in the sense of being discrete entities that the player fingers as such or that the listener perceives as such; many of them are really no more than notional points through which the music passes in the course of its ongoing motion, like Zeno's arrow. The attempt to capture Coleman's playing in notation, then, distorts what it is intended to represent, in that it imposes spurious divisions within what is in reality a continuous course of motion. Rather than being in any sense 'in' the sound or even in the perception of it under normal circumstances of listening, the separate notes shown in the transcription are, as Bruno Nettl puts it, 'convenient but sometimes misleading abstractions' (1983: 78); that is to say, they are products of the attempt to grasp the experience reflectively.

To transcribe music into Western notation is to assume, or at least to take as a starting-point, a division of the musical flow into a series of discrete rhythmic values, and a division of the pitch continuum into a series of discrete intervallic values. It is, in other words, to adopt a quite distinctive interpretational viewpoint, and one that is particularly likely to result in distortions when the music does not belong to the repertoire of Western art music. This problem is especially pressing for ethnomusicologists, for whom transcription is a basic methodological tool; and one of the means by which they have attempted to solve the problem, or at least to establish its nature and extent, has been the use of mechanical equipment that plots the fundamental frequency of a musical signal against time.[13] Nettl says about this that

the melograph, in questioning the basic assumption of the note as a unit of music, points out to us something of which, because of the constraints of Western notation, we are usually not aware. . . . It almost seems that ethnomusicologists are the victim of an analogue of the Whorfian hypothesis, according to which thought is regulated by the structure of

[13] Examples of such so-called melographic scores may be found in Seeger 1977.

language; musical hearing on the part of Westerners may be profoundly affected by the characteristics of Western notation. (1983: 78–9.)

When people listen to a rapid jazz improvisation in the ordinary way, is their perception of the music profoundly affected, as Nettl's remarks might suggest, by the characteristics of Western notation? Maybe this is true of ethnomusicologists, who are after all trained musicians. But it would be hard to maintain that it was true of the many jazz fans who do not read music; and even for an accomplished and literate jazz musician, to hear and to know a recorded improvisation in the ordinary way may well not be to have an image of it that is sufficiently specific for productional purposes—that is, for purposes of transcription or performance. David Sudnow (1978: 17) says of his early attempts to imitate the jazz he heard on the records:

Even when taking a portion of melody from a record where I thought I knew the improvised section well . . . a symptomatic vagueness in my grasp of these familiar improvisations was discovered. I knew the melodies only in certain broad outlines. Particularly with respect to the rapid passages, I found that, when singing along with a Charlie Parker recording, for example, I had been glossing the particularities of the notes in many of my hummings, grasping their essential shape perhaps but not singing them with refined pitch sensibility. It was particular notes that needed to be at hand to reproduce that stretch of music in its particularity, and the question arose: what had I in fact been listening to as a jazz fan all these years?

The kind of essential shape to which Sudnow refers became evident in some informal tests I administered, in which music students attempted to transcribe the Coleman passage shown in Ex. 39.[14] One student, for instance, began by writing down a skeletal plan of the first two bars, as shown in Ex. 40a. So far there was no problem; but when this student attempted to fill in some of the notes which appear in the plan as mere wavy lines, discrepancies began to appear between what was played and what was transcribed, and these were by no means simple errors of omission or approximation. Ex. 40b[15] shows how the space between the opening F♯ and the higher F♯ on the third beat of the

---

[14] These tests were carried out at Cambridge University in 1980. The subjects were 2nd-year music students.

[15] The beams and slurs in (b), (c), and (d), have been added in order to clarify the structures of the students' transcriptions.

Ex. 40

first bar was filled in; we can see a regularly constructed pattern consisting of three groups of three rising notes, contained within a four-note scale (F♯, G♯, B, C♯) which is consistent with the B major tonality of the opening bars of the solo. Other students, too, filled in this passage by means of regularly constructed sequential patterns, as shown in (c) and (d) of Ex. 40; and whereas each of these attempts at transcription is quite different (and none is very close to what Coleman actually plays), all three illustrate what Sloboda and Parker found in their tests of vocal recall, namely that the structure of the representation tends to be simpler and more consistent than that of the original.[16] It is in terms of notes conceived as discrete and abstract elements of design that these attempts at transcription possess the qualities of simplicity and consistency; and the results, while coherent, are coherent in a manner very different from the ongoing aural coherence of Coleman's performance.

If the students' attempts to grasp what they heard were influenced by considerations of abstract design based on the patterned disposition of notes, then equally they were influenced by the stylistic expectations with which they approached the task. Coleman's solo begins in B major and moves towards C major, in which key it cadences definitively at the end of the extract. Such a progression, within a single musical phrase, is rarely found in the art music repertoire with which these students were primarily familiar, and as a consequence the students either had difficulty in

[16] See p. 108 above.

detecting this progression or, if they did detect it, were reluctant to believe what they heard. One student simply transcribed the opening and the ending of the solo in B major, adapting what came in the middle so that the unexpected change of key was eliminated. Another at first transcribed the successive fourths in bar 3 quite correctly but then, realizing that this would lead the music altogether away from B major, transposed the passage so that the change of key was again avoided. And a third student realized that the final cadence was in a key other than the opening, but wrote it out in F sharp major, on the model of the traditional modulation to the dominant. In each of these cases, then, the structure of the music as it appeared in the transcription was to a large degree determined by what one might call the representational apparatus which the student brought to the task: that is to say, conventional musical notation and familiarity with a specific musical repertoire, both of which embody certain distinctive structural presuppositions. Indeed, one might say as a quite general principle that any transcription is an encounter between a musical phenomenon and an established representational apparatus; or as Pandora Hopkins describes it (1966: 311–12), 'a comparison of that which is unfamiliar to that which is familiar'. I should add, however, that the students were well aware of the discrepancies between what they heard and what they were able to capture in notation; like Sudnow, they ended up wondering just what in fact it was that they had been listening to.

Hopkins has herself conducted an unusual and instructive experiment (1982), the aim of which was to evaluate the influence of a musician's cultural background upon his musical perceptions. Three musicians participated: each was an expert performer, one in the field of Western classical music, one in Indian classical music, and the last in Greek popular music. Hopkins had each of the subjects listen repeatedly to recordings of music played on a type of Norwegian fiddle called a *hardingfele*, with which none of them was familiar, and they were asked to identify the recurrent three-beat rhythmic pattern that is characteristic of this style. As Hopkins says (1982: 146), the rhythmic pattern

is of such structural importance to the totality that not only the fiddler but also the audience foot-beats while the music is being played (much in the spirit of the Indian audience keeping the *tāla*). Indeed, the full effect of deliberately contrasting accentual patterns in the melodic line of a particular section (and their resolution) can best be felt by the listener who is experiencing this foot-beating.

However, she explains, record companies have not appreciated the significance of the foot-beating and have therefore carefully eliminated the sound of it from their recordings. In asking her three subjects to reconstruct the foot-beating pattern from commercial recordings of the music, then, Hopkins was testing their ability to grasp the music's rhythmic structure in more or less the same way that people perceive the structure from within the Norwegian fiddling tradition.

In the event, none of the subjects was very successful in this task. Their initial approaches clearly revealed the influence of their distinct musical backgrounds. The Western musician was perhaps the least successful, because of a basic preconception that rhythmic structure is to be understood as an aspect of, or consequence of, melodic and harmonic structure—something which is true of Western art music but not, it appears, of Norwegian fiddle music. The Greek musician had more success, trying to rationalize what he heard in terms of additive structures based on groups of two or three beats, much in the manner of Balkan music. On the other hand, the Indian musician did the opposite, listening out for extended rhythmic patterns such as are found in Indian music and then trying to resolve these into subordinate units. The musicians quickly found that the music did not present any recurrent pattern when heard in these ways, and 'they then began the task of restructuring in order to solve the problem that had been set before them.' (1982: 154.) That is to say, they attempted to focus on different aspects of the music, or tried out different hypotheses as to how its various aspects might relate one to another. But, Hopkins continues, 'this restructuring process was carried out by each musician according to the path already established in his or her initial responses to the material, determined, of course, by experience.' In other words, the basic interpretational framework that each musician brought to the task proved incapable of structural modification; all he could do was try out different ways of configuring what he heard within that framework. For instance, the Indian musician considered a number of alternative numerical schemes of subdivision, testing them against the music as it unfolded; but he was only able to conceive of these rhythmic patterns in terms of the specific types of rhythmic articulation characteristic of Indian music. Indeed, he was reluctant to believe that there really was a recurrent pattern in the music at all. As Hopkins explains, his scepticism 'derived from his expectation concerning the nature of a recurrent beat pattern; where he perceived an arbitrary unsteadiness, the *hardingfele spelemann* [player] perceives articulations within a consistently recurring pattern' (1982: 158).

In saying this, Hopkins allies herself to an interpretative approach which has had considerable influence in the analysis of the visual arts. This approach is particularly associated with E. H. Gombrich, who writes (and his words echo Hopkins's characterization of transcription) that 'All perceiving relates to expectations and therefore to comparisons.' (1969: 301.) From this principle Gombrich has derived an account of aesthetic perception in the visual arts which emphasizes precisely the features that emerged in Hopkins's experiment: a conscious or (more probably) unconscious framework of interpretation, and a problem-solving approach involving the construction of alternative perceptual hypotheses and their testing against the phenomena in question. The expectations that constitute the interpretational framework of perception, as Gombrich describes it, can come from various sources. They may be the products of the unconscious organization of the perceptual field that is the subject of Gestalt psychology (this corresponds to what Iser called 'autocorrelation'[17]). Or, more significantly for art history and criticism, they may embody conventions or beliefs that are specific to a given culture. In this case knowledge of such conventions may be acquired either through enculturation—a spontaneous learning process which is part of the normal experience of any culture member—or through some kind of specialized training, which is what distinguishes the connoisseur from the layman. Moreover, there are branches of art in which an adequate appreciation of what the artist intends is impossible unless the viewer is in possession of quite specific information, as for example in the case of the religious imagery and classical allusion that lie behind much medieval and Renaissance painting. Someone who does not understand this implied referential content will simply misunderstand the painting—that

---

[17] See p. 25 above.

is, fail to understand it as it was intended to be understood within the culture that produced it—and for this reason iconography, as the study of such referential content is called, is an essential aspect not only of art history but also of art criticism.

Now the general approach to aesthetic perception that is embodied in Gombrich's work can obviously be applied beyond the confines of the visual arts. Someone who sees an allegorical painting like Lorenzo Lotto's *Allegory*[18] as just a landscape, however much he may like it as such, is missing the point in much the same way as the child who reads Orwell's *Animal Farm* as a story about animals or Melville's *Moby Dick* as a story about whaling. As Iser says, reading a literary work is not a passive process in which the meaning contained within the text is conveyed to its readers, but an active process in which meaning is constituted because the readers 'adopt a position *in relation* to the text' (1978: 169); and the particular meaning that the text takes on for them will depend upon the particular expectations that each individual reader brings to his encounter with the text.

The most influential application of ideas such as these to music has come from the American theorist and analyst Leonard B. Meyer (1956, 1973), who like Gombrich has been heavily influenced by Gestalt psychology. Also like Gombrich, he sees aesthetic perception as being largely moulded by the nature of the listener's expectations, and he sees these expectations as being themselves largely moulded by the musical culture to which the listener belongs. For instance, if tonal music is to be understood by the listener, then he must recognize that a harmonic progression which begins and ends on the tonic is closed—no continuation is to be expected—whereas a progression that ends on some other chord, for instance the dominant, implies a continuation. A listener who was not acquainted with these stylistic norms, as Meyer calls them, would not be able to respond properly to the music; he might expect the music to continue when it had in fact reached a close, or think that it had finished when it had not, and so entirely fail to perceive the patterns of tension and relaxation that play so vital a role in the aesthetic effect of tonal music.

There are also cases in which, according to Meyer, even more specific information is required of the listener if he is to respond

---

[18] In the National Gallery, Washington, DC; reproduced in Gombrich 1969: 372.

properly. He quotes as an instance the opening of Beethoven's Sonata Op. 81a, 'Les Adieux', which is shown in Ex. 41, and comments (1973: 244) that

The use of horn fifths in the first measures . . . is unusual in almost every way. Instead of coming at the end of a fast movement, they are the beginning of a slow introduction; instead of being accompanimental, they are the main substance; and instead of reaching emphatic closure on the tonic, they end in a deceptive cadence which is mobile and on-going.

Now the importance of this, as Meyer sees it, is that the listener who is familar with the normal use of the horn-call will recognize just how deviant Beethoven's use of the pattern is in this particular instance. Thus, he says,

Because the schema is so well known and specific in its pattern, the effect of the alien, C-minor harmony is particularly powerful. This is no mere deceptive cadence: it strikes us as expressly anomalous. For this reason, we sense, though perhaps only intuitively, that it is significant. (p. 247.)

The musical effect, in other words, depends on the informed expectations that the 'competent listener', to use Meyer's term, brings to his experiencing of the music.[19] The listener who is unable to do this (Meyer does not actually speak of the 'incompetent listener') will in a literal sense hear the same sounds as his better informed partner; but he will be unable to hear them as music, and it is for this reason that Meyer writes that 'music is directed, not *to* the senses, but *through* the senses and *to the mind*.' (1967: 271.) It follows from this that listeners cannot respond properly to music with whose stylistic norms they are not acquainted; accordingly, speaking of non-Western musics, Meyer warns against 'the danger of reading Western meanings and expectations into passages where they are not relevant' (1956: 197).

Now there are certainly situations where an uninformed Western listener will miss some important aspect of non-Western music that he hears. One might cite as an example the Confucian ideal of musical listening as set out in the 'Records on Rites' (*Liji*)—an ideal which few Westerners could live up to:

The silk [chordophone] instrument sounds plaintive. Its quality is pure

---

[19] Subotnik (1981) refines this notion by distinguishing between the 'structural competence' required for the appreciation of classical music and the 'stylistic competence' required for romantic music.

Ex. 41

and intelligent, which enables the establishment of righteousness. A superior man hearing the sound of the *qin* and *se* [zithers] would contemplate on righteous ministers. The bamboo [aerophone] sounds mellow. Its mellow quality resembles the unity which brings together masses of people. A superior man on hearing the sound of *yu* [large mouth organ], *sheng* [small mouth organ], *xiao* and *guan* [vertical end-blown flutes] would recall the minister who treats his people magnanimously. (translated in Liang 1985: 179.)

But of course it might be rather naïve to treat such precepts as if they represented an account of actual musical listening. More to the point, then, is the example of Indian classical music, in which (as mentioned by Hopkins) it is the practice for audiences to keep the tāla—that is, to count the beats of the rhythmic pattern in the same way as the performers do, so that they can observe the deftness with which a singer or sitarist apparently loses his place in the rhythmic structure as he improvises, only to regain it miraculously at the last moment and land correctly on the downbeat; a listener who does not keep the tāla in this way cannot fully appreciate the performance. This is as much as to say that connoisseurship is widespread among Indian audiences—connoisseurship, that is, in the sense of the ability to keep track of the composition's unfolding in much the same manner as the performer (or, in the case of composed music, the composer) conceives it. So defined, the connoisseurship of these Indian audiences is quite comparable to that of the Western listener to Beethoven's Op. 81*a* who hears the opening in the manner that Meyer describes. And Op. 81*a* is not exceptional in this regard; many works of the classical tradition seem to have been written for an idealized listener—a listener who is able to keep track of the formal and tonal unfolding of the music, and so appreciate, for instance, the non-structural quality of the E flat 'false reprise' in the first movement of Beethoven's String

Quartet Op. 18. No. 2, and the way in which the beginning of the real recapitulation is inadequately prepared, resulting in the explosion of dissonance that takes place a few bars later.[20]

But as we saw in Chapter 1, keeping track of form in this way demands special training that most people do not have. That is not, of course, to say that the ability to do this may not possibly result in an enhancement of the listener's aesthetic experience. But it does mean that this kind of understanding cannot be the basis of the average listener's enjoyment of music; as I have said, it is one of music's most distinctive and significant characteristics that it is enjoyed by people who know nothing about it in any formal sense. However, such people may possess informal knowledge about music; Meyer could argue that the knowledge of the stylistic norms appropriate to a given style, which he sees as being required of the competent listener, is acquired not through any formal training but through enculturation.[21] For instance, we know that when Beethoven's First Symphony was originally performed, many people were surprised by its beginning on a dissonance, and one, moreover, that was foreign to the home key (it is the dominant seventh of the subdominant). In finding this opening surprising such people must have been consciously or unconsciously comparing it with the openings of other contemporary symphonies, and their ability to do so will have depended not on formalized study of the genre but simply on familiarity with a sufficient number of examples of it. Again, most twentieth-century listeners will hear a waltz as a waltz, a Charleston as a Charleston, and reggae as reggae without having to receive formal instruction in these matters; acquaintance with these genres is simply part of the normal experience of the adult Westerner (just as acquaintance with bourrées, courantes, gigues, and the rest will have been simply part of the normal experience of the genteel eighteenth-century listener). Similarly, most contemporary listeners will know, though they have never been formally taught it, that it is inappropriate to play Mendelssohn's Wedding March at a funeral, or Chopin's Funeral March at a wedding. The list could be extended almost indefinitely; people ordinarily possess a great deal

[20] A fuller acount of this passage may be found in Cook 1987a: 272–4.
[21] This is Subotnik's position as regards stylistic competence (1981: 86). See Edmonston 1969 for some empirical evidence concerning the relative roles of training and enculturation in the aesthetic response to music.

of knowledge regarding musical genres and their social function, most of which has been acquired simply through the process of enculturation.

But how important is knowledge such as this in relation to the listener's ability to derive aesthetic enjoyment from music? As regards genres, Dahlhaus has pointed out that these no longer have the importance for musical perception that they did in the eighteenth century and before; as I said earlier, we tend nowadays to hear works as individuals rather than as exemplars of a type, and this is one of the defining principles of the aesthetic attitude (Dahlhaus 1983: 13–14). It is for this reason that Dahlhaus remarks that, for us, 'every genre fades to an abstract generalization' (1982: 15). Or to put it another way, whereas genres were at one time musical facts, they are now merely musicological facts—that is, facts *about* music. And as regards social function, I have already quoted Alan Durant's argument that to perceive music aesthetically is precisely to perceive it as being detached from a particular social context; in other words, one dances to 'The Blue Danube' as a waltz, but listens to it as a musical composition.

But the most telling case is that of Beethoven's First Symphony. Nobody today will find its opening surprising, as contemporary audiences did, in consequence of simple enculturation. The frequent use of dissonant and tonally oblique openings in music written since Beethoven's time means that nowadays one can only find the passage surprising through an exercise of intellect—by preparing oneself to be surprised, in other words. In order to achieve this, one would have to make a study of the stylistic norms prevalent in Beethoven's day, so as to be able to respond to the First Symphony in the light of them. And this means that the music's surprisingness is again no longer a musical fact, but a musicological one. Theorists like Meyer, who believe that the listener's expectations and the composer's deviations from them play a foundational role in the aesthetic effect of music, argue that musical style changes through history because what was formerly surprising becomes normal, so that new methods for creating surprise (for instance, the use of ever more extreme dissonances) have to be found; as Dowling and Harwood put it, 'Art must change in order to maintain its power to move us.' (1986: 224.) And yet Beethoven's First Symphony still has the power to move us, even if we know nothing about the stylistic norms of 1800. It follows that, if what was surprising to Beethoven's audiences is no longer surprising to us, then such effects of surprise cannot have a very important role to play in the enjoyment of music.[22]

Meyer's concept of stylistic norms goes deeper than such effects of surprise, however, for it takes in all those habits or principles of combination and contrast that are specific to a particular style, and that are frequently described as its grammar or syntax. One would expect people to acquire knowledge of these norms, too, through enculturation rather than specific training. And one might therefore expect to see the importance of such knowledge for aesthetic perception with particular clarity in the difficulties encountered when a member of one culture attempts to respond to the music of another, for Meyer's position implies, as he puts it, that 'an American must learn to understand Japanese music just as he must learn to understand the spoken language of Japan' (1956: 62). Now there is no doubt that an American who wants to understand Chinese regional opera will need to learn the appropriate Chinese dialect, because the music is designed around not only the meanings but also the tonal inflections of the words; hence, as Liang Mingyue writes, 'when asked about the *Gaojia opera* from Fujian, a Shanghainese would probably not have a positive response unless he understands the Fujian dialect. One often hears the comment from a music conservatory student that it is easier to appreciate a Wagner opera . . . than it is to enjoy a Chinese opera, except one which comes from his own native region.' (1985: 233.) But Meyer is saying that what is true of the linguistically based style of Chinese regional opera is true of all music, Wagner's included. The psychologist John Booth Davies (1978: 71) concurs with this:

When we listen to music from a culture which does not use Western musical conventions, or with which we are very unfamiliar, it often sounds meaningless, and probably boring too. Oriental music or, to come nearer home, Scottish Pibroch, fall into these categories for many people. We cannot assume, however, that they are in some absolute sense really meaningless or boring, because they are neither of these things for the

---

[22] One work which does perhaps demand a knowledge of contemporary stylistic norms if it is to make its full musical effect is the first movement of Brandenburg Concerto No. 5; the extraordinary role that the harpsichord plays has to be heard against the background of the normal concerto grosso. But this is an exceptional case: it is really a theatre piece disguised as a concerto grosso.

Chinese or the Scots. The reason is simply that we are unfamiliar with the musical system and the set of conventions employed.

But is the matter as simple as Meyer and Davies suggest? It seems to me that it is simple only in the sense that for some people it is quite obvious that what Meyer and Davies are saying is right, whereas for others they are simply wrong.[23]

One of those for whom they are right would be Gerald Abraham. According to Abraham, 'Indian music . . . merely sounds to most of us like normal chromatic music played out of tune' (1939: 59), and this is presumably a straightforward description of his own experience. Now if I were to attempt to transcribe Indian music into Western notation, I would be implicitly comparing what I heard against the intervallic categories embodied in Western notation, and under such circumstances I might well be conscious of the discrepancies of tuning to which Abraham refers. But when I listen to Indian music in the normal way I simply do not hear it like this. It is not just a matter of familiarization; Indian music has never sounded to me like out-of-tune Western music, and the same presumably applies to the not insubstantial record-buying and concert-attending audiences for Indian and other non-Western musics that are to be found in most major Western cities. (Why would these people have persevered with such music if, like Davies, they found it meaningless and boring?) Maybe the reason for these irreconcilable views is that people like or dislike non-Western music for reasons similar to those why they like or dislike non-Western food: for reasons that have more to do with personality or upbringing than with perception. After all, if Peter likes trying new cuisines whenever

---

[23] This is a controversy that has been going on for centuries; see e.g. Sulzer's remarks in his *Allgemeine Theorie der schönen Künste* (trans. in Le Huray and Day 1981: 134) and Rousseau's comments in the *Essai sur l'origine des langues* (trans. in Lippman 1986: 329). Unfortunately there is little empirical evidence that can usefully be brought to bear upon this. Experiments in which Western students have been introduced to ethnic musics through programmed instruction (Heingartner and Hall 1974, and unpublished research by Flowers and Steele described in Haack 1980: 165–6) seem to reveal attitudinal shifts hardly distinguishable from those that occur in the case of Western music; and in any case it is difficult to be sure how far the knowledge transmitted by means of such instruction is equivalent to what would be acquired by a culture-member through enculturation. One seemingly promising experiment (Kessler, Hansen, and Shepard 1984), in which the responses of non-Western subjects to Western musical stimuli were tested and vice versa, is in my view compromised by the methodological problem mentioned in ch. 1 n. 23 above; see Cook 1987b.

he can and Paul does not, that is surely not because they perceive the tastes differently, or because Peter knows how to perceive
them and Paul does not. It is not really a question of perception at
all.

At all events, I would agree with John Blacking when he writes:

It is sometimes said that an Englishman cannot possibly understand
African, Indian, and other non-English musics. This seems to me as
wrong-headed as the view of many white settlers in Africa, who claimed
that blacks could not possibly appreciate and perform properly Handel's
Messiah, English part-songs, or Lutheran hymns. Of course music is not a
universal language, and musical traditions are probably the most esoteric
of all cultural products. But the experience of ethnomusicologists, and the
growing popularity of non-European musics in Europe and America and
of 'Western' music in the Third World, suggest that the cultural barriers
are somewhat illusory, externally imposed, and concerned more with
verbal rationalizations and explanations of music and its association with
specific social events, than with the music itself. . . . When the words and
labels of a cultural tradition are put aside and 'form in tonal motion' is
allowed to speak for itself, there is a good chance that English, Africans
and Indians will experience similar feelings. (1987: 129–30.)

I would only add that, in the case of music that is embedded in a
highly specific social context, cross-cultural enjoyment may be
facilitated by some basic awareness of this context: a few minutes
of video-film showing Aboriginal music being performed *in situ*
may well help listeners from other cultures to orientate themselves
towards what they hear on sound recordings. But even if it is true
that English, African, Indian, and maybe Aboriginal listeners
experience similar feelings, is this a sufficient basis for saying they
all understand the music? Can it not be argued, as Meyer would
maintain, that a Westerner's enjoyment of Indian music is likely to
be based on a misunderstanding of its real significance? Nettl says
that 'people often listen to Japanese, Javanese, Indian music,
making comments about it that would be totally unacceptable to
an Asian musician, but satisfied that they understand it because
they enjoyed it.' (1983: 44.) Now this is certainly true, and from an
ethnomusicological point of view it is no doubt important; but
that does not necessarily make it relevant to the issue of aesthetic
perception. For if the average Western listener is likely to say
things about Ravi Shankar's improvisations that are totally

unacceptable to an Indian musician, then equally he is likely to say things about Mozart or Chopin that are totally unacceptable to a Western musician. In other words, the ability to say things about music that are acceptable to a musician is simply not a useful criterion of aesthetic perception.

I said in the Introduction that the whole concept of aesthetic perception, as I employ it in this book and as it is embodied in the culture of contemporary Western art music, is not one that is found in all musical cultures, regardless of their time and place; rather, it is a product of Western society since the Industrial Revolution. It is almost inevitable that a Westerner will misinterpret the music of a foreign culture when he listens with pleasure to it, just as he will probably misinterpret the past music of his own culture, in that he will not understand it in total conformity with the manner in which the musicians who produced it understood it or expected it to be understood. In the case of music from a foreign culture, it would be perhaps possible for a Western listener to remedy this by immersing himself in that culture, as ethnomusicologists like Blacking attempt to; Martyn Evans argues that 'perhaps we can, in time, *adopt* the perspective of the Indian, or of the Venda, so that we really listen through it and not simply to it. But this means living their life.' (1985: 141.) To say this, however, is to miss the point of how and why Western listeners (unless, of course, they are ethnomusicologists) listen to Indian or Venda music. We listen to it not in order to understand it in the manner in which Indian and Venda musicians understand it, but to enjoy it. And we can do this without going to live in India or Africa, just as we can listen to Machaut's music, and enjoy it, without going to live in fourteenth-century France.

In so far as we listen to Indian music or Machaut's music as music, we are bound to misinterpret it, because our concept of 'music' is a contemporary Western one. According to Kenneth Gourlay (1984: 32), it is a specifically Western trait to conceive of music 'as particular configurations of sound that one either listens to or produces oneself', and our whole approach to the music of other cultures is moulded by this ethnocentric presupposition. It even dictates what music from other cultures is actually to be heard in the West: 'What in effect is happening,' he continues, 'whether intended or not, is that the opportunity for musical events from other parts of the world to be reproduced in Europe increases in proportion to the extent to which they conform, or appear to conform, to western conceptualization.' Now if this is true, it may give a false impression to Westerners regarding the nature and diversity of non-Western musics (which is the point Gourlay wants to make). But it does not mean that there is anything spurious within the Westerner's aesthetic enjoyment of the music he hears, or that he is misunderstanding what he hears in an aesthetic sense. The reason for this is simply that the aesthetic understanding, as it is embodied in the contemporary Western concept of 'music', is self-fulfilling: as Scruton puts it (1979: 87), it is 'characterized by no specific desire to "find out", no special preoccupation with facts, since while these may be a necessary pre-condition for its exercise, their knowledge is no part of its aim'. This is not just a technical philosophical definition: it is a description of the manner in which Western listeners generally approach music.

In other words—and this is the point I want to make—listening to music for the purpose of establishing facts or formulating theories and listening to it for purposes of direct aesthetic gratification are two essentially different things.

III

If by 'musical listening' we mean listening to music for purposes of direct aesthetic gratification, then we can use the term 'music-ological listening' to refer to any type of listening to music whose purpose is the establishment of facts or the formulation of theories.[24]

Sartre refers to the experience of leaving a concert and returning to the world of daily affairs in terms of 'the nauseating disgust that characterizes the consciousness of reality' (1972: 225). And Iser (1978: 140) not only describes the similar return to reality that occurs when one stops reading, but characterizes its essential quality very clearly when he says that this return

is always to a reality from which we had been drawn away by the image-building process. . . . The significance of this process lies in the fact that

---

[24] To forestall possible confusion I should mention that, in his 'Meta-Variations', Benjamin Boretz adopts a different terminology: his aesthetic listening more or less corresponds to what I call 'musical', whereas his 'musical' listening is closer to my 'musicological' (1970: 64–5).

image-building eliminates the subject–object division essential for all perception, so that when we 'awaken' to the real world, this division seems all the more accentuated.

It has often enough been said that one of the essential characteristics of musical listening is its non-dualistic quality; in Bruce Norton's words, music 'provides access to another, separate "layer of existence" or "order of reality". . . . It is an experience irreconcilably different from any in which a subject contemplates an object or distinguishes between that which lies within himself and that which lies without.'[25] Again, T. S. Eliot speaks in his *Four Quartets* of 'music heard so deeply | That it is not heard at all, but you are the music | While the music lasts.' And the truth of these observations is brought home by various experiences in which the non-dualistic consciousness of musical listening is disrupted through the unsought-for intrusion of the external world.

For instance, one's musical enjoyment of a televised concert can be disrupted by the kind of over-enthusiastic picture-editing in which the oboe cannot echo the clarinet's three-note motif without the two players appearing in turn upon the screen in monstrous close-up: the disruption of the musical experience is the result of the facticity, so to speak, and the spatial proximity of the players being thrust upon one. Similarly a sudden wrong note can put an end to the listener's absorption in the music at a concert, not because he cannot understand what he hears (hearing a note as wrong generally implies that one knows what it should have been), but because the mistake thrusts the performer's presence upon the listener; in Don Ihde's words, 'the flight of music into ecstasy is quickly lost if the instrument intrudes as in the case of having to listen to the beginner whose violin squeaks and squawks instead of sounding in its own smooth tonality.' (1976: 78.) Thomas Clifton (1983: 279) says something similar about the intrusion of any kind of extraneous sounds:

The relation between myself and these unwanted sounds can be described as being side-by-side: the sounds are in the same space I am in, be it a small room, a concert hall, or the open air. But this is the same relationship which exists between a chair which is next to, or side-by-side with, a table. These are objects: likewise, both the sounds and I have become

[25] 1975: 355. Norton is paraphrasing Victor Zuckerkandl's conception of music rather than stating his own.

objects, adjacent to each other. . . . On the other hand, music is experienced as such when a voluntary proximity of sounds is felt as opening toward: a condition *toward* which we use our freedom to effect the closure between ourselves and the music. From this it is clear that even the word 'proximity' has a purely phenomenal significance. The music need not be literally 'there' where I am. It could indeed be at a distance. But what makes sound remain merely sound is the absence of any bodily complicity with it.

In musicological listening, by contrast, what is experienced presents itself to the listener as a perceptual object, giving rise to some kind of judgement or behavioural response on the listener's part. As Sloboda (1985) and McAdams (1984) point out, the essential biological function of human hearing is to enable people 'to "parse" the acoustic environment effortlessly' (Sloboda, p. 155), that is, to separate out the different sounds that are heard. Musicological listening achieves much the same in the case of musical sounds. To hear a complex sound musicologically is to hear it in terms of the particular pitches that are played and the particular instruments that play them; it involves the co-ordination of what is heard with some scheme of representation that is adapted to the purpose in hand. For instance, recognizing an example in a class test as a major seventh played on a viola entails the listener co-ordinating what he hears with a pre-existing knowledge of intervallic types and musical instruments; recognizing a sequence of notes as belonging to a particular note-row requires that the listener co-ordinates what he hears with some kind of abstract representation of the note-row. Pandora Hopkins's perplexed subjects, too, were listening musicologically—that is, they were listening to the *hardingfele* music not for its own sake, but in the hope of being able to discover its recurrent rhythmic pattern. And as these examples illustrate, it is a defining quality of any such act of perception that it completes itself in the judgement or behavioural response to which it gives rise.

It is mainly listening of this sort that has been the focus of experimental psychological research, involving as it does judgements of the identity or non-identity of pitches or intervals, the grouping of notes according to one organizational principle or another, the recognition of melodic contours under various transformations, and so forth. In each case the experimental conditions give rise, whatever the nature of the musical stimulus, to a perception which completes itself in the required judgement or behavioural response. Now there is no reason to doubt the validity of such research as a means of gaining information on the perception of non-verbal auditory stimuli; but whether it tells us much about musical rather than musicological listening (in the sense that I have defined it) is another matter.[26] Sloboda remarks, playing devil's advocate, that 'In defence of such research one may, of course, argue that music is made up of a large number of small fragments chained together, and that music perception is simply a concatenation of a series of perceptual acts on such fragments.' (1985: 152.) But this argument quickly runs into absurdity.

Consider what happens when someone hears a rapid harp glissando. Are we to believe that his perception of the characteristic rising swoosh of sound results from the integration of a large number of perceptual acts, each corresponding to the identification of a separate note? What about listening to a rapidly played scale on the violin, or to Coleman's improvising on the saxophone, where portamento or pitch-bending may so run the notes together that there are no real boundaries between them: in these cases what would the basic units be on which the perception of the music was based? It seems clear that here, at least, the perception of the musical event as a whole—the swoosh of the harp, the violin scale—is a primary perceptual construct rather than the concatenation of a series of fragmentary perceptual acts, and the term 'global precedence' has been coined to refer to this phenomenon (Watkins and Dyson 1985: 109). And if this argument is generalized, it leads to the conclusion that, as Mary Louise Serafine says, 'the perception of single pitches does not necessarily precede the perception of groupings of multiple pitches. In other words, the discernment of single pitches is not the prerequisite to the perception of musical wholes.' (1988: 63.)

Serafine's argument (for which she marshals considerable evidence) turns on the distinction between what I call musical and musicological listening, for she is saying that the discrete pitches we see in scores and talk about in analysis classes 'arise only as a result of reflection *upon* music and notation *of* it' (1988: 60). That is, they can be made the objects of a musicological listening which is

---

[26] On this issue see Sloboda 1985: 151–4, McMullen 1980: 183–6, Serafine 1988: 52–67, and Randall 1972: 116–22.

structured in terms of musical notation and in consequence constitutes what is heard as a completed perceptual object, and this is what is done in an aural training or music theory class; but they are not heard as completed objects of perception in the course of ordinary musical listening.[27] Or to put it in terms of Merleau-Ponty's metaphor,[28] scores represent the back of the musical fabric: and whereas from the player's point of view the score is prehistoric to the performance, because (as I have said) it is abolished in the act of performance, for the listener it simply does not exist. And it is here, as I see it, that the crucial distinction lies, from a critical point of view, between music on the one hand and the literary or pictorial arts on the other. Reader-response criticism shows how the literary experience emerges in the reader's imaginative activity as he 'bridges the gaps' in the text, to use Iser's phrase;[29] Gombrich's account of the psychology of representation shows how pictorial meaning emerges from the beholder's imaginative activity as he interprets and reconstructs what he sees. The signs embodied in the literary text and in the painting play a genuine role in the aesthetic process, which goes beyond them in the same sense as the performance goes beyond the notational symbols of the musical score. But this is not the same as what happens in musical listening. Listeners do not bridge the gaps between the notes, as readers bridge the gaps between the words, because notes simply do not exist for the listener in the sense in which words exist for the reader.

The failure to appreciate this has led to a lot of theoretical confusion, a representative example of which can be found in the work of the pioneering psychologist of music, Carl Seashore. In the 1920s Seashore carried out a series of experimental investigations into musical performance. He devised mechanical techniques for recording the precise pitches and rhythms produced by singers

[27] Hanslick says that 'music begins where . . . isolated auditory impressions terminate' (trans. 1957: 80), while Ingarden (1986: 44–5) writes: 'The melody . . . is what we directly hear as a qualitative whole where only an analysis is capable of discovering the individual sounds. Whoever moves away from the melody perceived in this manner to "a relation of pitch" abandons the realm of artistic products or aesthetic objects given us in experience and instead reflects upon the equivalence of certain mental operations that at best are in a certain way of conformity with aesthetic objects. This is a move from an organized, harmonized unity of the perceived whole to an atomized multiplicity of elements received only hypothetically but not appearing as palpable elements in a musical work.'

[28] See p. 135 above.

[29] See above, p. 18.

and violinists, and was amazed on analysing the resulting data to find that highly skilled musicians played out of tune and out of rhythm most of the time—out of tune, that is to say, in terms of equal-tempered or indeed any other theoretically formulated scales, and out of rhythm in terms of the relationships of half as long and twice as long that are shown in the score. On the basis of these results he developed an influential theory according to which the artistic value of musical performance derived largely from the kind of expressive deviations from normal values which he had discovered (Seashore and Metfessel 1925). Now from a productional perspective—for instance in terms of instrumental tuition—this is a useful theory, because instrumental technique is generally acquired through rather mechanical exercises, and many budding performers have to learn how to liberate themselves from an over-rigid adherence to notational values. But the theory makes no sense as an account of aesthetic perception. This is because the normal values that define the 'deviations' in performance as such have no existence in what is heard; the deviations come into being only through the act of making a comparison between what is heard and the notational values—and this is a comparison that the musicologist or psychologist makes, not the listener. As Pandora Hopkins (1966: 311) says, speaking in general of the deviations from theoretical values that are to be observed when music is transcribed, 'The concept of "deviation" was surely not in the original piece but exists only in the transcription of it.'[30]

In *The Concept of Mind* (1973: 216), Gilbert Ryle falls into a similar kind of confusion when he tries to describe what happens when someone hears some waltz for the first time. He says of this listener that

he does not know how this tune goes, but since he knows how some other waltz tunes go, he knows what sort of rhythms to expect. He is partially but not fully prepared for the succeeding bars, and he can partially but not completely place the notes already heard and now being heard. He is wondering just how the tune goes, and in wondering he is trying to piece out the arrangement of the notes. At no moment is he quite ready for the note that is due next. That is, he is thinking in the special sense of trying to puzzle something out.

---

[30] For further consideration of the fallacy illustrated by Seashore's theory see below, pp. 225–6.

Cognitive psychologists, to be sure, model perceptions in terms of the unconscious weighing of probabilities. But one cannot sensibly talk of 'unconscious wondering'; Ryle's terminology seems to imply a reflective awareness of the music, a stepping out of what Schutz calls the musical flow, and it is this that makes what Ryle says so oddly untrue to the real-life experience of hearing a waltz. And the same applies, rather surprisingly, to Schutz's own so-called phenomenological analysis of a series of notes, according to which, when we hear two notes, 'we are referring the second one to the first and say: That is an interval of the second upwards.' (ed. 1976: 47.) But who is this musicological homunculus who does the referring and saying of which Schutz speaks, and the wondering that Ryle describes? And where does he find the time to do it? In both cases the descriptions are clearly pre-phenomenological in that they are formulated in terms of perceptual objects which are constituted not by musical listening but by reflection upon it.

I am not, of course, saying that people are never aware of notes, intervals, motifs, themes, structural sections, or points of closure when they listen to music in the ordinary way. But the kind of perceptual acts through which notes, intervals, and the rest are constituted as perceptual objects do not play a foundational role in the aesthetic experience of music. Indeed, far from being a prerequisite for aesthetic perception, listening to music in terms of such completed musicological perceptions can become detrimental to aesthetic perception or even incompatible with it; as Maurice Halbwachs put it (1980: 181), it can lead the listener to 'become too preoccupied in the music', and so cease hearing it as music at all. Thomas Clifton goes into more detail:

How easy it is to slip out of music and listen instead to the performer's instrument, or the tone row, the pitch classes, etc. On the other hand, one can intend to listen for all these things, and suddenly become caught up in the music![31]

This separation between the musical and the musicological

---

[31] 1983: 282. This is another viewpoint with an 18th-cent. pedigree; Sulzer says that in aesthetic perception 'the object must be comprehended as an entity, our attention must not be drawn to the individual details so that these become the object of our contemplation. Anyone who analyses an object, contemplating and consequently examining each of its separate parts to discover how it is constructed, does so completely dispassionately; if we are to feel, our efforts should be directed not towards the contemplation or analysis of the object but towards the effect that it has on us.' (Le Huray and Day 1981: 124.)

experience of music became very evident during the students' attempts to transcribe the Ornette Coleman improvisation, mentioned above: in trying to figure out what note followed what, or within what interval a particular flurry of notes was contained, they stepped out of the ongoing experience of the music and built up static representations of it instead,[32] developing and refining these in the course of a sequence of hearings. And yet these evolving musicological experiences of the music seemed completely detached from the original experience of the music as music, as jazz improvisation—an experience which re-established itself every time the music was heard for itself and not for an ulterior purpose, and which seemed completely unaffected by the successive attempts at transcription. Maybe this Coleman improvisation is an extreme case. But the point it illustrates—that hearing notes, intervals, and note-rows is not the same as hearing music—is a general one.

W. Jay Dowling writes (1982a: 423) that 'when pitches are coded at the psychophysical level or the level of tonal material outside of a tonal context, listeners find it difficult to integrate them into higher order units.' He is referring to relatively low-level perceptual processing, but it seems to me that his words can be applied to higher levels as well. To hear a note, an interval, or a note-row as the object of a completed perceptual act is, or at least can be, to disrupt the perceptual integration of the music that gives rise to the aesthetic experience. To listen to music too hard—to hear it in terms of its component sounds, and to co-ordinate these with some production-orientated scheme of representation—is to risk not hearing it as music at all; and conversely, to hear music aesthetically may be to hear hardly anything in production-orientated terms. Halbwachs has a beautiful image which bears upon this: when we leave a concert, he says, we may find we remember 'almost nothing of a piece just heard for the first time. The melodic themes break up and notes scatter like pearls from a necklace whose thread has broken.' (1980: 160.) Similarly, Sloboda (1985: 59) cites the instance of

someone who has just listened to a performance of a long and complex

---

[32] Pandora Hopkins remarks, using a singularly American metaphor, that in transcribing music, we 'freeze our findings much as one would freeze orange juice or chocolate cake' (1966: 311).

symphonic work. It is quite possible that he or she cannot recall a single theme from the work (I have often been in this situation myself), yet he or she certainly remembers *something* about the work, and can make some appropriate response to it. When this response is expressed in words it characteristically contains remarks about the substance of the music which are neither descriptive ('it was loud') nor reactive ('I liked it') but embody an attempt to *characterize* the music through metaphor ('It had the feeling of a long heroic struggle triumphantly resolved'). It seems less significant that people often disagree about their characterizations than that they nearly always have *some* comment to offer. This is not an arbitrary reaction, but a genuine attempt to describe some real thing or experience.

When this happens, it is the affective content conveyed, however inadequately, by means of such descriptions, and the sense of satisfaction engendered through absorption in a piece of music, that is the real object of the listening process, and not the sound of the orchestra, nor the score, nor any musicological representation of what was played.[33]

3.2   APPRECIATION AND CRITICISM

I

Alfred Schutz condensed into one sentence the argument I have been putting forward in the preceding pages. 'The listener', he wrote (ed. 1976: 26), 'responds neither to sound waves, nor does he perceive sounds; he just listens to music.'

A number of writers have tried to characterize this 'just listening'. One feature that is widely agreed to be basic to it is its effortless quality; the psychologist Leon Crickmore, for example, says that 'in the moments of profoundest involvement the

---

[33] Wittgenstein would not have agreed: 'Suppose there is a person who admires and enjoys what is admitted to be good [music] but can't remember the simplest tunes, doesn't know when the bass comes in, etc. We say he hasn't seen what's in it. We use the phrase "A man is musical" not so as to call a man musical if he says "Ah!" when a piece of music is played, any more than we call a dog musical if it wags its tail when music is played.' (ed. 1966: 6.) But when we call someone musical we are generally talking about their ability to produce music, or to grasp it in productional terms; it is in these terms, and not in terms of aesthetic perception, that Wittgenstein's listener hasn't seen what is in the music. His real aim in this passage is to discredit the idea that understanding music means having certain inner experiences; it is this that leads him to put forward particular public reactions as the criterion for an adequate response to music.

enjoyment of music is felt as a kind of effortless awareness, more passive or receptive than active—an intuitive act which involves no discursive or reflexive process.' (1968a: 239.) Eric Blom coined the term 'overhearing' to refer to just this kind of involvement with music. He called it a 'delicious sense of effortless absorption' and described it as

a kind of hovering on the brink of receptiveness, an absorption of the musical impression without any conscious effort. We may be keen, but tired. Nothing else will hold us more than the music . . . yet the music cannot quite move us out of our listlessness. But once the lassitude has worn off, we shall find that the impression has remained—nothing very definite, perhaps, only a sort of afterglow, but something compelling and endearing just the same. It is rather a blessed state to find oneself in at a concert, and afterwards the felicity, felt to be undeserved, is perhaps for that very reason the more welcome. The only trouble is overhearing cannot be cultivated. It is a delight that comes rarely, a gift of the gods to accept thankfully, but it must not be expected too often. When most expected it will be least likely to produce itself.[34]

However, these positive evaluations of the immediacy and spontaneity of 'just listening' have by no means been universal. Kant and Hegel spoke with disfavour of the invasive quality of music, while Hanslick described as 'pathological' any experience of music in which the listener did not constitute the music as an imaginative object held at an aesthetic distance, but instead reacted to the sound in a directly physiological or psychological sense.[35] Heard in such a manner, Hanslick says, music becomes no more than a drug: it 'loosens the feet or the heart just as wine loosens the tongue' (trans. 1957: 93). In this way it degrades the listener; Hanslick even speculates that it 'may prevent the development of that strength of will and power of intellect which man is capable of' (p. 94). This sense of music being somehow threatening seems to be a widespread one, for it is also to be found in such legends— or maybe cautionary tales would be a better description—as those of the Sirens and the Pied Piper. Even the nursery rhyme 'Tom,

[34] Blom ed. 1977: 739. Hanslick describes a similar experience, but comments that it cannot have a foundational role for the aesthetics of music, because 'A purely aesthetic factor appeals to our nervous system in its normal condition, and does not count on a morbid exaltation or depression of the mind.' (trans. 1957: 78.)

[35] Hanslick trans. 1957: 12, 90. Naturally Hanslick considered Wagner's work to be the prime example of a music designed to be experienced 'pathologically', offering what Adorno disparagingly saw as a ready-made sensual experience.

Tom, the Piper's Son' has people dancing to his music against their will, while something of the sort entered the pages of history in the phenomenon of the tarantella that was widespread in fifteenth- and sixteenth-century Europe. And nowadays such concerns still appear in the distrust of the demagogue whose 'musical' voice turns people's heads and addles their minds,[36] and in the worries that people sometimes express regarding the deleterious effects of pop music upon the young—worries that have a pedigree extending at least as far back as Plato.

Writing not long after the definitive emancipation of instrumental music from a position of inferiority to vocal music, but unwilling to accept this development, Hegel praised the function of the text in defining the boundaries of the musical experience:

A text provides from the start definite conceptions and thereby rescues consciousness from that dreamier element of feeling without concepts in which we may allow ourselves to be led hither and thither without interruption and may preserve our freedom to feel anything we choose in a piece of music and to feel moved by it in any way we choose.[37]

A text, in other words, mediates between the listener and the inchoate or uncontrollable qualities of the musical experience; it not only, as it were, holds the music at a distance, but also subjects it to the authority of reason. Now I would argue that the aesthetic approach to musical listening that I outlined in the opening chapter of this book—the aesthetic prefigured in Hanslick, implied in the analytical and theoretical writings of Schenker and Schoenberg, and set out explicitly by Collingwood, Hampshire, and Scruton— sets out to fulfil for instrumental music essentially the same role as the one Hegel saw the text fulfilling for vocal music.[38]

Collingwood and Hampshire emphasize the need for the listener to constitute the music as an intentional object as he hears it; Scruton contrasts an aesthetically adequate experience of the music with a mere passive response to it, and underlines the role of critical reasoning in giving rise to such an aesthetic experience. In

[36] Perhaps the classic description of this is Tolkien's account of Saruman in *The Lord of the Rings*.

[37] Trans. from *Aesthetics: Lectures on Fine Art (Ästhetik oder Wissenschaft des Schönen)* in Dahlhaus 1982: 29.

[38] In *The Beautiful in Music* Hanslick repeatedly attacks Hegel's views on music, stressing the foundational role of instrumental rather than vocal music from the point of view of musical aesthetics (trans. 1957: 29–30, 120).

each case the essential demand is that the listener's experience of the music should be mediated by some kind of voluntary and rational representation of what he hears; the difference between Hegel on the one hand and Collingwood, Hampshire, and Scruton on the other is that whereas Hegel sees this representation in terms of textual semantics, his successors see it in terms of what is essentially some kind of abstract representation of the music's structure. And the importance for real life of the philosophical ruminations of Collingwood, Hampshire, and Scruton is that they provide the rationale for what is possibly the most significant educational movement in musical history:[39] the movement Virgil Thomson (1939) called the 'Appreciation-racket', the origins of which can be traced back to the time when instrumental music was achieving its emancipation,[40] but whose current scale of operations is the product of twentieth-century educational thinking in North America.

The courses of instruction and programmed listening that are offered in American schools and colleges under the title 'Music Appreciation' have the basic aim of inducing in the listener certain types of representation which are believed to result in a heightening of the aesthetic experience. These representations are primarily formulated in productional terms, even though their application is to reception rather than to production. In a casual and apparently rather surprised remark, the educationalist Robert Petzold (1969: 86–7) betrayed a presupposition underlying much work in the field of music appreciation, which is that productional categories are the only ones in which music can be adequately represented; reporting on the results of an extensive series of tests in which children were required to respond in a variety of ways to musical stimuli, he wrote:

Children need to learn how to think musically, how to analyze and evaluate the factors that are present in a musical situation. The fact that performance accuracy is not inhibited when certain of the basic elements of music are presented in combination (i.e. melody–rhythm, melody–harmony, timbre–melody) indicates that children are capable of

---

[39] The link between the philosophical rationale and its educational application is particularly clear in the work of Percy Scholes; see Jorgensen 1987: 144.

[40] Parakilas traces it back to the 1820s (1984: 16). Hanslick played a major role in its development; for nearly 40 years he gave lectures on music appreciation at Vienna University.

responding to the more complete musical situations. Children will respond to that which they are asked to respond to, even in complex auditory situations, and it may not be necessary to treat each of these elements as separate entities to be combined into musical wholes at some later time.

Why, one might ask, would anybody have thought in the first place that listeners need to be introduced to the various parameters of music one by one? The answer is clear: it is the result of an inappropriately reified view of music, in which timbral values, pitch relations, and the rest are seen as things to be communicated through sound.[41] For as I have tried to demonstrate, these things are not in reality intrinsic to the phenomenon of musical listening at all; Petzold is confusing the two sides of the musical fabric—or, rather, he is just beginning to discover the distinction between them.

The 'Appreciation-racket' does not simply involve the idea that musical listeners should formulate representations of what they hear; it assumes that they should do so consciously. (Virgil Thomson was particularly scathing about this, describing the assumption that 'the conscious paying of attention during the auditive process intensifies the favorable reaction' as 'false, or at least highly disputable'.[42]) In other words, the idea is that it is desirable to observe things consciously rather than simply to respond to them passively, or maybe not to respond to them at all. Here it is perhaps useful to consider a specific example. I knew and played Schumann's 'Vogel als Prophet'[43] for some years before, happening to work through the piece for a class, I noticed that it contains the short passage of strict canonic imitation marked in Ex. 42. This surprised me, not because one does not expect to find canonic devices in Schumann (they are in fact rather characteristic of him) but simply because I had been unaware of it for all that time; the canon is, as it were, absorbed into the texture of the music—it is there, but one doesn't easily hear it. And that is why most listeners would have to have it pointed out to them if they were not to overlook its existence.

[41] See below, p. 226.
[42] Thomson 1939: 125. This assumption goes back to Hanslick, according to whom 'The aesthetic appreciation of music . . . is only possible when our mind is fully awake; when we are "conscious" of the music and perfectly realize all its points of beauty.' (trans. 1957: 99.)
[43] From *Waldscenen*.

Ex. 42

But what difference does it actually make whether or not one is aware of this little bit of canon, seeing that Schumann has written the music in such a way that it is not readily audible? The answer depends on what one is trying to do with the piece. If one is trying to understand it in terms of Schumann's compositional thinking— by which I mean not only his technical procedures, but also his literary and philosophical orientation towards the work—then undoubtedly the canon is important. But if one simply wants to enjoy the music, then I would say that it is nice to know the canon is there, but that the very fact that it has to be explained to the listener means it is not of any great importance. In defence of this opinion I would quote Debussy's view that music should 'procure for us immediate pleasure, and either impose or insinuate itself in us without our having to make any effort to understand it'.[44] I would cite, too, Aaron Copland's statement (1961: 13–14) that

From self-observation and from observing audience reaction I would be inclined to say that we all listen on an elementary plane of musical consciousness. . . . We respond to music from a primal and almost brutish level—dumbly, as it were, for on that level we are firmly grounded . . . and all the analytical, historical, textual material on or about the music heard, interesting though it may be, cannot—and I venture to say should not—alter that fundamental relationship.

[44] From an article in *La revue bleue*, 1904, trans. in Jarocinski 1976: 97.

Now Copland is not saying that analytical, historical, or textual knowledge can play no part in musical listening; the listening of the connoisseur, after all, is defined by just such knowledge. He is saying that such knowledge does not play a foundational role. If I enjoy the 'Eroica' Symphony, say, it is because I like the music and not because I have an analytical appreciation of it. (Indeed, I would hardly be drawn to analyse the music if I did not like it in the first place.) On the other hand, if I do not enjoy a piece, then 'understanding' it in a production-orientated sense is no more a substitute for enjoying it than 'understanding' the behaviour of people I dislike is a substitute for liking them. If I dislike Schoenberg's Piano Piece Op. 33a, then knowing about serialism will help me to understand why Schoenberg wrote the piece as he did, just as knowing about the historical background will help me understand why Schoenberg chose to give the work a neo-classical form and an abstract title; but this is not an adequate substitute for a direct response to the music. I am not denying that a technical analysis may uncover aspects of the musical construction that are interesting or elegant or even, in their own way, beautiful. But we are dealing here with a musicological rather than a musical beauty. To adapt Kathryn Bailey's remark about Webern's Symphony,[45] it is the visual, intellectual Op. 33a—the piece for the analyst—that is beautiful and not (for me) the aural, immediate one.

The result of this kind of analysis, then, is not musical but musicological appreciation. Now there is nothing wrong with musicological appreciation. When one can respond directly to a piece of music, knowing something about it as well (as in the case of the canon in 'Vogel als Prophet') can add an extra dimension of interest or enjoyment to the experience; it helps to open the music up to reflective thought, and some people—though not others—find that this significantly enhances their pleasure. And when someone knows a piece so well that it has gone stale for him, he may find his response to it renewed and refreshed if he learns about its historical background, or thinks about it from an analytical point of view. This is because the very discrepancy between grasping a piece in musical terms and in musicological terms means that the one can strike sparks off the other; it is rather like a metaphor which presents a familiar object in a new light through

[45] See above, pp. 58–9.

the illuminating collision of two apparently unrelated ideas. Even following a score while listening to a familiar piece can provoke new insights, because it leads one to approach the music from a new angle, to 'see' the sound in a different way; the musician who listens with a score is indulging in a strange, dual-level art form in which hearing and vision run sometimes in parallel, sometimes at tangents to each other, and sometimes in opposite directions.

But all this makes sense only on the basis of an established response to the music. The problem with musicological appreciation is that it is likely to be counter-productive if it is regarded, as it often is, as a way of introducing people to music that is unfamiliar to them. Schoenberg, who emigrated to the USA in 1933, inveighed against the shallow knowledge retailed by the music appreciation texts that he found there, giving the example of a student who has read that Schumann's orchestration is gloomy and unclear, and who as a result 'will never listen to the orchestra of Schumann naively, sensitively and open-mindedly' (ed. 1984: 114). As Schoenberg points out, it is when the student has no experience of the music in question that this kind of vicarious knowledge becomes most dangerous; instead of enhancing his response to the music, it becomes a substitute for it, leading to a kind of narrow-mindedness in which everything is rejected that does not conform to his preconceived notions. Schoenberg, of course, had plenty of experience of this kind of narrow-mindedness. One need only think of the committee that turned down Schoenberg's *Verklärte Nacht* because it contained one dissonance that was not to be found in the harmony books, or the director of an Italian conservatory who loudly protested at *Pierrot lunaire* because there were no triads in it (ed. 1984: 131, 97). In such instances, people's musicological responses were evidently getting in the way of their musical ones. I shall return to this in the next section.

If the conscious representation of musical structure is one main element in the 'Appreciation-racket', the other is a kind of explicit hermeneutics: people are encouraged to experience music in the light of a reflective awareness of what it means, either in terms of the social or personal values it symbolizes and communicates or in terms of some kind of expressive or representational content. Now when he sees a piece of music in terms of a reflective awareness of its meaning, the listener is (to use Iser's phrase) adopting an interpretative position in relation to it.[46] For instance, the listener can adopt a position in relation to Mozart's *Marriage of Figaro* or Beethoven's Ninth Symphony, because these works can be seen from various possible interpretational perspectives, and the position that he adopts in relation to such a work will modify his experience of it. Someone who perceives *Figaro* as a domestic comedy will experience it in a distinctly different manner from someone who perceives it as a political document; and this does not simply mean that they will hear and see the same things but interpret them differently. It means that they will actually perceive different things; and as Roger Scruton argues, the critic's (or appreciation teachers') importance lies in his capacity to modify the aesthetic experience through his interpretation of the work.[47]

But to say that the listener can in this way take up an interpretative position in relation to *Figaro* or the Ninth Symphony is precisely to identify what we generally call the 'literary' aspect of these works—that is, the aspect in which they are possessed of an extra-musical meaning which is capable of critical exegesis and interpretation.[48] Both these works embody social and political aspirations and are misinterpreted, or at any rate incompletely interpreted, if they are heard just as music; that is why it makes sense to speak of adopting a position in relation to them. In a similar though more extreme way, Wagner's music-dramas require the listener to follow and interpret the action quite consciously if he is fully to grasp what is going on in the music: hence the little guides to Wagner's works that Stravinsky described as making 'the neophyte attending a presentation of *Götterdämmerung* resemble one of those tourists you see on top of the Empire State Building trying to orient himself by spreading out a map of New York' (1947: 80).

Götterdämmerung, *Figaro*, and even the Ninth Symphony have texts: to this extent they are all literary as well as musical works. But there are examples of purely instrumental music that demand

---

[46] See above, p. 143.

[47] See above, pp. 19–20.

[48] And possibly an intra-musical one too. Treitler (1980) argues that the meaning of the 9th Symphony derives largely from its manipulation of the traditional musical genres, and offers a critical exegesis based on this. Here, then, genre would constitute more than the 'abstract generalization' to which Dahlhaus refers (see above, p. 147). But of course the 9th Symphony is exceptional in this, as in other respects: as Treitler says, 'more than any other work of the Tradition, it *demands* interpretation.' (1982b: 161.)

the same kind of conscious interpretation on the listener's part. One such example, which Peter Kivy discusses, is bars 14–16 of Bach's Chorale Prelude *Jesus Christus, unser Heiland* (BWV 665).[49] Kivy comments on the 'peculiarly jagged, leaping and percussive' nature of the melodic figure in this passage, and argues (not wholly convincingly, in my view) that in purely musical terms this figure makes very little sense. What makes sense of it, he says, is the text of the chorale on which BWV 665 is based. As he explains, 'It is only by knowing, through the text, that . . . it is a "representation of the strokes of God's wrath" that we can make *musical* sense of its appearance.'[50] Again, then, a literary interpretation is called for; it is just that the text has gone, so to speak, underground.

And yet there are some pieces of music which do not in any way involve a text, and which still seem to require the same kind of interpretative stance on the listener's part if they are to make sense in musical terms (and not just analytically or historically). A case in point is Charles Ives's *Central Park in the Dark*. Would this piece make musical sense if someone were to listen to it under the misapprehension that its title was, say, *Appalachian Spring*? Perhaps not. For Ives's title, with its suggestion of different night sounds coming from different directions, does not just tell us what the composer himself had in mind: it indicates to the listener the manner in which he is to 'parse' what he hears into distinct, superimposed strands of sound. This means that, as with the Bach, a specific interpretative stance is required if the piece is to be heard properly. (Or might it be argued that it is only when we stop hearing it as night sounds, and instead hear it simply as music, that we can grasp the full power and modernity of Ives's conception?) In the same way, one might say that Stockhausen's *Hymnen* has to be heard in terms of the national anthems from all over the world of which it is constructed; here what is involved is not just an aural parsing of the sound, but also the message that is expressed by the superimposition and interpenetration of the anthems—the message of man's universal brotherhood.[51] (Or might it be argued that it is only when we stop hearing the work as being constructed of different musics, and instead hear it as 'a higher unity, a universality

---

[49] Ex. 28 in Kivy 1984.
[50] 1984: 148–9. The quotation is from Schweitzer.
[51] Maconie 1976: 219–20.

of past, present and future, of different planes and spaces'[52] that we can understand *Hymnen* properly?)

These examples from Bach, Ives, and Stockhausen all lead the listener to adopt a specific interpretative position in relation to them: they each demand, in certain respects at least, to be heard in a specific way. But in each case this position is so specific—the music is either interpreted in the appropriate manner, or misinterpreted—that it no longer really corresponds to what Iser has in mind. For in Iser's eyes it is only pulp literature or propaganda that insists on being interpreted in a specific, predetermined manner (and indeed it might be argued that *Hymnen* does tend towards propaganda, of however high an order.[53]) True literature, for Iser, is not like this: it gives the reader the freedom to interpret the text as he wishes, and so to play an active role in the constitution of the literary work. Now most music does in fact bestow a great deal of freedom upon the listener. Indeed, it bestows more freedom upon the listener than literature generally does upon the reader. When someone reads a novel, after all, his freedom of thought is constrained by the narrative structure of the work, by the need to understand what is going on. (I cannot properly enjoy a Jane Austen novel if I do not remember who the main characters are, or get them muddled up with characters from some other novel.) But in general the musical listener is free, within broad limits, to think or imagine or focus on whatever he likes.

I can think of Till Eulenspiegel's merry pranks or listen to Strauss's symphonic poem as absolute music; I can track the evolution of the work's form or see shapes moving in space; I can listen to the E flat clarinet or listen to nothing in particular. Or, to take an example that is comparable with *Central Park in the Dark*, I can hear the night sounds in the third movement of Bartók's *Music for Strings, Percussion and Celesta* as night sounds—which is to say that I hear them as both music and night sounds—or I can hear them just as music, perhaps not even knowing that they have any other connotation. (Would it in fact have occurred to anyone to

[52] These words come from Stockhausen's sleeve-note for *Telemusik* (DGG 137012) and refer to that work, not to *Hymnen*.

[53] But see Maconie 1976: 222. Cone discusses the quotation from 'La Marseillaise' in Debussy's *Feux d'artifice* (from Book 2 of the *Préludes*), which must be heard as representing the band playing at a firework show—it makes no other musical sense—and comments: 'On this literal level the passage is effective and amusing, but it limits the possible significance of the music and discourages one from taking it very seriously.' (1974: 169.)

hear them as night sounds if Bartók had not given the title 'Night Music' to the first piece he wrote in this particular style, in the piano suite *Out of Doors*?) From an aesthetic point of view it does not seem to matter greatly which I do; certainly it is nice to hear Bartók's night sounds as night sounds, just as it is nice to hear the canon in 'Vogel als Prophet' as a canon, but as in that case it is not very important. It is not as if the piece made sense one way but not the other, as if one would be likely to enjoy it if one knew about the night sounds but not otherwise. Again, would it really matter very much if someone got the record-sleeves mixed up and listened to *Ein Heldenleben* under the impression that he was hearing *Symphonia Domestica*? (Felix Weingartner thought not.) Did it really matter when certain nineteenth-century critics misinterpreted Beethoven's 'Les Adieux' Sonata as a depiction of the parting and reunion of two lovers, instead of the departure and return of the Archduke Rudolph (Hanslick trans. 1957: 61–2)? I see no reason to think so: and if it does not matter so very much when a work like *Ein Heldenleben* or Op. 81*a* is misinterpreted in such a manner, then it follows that interpreting it cannot be so important in the first place.[54]

All this suggests that, for the ordinary listener if not for the connoisseur, listening to music is not, in fact, very similar to reading a work of literature (at least as Iser describes it). When the interpretative position adopted by the listener matters in a musical sense, as is perhaps the case in *Central Park in the Dark*, he has little if any freedom of interpretation. On the other hand, when he does have this freedom, his interpretation does not seem to be so important for the aesthetic experience. To be sure, he is free to prevent an aesthetic experience from happening at all, for instance by listening too hard to the instrument, the note row, or the pitch-classes (as Clifton said), or by thinking too hard about an imminent tax demand. But there seems to be less scope for him to determine what *sort* of aesthetic experience he will have, by choosing to hear the music in one way or another, than Iser maintains is the case in literature. And I would argue that it is because music offers the

---

[54] It was a younger contemporary of Beethoven, Fétis, who wrote that music should 'excite us, and it is enough. But upon what subject? It is of no consequence. By what means? I know not; and, further, I care not.' (1842: 289.) And Kivy concludes his book on musical representation, 'When one knows *only* what a musical composition might picture or represent, one doesn't know so very much'. (1984: 216.)

listener only limited scope for deciding what sort of aesthetic experience he will have that music criticism occupies a less prestigious—and indeed less significant—role than does literary criticism.

I am referring here to the kind of music criticism that aims at general intelligibility rather than being expressed in technical terms and addressed to experts. It is hard for such criticism to advance beyond the essentially redundant role of morning-after journalism without becoming involved in some kind of hermeneutics; but if the critical interpretation is to consist of anything more discursive than an apt image or an illuminating metaphor—such as E. M. Forster's association of the scherzo from Beethoven's Fifth Symphony with 'a goblin walking quietly over the universe'[55]—then the danger of eccentricity and irrelevance seems never to be far off. A classic illustration of the kind of eccentricity I have in mind is Arnold Schering's interpretations of Beethoven's instrumental works as being based on specific works of literature; he thought, for instance, that the String Quartet Op. 59 No. 3 was based on *Don Quixote*, in such a way that the melodies were settings of Cervantes' words, the motifs represented different characters, and so forth. There is, of course, not a shred of evidence that Beethoven intended anything of the sort. But that is not in itself a fatal objection. As Bruno Nettl comments (1983: 202), 'If the association of Beethoven and Cervantes is not to be found in Beethoven's life, it may nevertheless become a valid association in the mind of the believing listener, and in other ways it might possibly provide a guide for understanding the musical work.'

Schering's interpretation of Op. 59 No. 3 is certainly an example of adopting a position in relation to a work, and with a vengeance; but is it really possible, as Nettl suggests, that it could lead a listener to an aesthetic experiencing of the work where previously there was none, or even that it could render more profound an already existing aesthetic response? For it is precisely in its power to do this that the significance of, say, Leavis's interpretation of *Paradise Lost* lies; it is not really to the point to ask whether or not his ideas correspond to what Milton intended, because Milton is dead and what matters now is the aesthetic experiencing of Milton's text to which Leavis's interpretation may

---

[55] Helen makes this association in ch. 5 of *Howards End*.

lead the reader. In the same way, as Hanslick argued, 'Aesthetically speaking, it is utterly indifferent whether Beethoven really did associate all his works with certain ideas. We do not know them, and as far as the composition is concerned, they do not exist.' (trans. 1957: 60.) The trouble with Schering's interpretations of Beethoven, then, is not that Beethoven did not intend them but that they do not contribute to the listener's aesthetic experience; they just get in the way. One cannot hear the music in terms of them, or at any rate not in the natural and unforced manner in which one can hear the scherzo from the Fifth Symphony in terms of Forster's metaphor,[56] or in which Schumann found he could hear Berlioz's *Symphonie fantastique* in terms of its programme.[57] At most, interpretations such as Schering's can give rise to an intriguing experience of the music in which (as in the case of technical analysis) musical and musicological responses strike sparks off one another. But this falls far short of the mutual reinforcement and ultimate merging of critical interpretation and aesthetic experience that give Leavis's writings their value. And if the comparison of Schering with Leavis is not really a fair one, nevertheless I think it does locate a decisive imbalance between what discursive criticism can achieve in music and what it can achieve in literature. One might even maintain that whereas critical interpretation is or can be intrinsic to the literary experience, the meaning that a critic discovers in music arises not from the musical experience as such, but from critical reflection *about* it; that is, the meaning is not musical but musicological. To adapt another phrase of Iser's (1978: 54), what the listener is basically concerned with is not the meaning of the work but its effect; and this is something that requires no mediation and indeed brooks none.

II

I have tried to suggest some reasons for being suspicious of the whole concept of 'music appreciation' as a matter of principle. And in practice there is little hard evidence that programmed

---

[56] Even so, Helen's sister Margaret complains a few pages later that, when she listens to the 5th Symphony, Helen 'won't let it alone. She labels it with meanings from start to finish; turns it into literature. I wonder if the day will ever return when music will be treated as music.'

[57] See above, p. 14.

instruction in music leads to an enhanced enjoyment of it, over and above the undoubted effects of repeated hearings. (I am not, of course, denying that people may derive lasting pleasure from their exposure to music as a result of music appreciation classes; what I am questioning is the role of the instruction that is offered in them.) For every empirical study that seems to show a clear positive effect of instruction upon aesthetic enjoyment (e.g. Bradley 1972), it is possible to cite one that suggests that it has little or no effect (e.g. Prince 1974). Indeed, there are indications that instruction can actually have a negative effect; summarizing an unpublished thesis by D. Steele, Paul Haack (1980: 166) says that the author

found that it was possible to program instructional activities relating to ethnic musics in such a manner that significant improvement in factual knowledge and stylistic identification skills could be brought about. However, the instructional tapes and related activities failed to yield any attitudinal gains, and, in fact, it appeared as though there could be a slight tendency toward attitudinal decline over the period of instruction.

And Crickmore cites the example of a student, who scored highly in the Wing Standardized Test of Musical Intelligence, saying of his former music master that 'He kept breaking the pieces up and explaining why each movement was so constructed; I disliked this intensely. When listening to music I like to be quiet and not have it broken up and analysed. Because of this "forced" method of teaching my reactions are unfavourable towards classical music.' (1968b: 293.) This student would evidently have agreed with what, over twenty years ago, Max Kaplan called his 'outdated but firm belief . . . that music, like poetry or painting, is best served by exposing them to young people with a minimum of teacher-interference' (1966: 120).

It seems, then, that instruction which leads to increased knowledge about music does not, or at any rate does not automatically, lead to enhanced enjoyment of it. In fact it seems that instruction may not even enhance people's observation of what they hear. Patricia Flowers (1983) carried out an experiment in which students were taught a basic musical vocabulary of forty-four technical terms. She found that their powers of observation were no greater after instruction than before it; verbalization did not enhance the acuity of their perceptions. Geringer and Nelson (1980) carried out tests in which students had to write down answers to questions about a piece of music while listening to it, and found that their observation of the music was no better than that of students who just listened. These negative findings seem to extend to higher levels of musical education, too. In another unpublished thesis, the primary purpose of which was to relate the way people described music to their musical background, Bar-Droma found that

> while the laymen often were able to demonstrate considerable insight into new pieces of music, and the outstanding young musicians were able to reveal insights into unfamiliar and familiar pieces but more into the former, music majors demonstrated a notable inability to reveal new relationships in familiar pieces of music.[58]

Lucy Pollard-Gott (1983) discovered a similar phenomenon in the course of experiments in which listeners with differing degrees of musical expertise had to compare different passages from Liszt's B minor Sonata: as she explains (p. 81), for the experts,

> theme was the most important basis for similarity judgements. . . . One expert commented that after the similarity task was over, he realized that there might have been other criteria for judging similarity such as relative loudness. Yet when he heard the passages, their thematic relations were compelling and seemed to be the only natural basis for comparing them.

Listeners with less expertise were, however, more open in their approach, simply because their responses were not mediated, as the experts' were, by some kind of pre-established musicological representation.[59]

In an essay on musical criticism, Karl Aschenbrenner discusses the use of such terms as 'lucid', 'florid', and 'prolix', pointing out that they can serve to draw attention to aspects of the musical experience that might otherwise be overlooked; and he concludes

---

[58] Haack 1980: 143–4.

[59] A possibly related finding is that of Haack, who tested the effect of programmes designed to enhance certain music perceptual skills upon children with varying degrees of experience in playing instruments. He found that less experienced players achieved 'significantly higher gain scores than the more experienced instrumentalists, and it was speculated that extensive instrumental experience as it generally exists at the secondary school level may tend to inhibit the perceptual listening skills under study.' (1980: 162.) Again, Serafine concluded from an extensive series of experiments that 'music cognition results from normal cognitive growth and everyday experience with music, and not from learning in the narrow sense. At the least, musical understanding . . . does not grow out of the ability to perform learned music on an instrument.' (1988: 234.)

that 'To hear music equipped with a generous fund of critical concepts is to realize it as a genuine value experience.' (1981: 109.) But I wonder if the opposite is not just as true. For, paradoxical as it may seem, it is really quite logical to suppose that, if listeners' responses are mediated to a significant degree by verbal or other representations of what they hear, then they will hear or at least respond to less than would otherwise be the case—especially if they are listening to music that is unfamiliar to them. This is not just because of the familiar difficulties of formulating musical experiences in terms of words and other symbols for, or images of, music: it is because such words and symbols and images inevitably become sedimented. As a result the critic, whose listening naturally tends towards verbal representation, can easily find his musical responses becoming rigid and inflexible through being framed in what are, literally, musicological terms.[60] One has only to browse through Nicolas Slonimsky's *Lexicon of Musical Invective* to see the results of this: critics (who, after all, are not in reality malicious numskulls, but people with extensive musical knowledge and experience) have time and again failed to recognize the aesthetic qualities of genuinely new music when they heard it, preferring in its stead music that half a century later everyone recognizes to be conservative hack-work.[61]

[60] Dahlhaus, following Adorno, argues that a fresh and unprejudiced hearing of a piece of music 'relating "immediately" and free of dogmas to the object can hardly be achieved except by the detour of emancipation from the ingrained—an emancipation which employs the tool of reflection about music mediated by notation' (1983: 54–5). This argument is consistent with the view that musical literacy is a prerequisite for fully adequate aesthetic appreciation (see p. 17 above); but I believe it underestimates the degree to which notation itself is sedimented and embodies, or encourages, possibly irrelevant interpretational criteria.

[61] Examples are perhaps unnecessary, but I cannot resist quoting the critic in the *New York Post*, who after hearing *La Mer* in 1907 pronounced: 'Debussy's music is the dreariest kind of rubbish. Does anybody for a moment doubt that Debussy would not write such chaotic, meaningless, cacophonous, ungrammatical stuff, if he could invent a melody? . . . Even his orchestration is not particularly remarkable. M. Loeffler of Boston is far more original from this point of view.' (Slonimsky 1965: 94.) And an entry that Tchaikovsky confided to his diary (which is surely a better place to write such things than a newspaper) reads: 'I played over the music of that scoundrel Brahms. What a giftless bastard! It annoys me that this self-inflated mediocrity is hailed as a genius. Why, in comparison with him, Raff is a giant, not to speak of Rubinstein, who after all is a live and important human being, while Brahms is chaotic and absolutely empty dried-up stuff.' (Ibid.: 73.) It follows from my argument that composers are likely to be particularly bad listeners, simply because they are so accustomed to experiencing music in terms of procedurally orientated representations, and highly characteristic ones at that: if one attempts to imagine what it would be like to hear Brahms's music 'as' Tchaikovsky, one can perhaps envisage the sense in which it would seem chaotic and dried-up.

The problem is not that these critics did not listen hard enough to the new music, and so failed to hear what was new in it: it is that they listened too hard, and consequently heard only what they were musicologically prepared to hear. A vivid illustration of this is provided by Hanslick's complaint about the 5/4 time signature of the second movement of Tchaikovsky's 'Pathétique' Symphony: 'it is disturbing to listeners and players alike. The ear is always substituting more comfortable measures, dividing five-four into two and three parts, or into three and two—an intolerably worrisome procedure. It is, moreover, superfluous, since the piece could be adapted to six-eight time without damage.' (trans. 1963: 302.) Hanslick was evidently too involved, in a musicological sense, with what he heard to be able to experience the music naïvely and open-mindedly; a less professional listener would not have been likely to encounter the same problems.[62] It is the same professionalism that explains why the critics could not come to terms with *Pierrot lunaire* when they first heard it, unlike the hotel lift-attendant who told Schoenberg in 1930 that he had heard the work's first performance, nearly twenty years before, and still had the sound of it in his ears (ed. 1984: 98–9). And it is why, throughout musical history, significant innovations in style have time and again established themselves not in the concert-hall, where listeners focus their attention on what they hear, but rather in the theatre, the opera-house, the ballet, or the cinema—all situations in which the listeners' conscious attention is diverted elsewhere.[63] Under such circumstances, it seems, what is musicologically difficult or impossible to understand may be understood

---

[62] Cf. Bernard Shaw's argument that Wagner's music is 'easy for the natural musician who has had no academic teaching. The professors, when Wagner's music is played to them, exclaim at once "What is this? Is it aria, or recitative? Is there no cabaletta to it—not even a full close? Why was that discord not prepared; and why does he not resolve it correctly? How dare he indulge in those scandalous and illicit transitions into a key that has not one note in common with the key he has just left? Listen to those false relations! What does he want with six drums and eight horns when Mozart worked miracles with two of each? The man is no musician." . . . The unskilled, untaught musician may approach Wagner boldly; for there is no possibility of a misunderstanding between them. . . . It is the adept musician of the old school who has everything to unlearn; and him I leave, unpitied, to his fate.' (1899: 3–4.)

[63] As Glenn Gould remarked, 'If you really stop to listen to the music accompanying most of the grade-B horror movies that are coming out of Hollywood these days, or perhaps a TV show on space travel for children, you will be absolutely amazed at the amount of integration which the various idioms of atonality have undergone in these media.' (ed. 1987: 120.) But this is not the case in the concert-hall.

quite easily in a musical sense. How else is one to explain the phenomenon of *2001: A Space Odyssey*, whose audiences flocked to their local record shops in order to buy the sound-track—a sound-track consisting largely of avant-garde music by Ligeti, which the same audiences would as likely as not have rejected as much too 'difficult' had they encountered it in the concert-hall or on a radio channel devoted to serious music?

III

There is a theory, which I do not believe, that new music is always 'difficult'. Apologists for 'modern music' have for years argued that serial and post-serial styles will in time become generally established, as audiences became familiarized with them; that is to say, that the 'difficulty' of modern music is a temporary phenomenon which will eventually wear off.[64] Yet the date-line for 'modern music'—music generally regarded as 'difficult' by audiences and concert promoters—has for years remained stubbornly stuck with Schoenberg's innovations of the early 1920s; if this were merely a matter of time-lag, then it would be as if Chopin's music had remained incomprehensible to the general public throughout the entire nineteenth century and even into the twentieth. The time-lag theory seems to me not only wrong, but misleading, for it involves the assumption that Schoenberg and his followers and successors wanted their music to be widely accepted like that of Chopin or Verdi or Richard Strauss. I would prefer to argue that one of the main forces underlying the apparently puzzling evolution of modern music is in fact a profound distrust of the popular.

For the Marxist sociologist Theodor Adorno, writing in the years immediately following the Second World War, mass culture was an instrument of bourgeois repression. In his *Philosophy of Modern Music* Adorno threw his weight behind Schoenbergian serialism because, as he saw it, the inflexible rationality of serial organization helped to render it impervious to political manipulation. He reserved his most scathing attacks for what, in a rather odd choice of term, he called the 'intellectualist' composer: that is, the 'moderate modernist' whose music is simply an attempt to give the

---

[64] Schoenberg is the main source of this idea; see for instance ed. 1984: 285.

public what they want through creating effects of 'enticement and banality'.[65] Adorno's politically motivated distrust of popularity in music coincided with the widespread reaction in post-war Europe against a climate of subjectivity and emotionalism which had become suspect or even disreputable through its association with nationalism, racism, and mass hysteria—and which was epitomized by Wagner's works and by Hitler's adoption of Wagner as the spiritual ancestor of the Nazis. In a recent book Peter Franklin writes that the pioneers of modern music 'may now claim the horror of two World Wars and the knowledge of Auschwitz to support their assertion that no harmony of style and idea with subjective expressive intention in music can have any valid basis beyond that of evasion and self-indulgent nostalgia' (1985: 115). And the composer Ernst Krenek specifically linked this reaction against compositional subjectivity with the attraction of the serial method when he described the purpose of post-war total serialism as being 'to set up an impersonal mechanism' in place of an inspiration that had become discredited 'because it is not really as innocent as it was supposed to be, but rather conditioned by a tremendous body of recollection, tradition, training and experience' (1962: 90). Part of the motivation for total serialism and all that went with it was undoubtedly a desire to wipe the slate clean.

I would argue that the musical events following the Second World War merely expressed, in a particularly explicit manner, currents of feeling that went back to the First World War and even earlier. The prolonged compositional crisis that Schoenberg went through at the time of *Die Jakobsleiter* coincided with the closing years of the First World War, and was resolved in the invention of serialism; not only in their compositional technique, but also in their neoclassical textures and forms, the serial works of the 1920s can be seen as constituting a critique of the extreme subjectivity of Schoenberg's pre-war masterpieces. And if these works aimed at a new kind of objectivity in terms of style and compositional method, they implied a manner of listening equally different from the kind of essentially passive emotional response elicited by the works of Wagner and the Wagnerians (or, for that matter, of the young Schoenberg). Consequently, and perhaps influenced by

---

[65] Adorno trans. 1973: 12. Schenker uses the term 'rationalist' in a sense similar to Adorno's 'intellectualist' (Kalib 1973: ii, 216).

Hanslick's thinking, Schoenberg demanded of his audiences not an immediate (that is, 'pathological') emotional response to the music, but one in which emotion was the product of some kind of higher-level comprehension of the work's structural organization. Schoenberg (ed. 1984: 215) described this more objective kind of listening when he wrote in 1941:

Form in the arts, and especially in music, aims primarily at comprehensibility. The relaxation which a satisfied listener experiences when he can follow an idea, its development, and the reasons for such development is closely related, psychologically speaking, to a feeling of beauty. Thus, artistic value demands comprehensibility, not only for intellectual, but also for emotional satisfaction.

Moreover, in his writings Schoenberg is constantly harping upon the difficulties that the listener may encounter in comprehending what he hears, and the need for composers to bear these difficulties in mind. In a particularly telling passage, dating from 1931, he writes:

If a musician, feeling not that he must, but that he ought, should be inclined to write a piece whose expression is to be popular, i.e. generally comprehensible, let him reflect on the following: (1) One understands only what one can take note of. (2) One can easily take note of something only if it is (a) clear (characteristic, plastic, sharply contoured and articulated); (b) frequently repeated; (c) not too long . . . (p. 267.)

—and he continues in the same vein, up to a total of twelve points. It is hard to be sure to what extent he could himself have been in sympathy with such an aim;[66] but he does record that he went to special pains when composing the First Chamber Symphony so as to ensure that the music would be comprehensible to the listener. The problem, as he explains, was the over-abundance of motivic and motivically derived material. Consequently, he continues, 'The task . . . was to retard the progress of development in order to enable the average good listener to keep in mind what preceded so as to understand the consequences.' (p. 61.) Composing, in other words, involves making things comprehensible to the listener by accommodating the music to the speed at which he can take things in, to the number of distinct musical figures that he can remember,

[66] In 1946 Schoenberg wrote that, of all types of pandering to popular tastes, the 'most deplorable is the acting of some artists who arrogantly wish to make believe that they descend from their heights in order to give some of their riches to the masses. This is hypocrisy. . . . There is only "l'art pour l'art", art for the sake of art alone.' (ed. 1984: 124.)

and to the complexity of the connections between them that he can grasp; in this way, as Schoenberg puts it, 'The language in which musical ideas are expressed in tones . . . must be proportionate to the intellect which it addresses.' (p. 399.)

It seems strange to find Schoenberg, of all people, offering advice on how to write music of popular appeal, and despite his pains the development of the First Chamber Symphony is extremely hard to follow in the kind of way that he describes. I would suggest that both the difficulty from the listener's point of view and the conscious concern that Schoenberg consequently shows for the listener (a concern unmatched by any earlier composer) have the same root cause: Schoenberg is himself thinking of the music in terms of its meaning rather than its effect, that is to say in terms of productionally conceived structures to be communicated through sound, rather than in terms of intended effects to be created by appropriate musical means.

Composers before Schoenberg had, of course, conceived of their music as a form of communication, in that they intended their works to convey programmatic or emotional contents, political or social values, or—more relevantly to Schoenberg—some kind of architectonic idea. Beethoven's (or Schlösser's) account of the fundamental idea that never deserted him indicates one of the sources of Schoenberg's own concept of the musical idea,[67] and Schoenberg considered the communication of this idea to the listener to be the primary purpose of a composition. Hence, he wrote, 'The effort of the composer is solely for the purpose of making the idea comprehensible to the listener.' (p. 285.) But what makes Schoenberg's concept of the musical idea different from that of the nineteenth century is his view of it as something that can in principle be specified in technical terms; thus he said that 'An idea in music consists principally in the relation of tones to one another' (p. 269), and explained that even in his pre-serial music he was 'always occupied with the aim to base the structure of my music *consciously* on a unifying idea, which produced not only all the other ideas but regulated also their accompaniment and the chords, the "harmonies" '.[68] Correspondingly, if the listener is to compre-

---

[67] See above, p. 114. Another source is Schopenhauer (White 1984).

[68] J. A. Smith 1986: 196. Schoenberg's use of the term 'idea' is not, however, consistent; for an account of the various, and sometimes contradictory, senses in which he used it see C. M. Cross 1980.

hend the music as he hears it, to understand the idea that the composer is trying to communicate, he must be able to grasp the notes and their relations to one another: he must be able to remember motifs and themes and observe their repetitions, follow harmonic progressions and successions of keys, and keep track of the unfolding of the musical form. 'For instance', says Schoenberg, referring to music in the traditional tonal forms, 'the listener with a schooled musical ear will recognize the reprise of the theme through the return to the original key; he will also feel that so long as foreign keys are present the main theme is less likely to recur, but rather secondary themes or developments.' And he adds: 'Such trained listeners have probably never been very numerous, but that does not prevent the artist from creating only for them.'[69]

In saying this Schoenberg reveals that the source of his basic conception of the relationship between composer and listener lies in nineteenth-century beliefs as to the composer's ultimate purpose or mission (it is worth noticing that on occasion he reverts to a favoured nineteenth-century term for the composer: the 'musical poet'.[70]) For it was one of the basic principles of Schoenberg's conception of artistic morality—which he shared with, or adopted from, Karl Kraus—that, as Franklin puts it, the artist's first duty is 'to find and define an image of *himself* which corresponds most comprehensively to the "truth" that he feels within himself' (1985: 62). That is why Schoenberg believed that

Those who compose because they want to please others, and have audiences in mind, are not real artists. They are not the kind of men who are driven to say something whether or not there exists one person who likes it, even if they themselves dislike it. They are not creators who must open the valves in order to relieve the interior pressure of a creation ready to be born. They are merely more or less skilful entertainers who would renounce composing if they did not find listeners. (ed. 1984: 54.)

In other words, real compositions are not designed to be perceived

---

[69] Ed. 1984: 278–9. Schoenberg's comments about the trained listener should be read in the light of his statement elsewhere that 'in my youth, living in the proximity of Brahms, it was customary that a musician, when he heard a composition for the first time, observed its construction, was able to follow the elaboration and derivation of its themes and its modulations, and could recognize the number of voices in canons and the presence of the theme in a variation; and there were even laymen who after one hearing could take a melody home in their memory.' (pp. 120–1.) He cites Hanslick as an example of such a trained listener.

[70] See for instance ed. 1984: 220.

at all: a work's perceptual qualities are no more than, so to speak, the epiphenomena of a creative act which obeys its own laws of inner necessity.[71] Or to put it another way, a work of music is fundamentally a moral entity and not a perceptual one. And this is little more than a twentieth-century adaptation of the concept of 'art-religion', as Heine called it, which, Dahlhaus writes, 'demands of listeners contemplation, self-forgetting study' of the work of art (1982: 13.) In one of his earliest writings, Schenker spelt out just what these demands entailed: ' "Laws" derive only from the sacred caprice of creative artists, and these one must gratefully accept even at the expense of enjoyment' (trans. 1988: 134). Such thinking is the principal source of Adorno's belief that for the artist to give his audiences what they want is simply a betrayal of his artistic integrity; it is the principal source of the deep distrust of popularity that character-izes modern music.

In order to put this into perspective, we have to remember that art music designed to appeal to mass audiences is a relatively recent phenomenon. It could hardly have developed until the second half of the nineteenth century, when theatres and concert-halls seating audiences of a thousand or more began to become common; Wagner was perhaps the first composer whose most serious productions gained a mass following among the urban middle classes in his own lifetime. Indeed, Thomas Mann's critique of Wagner centred precisely on the fact that he had 'found both a style and a form of artistic expression that broke the sanctity of art as possession of the few and the educated' (Botstein 1987: 96). In view of this it is ironic that the solution that Schoenberg and his contemporaries adopted to the problem of popularity had a precedent in Bayreuth. For rather than attempting to win the affections of the mass audiences they distrusted,[72] the musicians of the modern movement set about creating their own audiences—

---

[71] The artist, says Schoenberg (ed. 1984: 121), is 'ceaselessly occupied with doing justice to the idea. He is sure that, everything done which the idea demands, the external appearance will be adequate.'

[72] Schoenberg wrote that if a work 'is art, it is not for all, and if it is for all, it is not art' (ed. 1984: 124), and quoted with evident approval 'Schopenhauer's story of the surprise of one ancient Greek orator who, when he was suddenly interrupted by applause and cheers, cried out: "Have I said some nonsense?" ' (p. 114.) Schenker expressed even stronger views on the subject, saying that 'an unbridgeable chasm has always existed and will continue to exist between art and the people.' (trans. 1979: 106.)

audiences which were set apart from the masses and which were committed to the cause of modern music. The first of these was created by the significantly named Society for Private Musical Performances, which Schoenberg set up in Vienna in 1918. Details of its programmes were not announced in advance, and admission to concerts was restricted to members of the society. Both applause and demonstrations of disapproval were strictly forbidden, as was the publication of reports or criticisms of concerts in the press.[73] Though the society only lasted for three years, it set the pattern for the exclusive audiences on which the new music has since then depended, such as those of the regular festivals at Darmstadt in Germany and Tanglewood in the United States.

Because of their commitment to the new music, such audiences have been willing to work in order to understand it in the manner in which it demands to be understood; there has always been a strong educational component in modern music, with composers being ready to talk in public about their works, or to supply informative programme-notes. Berg described the activities of the Society for Private Musical Performances as 'semi-pedagogic', and remarked: 'If joy and pleasure in some of the performed works are awakened . . . this must be considered to be a side effect. . . . In the planning of programs, no attention can be paid to this . . . because our purpose is restricted to giving as perfect a representation [of modern music] as possible.' (Meibach 1984: 164.) In accordance with this, it was one of the society's stated aims to provide repeated performances of new works so as to enable the listener to grasp these works on their own terms, so to speak, rather than his. And in 1939, eighteen years after the society went out of existence, Gerald Abraham made a quite unambiguous statement of the duty that modern music imposes on its audiences to prepare themselves for the listening experience: 'If you are not prepared to tackle the difficulty of the modern musical idiom in the same spirit that you would tackle the learning of Spanish, if you decided to take up Spanish as a hobby, you must resign yourself to the fact that modern music is not for you.' (1939: 22.) And that, of course, is exactly what most people have done.

---

[73] See Berg's statement of the society's aims, trans. in Meibach 1984.

IV

My purpose in tracing these aspects of the evolution of modern music has been to indicate some of the sources of Collingwood's, Hampshire's, and Scruton's views about the nature of musical listening, and to suggest that such views have no special claim to universal validity. On the contrary, the insistence of these critics, and of educationalists in general, that the aesthetic appreciation of music means something quite different from an immediate enjoyment of it reflects the profoundly anti-popular orientation of modern music: it is itself a historical phenomenon. To turn this into a general principle, supposedly applicable to all music, is to render problematic a type of aesthetic experience which might otherwise be distinguished by its remarkably effortless nature and availability to practically anyone who cares to listen; it is, in fact, to create the very problem that the 'Appreciation-racket' is meant to solve. It is also, it seems to me, to introduce an element of falsity into the relationship between the musician and the general public. For, as Bruno Nettl says, 'The fruits of music, like science, are enjoyed daily by practically all of the population, but the academic musical establishment has made the lay public feel that without understanding the technicalities of musical construction, without knowledge of notation and theory, one cannot properly comprehend or deal with music.' (1983: 135.) Hence the feeling of inadequacy I mentioned in the Introduction.

Even the musician, however, might begin to wonder what it means properly to comprehend or deal with music when he reads Leonard B. Meyer's statement that 'neither memorization nor performance necessarily entail understanding. . . . It is possible to read, memorize and perform music that one does not really understand.' (1967: 291.) One wants to add: and to compose, listen to, and write about it too! For, with these additions, Meyer's statement takes on a new meaning. Music is, as John Blacking says (1973: x), 'too deeply concerned with human feelings and experiences in society . . . for it to be subject to arbitrary rules, like the rules of games'; that is why symbols and images of music can never fully embody the coherence and quiddity of a piece of music (and why the Martians will never achieve that authentic performance of the E minor Prelude). To be sure, it is through these symbols and images that we can understand music in a productional sense. But this is a partial understanding, an understanding that remains on the wrong side of the musical fabric and so is really no understanding at all, unless it is completed through some kind of aesthetic participation—through reading, memorizing, or performing music, or through composing it, or just through listening. To think that one can understand music in some abstract, symbolical sense that can be separated from such aesthetic participation is simply to misunderstand the whole nature of the enterprise. And this means that the very concept of 'really understanding' music becomes vacuous; there is only reading it, memorizing it, performing it, composing it, and listening to it—in short, loving it.

Such at least is the testimony of Artur Rubinstein, according to whom ' "understand" is a word one shouldn't apply to music; there's nothing to be *understood*—for me, music must be felt.'[74] Igor Stravinsky used almost the same words when he remarked, 'I haven't understood a bar of music in my life; but I have felt it.' Further comment seems superfluous.

[74] Quoted in Mitchell 1966: 19.

4 Composition and culture

4.1 COMPOSITION VERSUS PREDICTION

I

Stravinsky wrote *Les Noces* while staying in a small village in Switzerland. His friend and collaborator C. F. Ramuz, describing the house in which the composer lived, records

> how Stravinsky turned one of the attic rooms into a studio, reached by a half-hidden wooden staircase well barricaded by doors, and how of a summer afternoon the sound of the composer at his piano and percussion instruments could be heard in the little square outside, where two or three women were usually to be found on a bench, knitting in the shade of the trees. These would raise their heads for a moment in bewilderment, and then with an indulgent 'C'est le monsieur russe!' resume their knitting.[1]

And one can understand the women's bewilderment, for the sounds that composers make as they compose at the piano (not to mention the battery of percussion) can be strange indeed. The reason is, of course, that when a composer composes at an instrument, he does not always listen to what he is playing in quite the manner in which a performing musician does (or in which the composer himself would when performing). Suppose, for example, that a composer is working on an adagio for strings. He may use the piano as he elaborates the harmonies or lays out the textures of the music. But what the composer actually plays on the piano might well sound strangely insubstantial and unsatisfactory to anybody who happened to overhear him at work: there might, for instance, be disconnected plinks in the highest register, swamped by the disproportionate weight of the sustained notes in the lower registers. But the composer would not hear what he was playing like this: he would be hearing those disconnected plinks in terms of the soaring, sustained sonority of high violins, and so for him there would be no imbalance between the registers. In other

[1] Trans. in E. W. White 1979: 253.

words, he would be hearing the sound not as piano music, but as a model of the intended music for strings.

There is, of course, a certain danger in hearing sound as subjectively as this. It can happen that a composer will hear a connection or a directed motion in his music that nobody else hears, or fail to hear something that is audible to everyone else (for instance an unintended tonal inflection in an atonal work), because he hears the music as he imagines it in his 'inner ear', rather than as it is actually being played. Composers sometimes make bad performers for this reason: as Ralph Kirkpatrick says, 'the role of the inner ear can be pushed much too far, or rather it can be pushed further than it should go without the support of the outer ear. We know how atrociously some composers with splendid inner ears can perform on their long-suffering instruments.' (1984: 110.) These problems arise from a failure to distinguish real sound from imagined sound; Gerald Abraham has criticized as eminent a composer as Schumann for confusing the two when writing for orchestra, arguing that he never really wrote orchestral music at all, but rather piano music arranged for orchestra (1974: 57). In other words, when Schumann was working at the piano on an orchestral piece, he was always hearing what he played too literally, as piano music, and not as a model of the piece for orchestra.

To use piano sound as a model of orchestral sound—to sketch at the piano—is to attend to certain aspects of the sound and to ignore others. Actually the same applies to all models. When an architect makes a model of a building he is working on (and this applies to a computer-generated model as well as to the traditional type), he uses it as a means of making empirical decisions about the appearance of the building. He can rotate the model to see how it looks from different angles, or try out different configurations of windows and choose the one that looks best. And in doing this he sees the model as a building; that is to say, he ignores its physical aspects and instead attends to those aspects that translate reliably and usefully into real life, such as the spatial configuration of its various elements. In the same way, a composer who is sketching an orchestral piece at the piano ignores certain properties of piano sound (the rapid decay of the high notes, the specifically pianistic properties of the lower register) while attending to the effect of a particular harmonic progression or textural layout; for within certain constraints—and learning what these constraints are is an important part of learning how to write for orchestra—the properties of harmonic progressions and textural layouts translate reliably and usefully from piano to orchestra. There are also a number of other modelling transformations, as one might call them, that composers use when they sketch their music. One of these is the transformation from slow to fast: again, within certain constraints, progressions and textures (and even figurations and forms) that make aural sense when played fast will continue to make aural sense when played slowly, which means that rapid passages can be worked out slowly with some confidence that they will continue to sound right when played up to speed. But by far the most important of these modelling transformations is that from the simple to the elaborate.

It is one of the characteristics of tonal music that simple but coherent tonal structures continue to sound coherent when they are elaborated, or—to put it the other way round—that elaborate musical structures can be reduced to simple melodic and harmonic prototypes which continue to make aural sense in their simplified form. In this lies the possibility of modelling tonal music at different levels of elaboration, and these different levels of elaboration are easiest to see when they correspond to a division of labour in the compositional process. In some music from the Baroque period, for example, responsibility for the most highly elaborated stage in the compositional process fell not upon the composer but upon the executant. In their instrumental sonatas composers like Corelli, Geminiani, and Handel sometimes supplied the performer with only the skeleton of the music that was to be played; the ornamentation, which contributes crucially to the music's effect, had to be provided by the performer. However, there are a few instances in which the composer, or a performer, wrote down a version of one of these movements as it was meant to be played. Ex. 43 shows the beginning of Geminiani's playing version of the final movement of Corelli's Violin Sonata Op. 5 No. 9. His elaborated version of the violin part is shown in the top stave; the lower two staves show what Corelli originally wrote.[2]

---

[2] Geminiani's playing version is given in Hawkins ed. 1875: ii, 904 ff. In both this example and Ex. 44 I have modernized Corelli's notation of accidentals (i.e. added a 3rd sharp sign to the key signature), to match Geminiani's.

Ex. 43

Tempo di Gavotta Allegro

It is possible to play the music as Corelli wrote it, of course. But it sounds, if not incoherent, then thin and arbitrary, with its monotonous quarter-note rhythms and ungainly leaps. The sense of the music emerges not when it is performed as written, but when it is used as the basis for a performance. Geminiani's version represents such a performance. It retains not only the form and the harmonic pattern, but also almost all the notes of Corelli's violin line; however, they are absorbed into a quite new melodic organization. With its characteristic rhythmic pattern, Geminiani's opening is a tune in a way that Corelli's is not. And as such it has structural characteristics different from those of Corelli's original. Ex. 43 provides an instance of this: whereas in the original version the first four bars consist of an undifferentiated stream of quarter-notes and make up a single phrase, Geminiani's version has three sequential repetitions of a distinctive one-bar phrase and a contrasted closing phrase, producing a strongly accented down-beat quality. But the way in which this version involves a reinterpretation of the music's structure can be seen more clearly in Ex. 44, which shows the middle section of the movement together

Ex. 44

with the first four bars of the final section. In Corelli's score the final section is an unaltered repeat of the first (compare the last four bars of Ex. 44 with the first four bars of Ex. 43). But this is not the case in Geminiani's version. As before, Geminiani incorporates virtually all the notes of Corelli's score into his version, but the way in which he does it is quite different. The tune that gave the opening its particular character never reappears. It goes underground: the surface of the music consists of a chain of suspensions with double-stopping and, towards the end of the movement, triple- and quadruple-stopping. And whereas in Corelli's score the return of the opening idea (bar 35, marked forte) is an important structural point, Geminiani goes out of his way to disguise it, treating it almost identically to the preceding four-bar section (marked piano). Geminiani, in other words, is making a different kind of piece out of what Corelli wrote. Corelli's score shows a symmetrical ABA structure, in which the beginning of the B section forms a contrast to the material of the A section, and in which the beginning of the final A section is projected as an important point of arrival. By contrast, Geminiani's piece does not really come over as an ABA structure at all. His B section contains clear references to the rhythmic pattern of the opening (see in particular bars 21 and 27), whereas his final section retains only its underlying linear–harmonic structure. The progressive liquidation of the thematic material, together with the thickening textures and multiple-stopping, mean that Geminiani finishes the movement (and with it the sonata) in a climax of virtuosity that is quite foreign to Corelli's original conception. In a real sense, then, we have not so much two different versions of the same piece as two different pieces, each of which serves a different purpose. Geminiani's is for playing. Corelli's, on the other hand, is to be read, and reflected on, and experimented with, leading in due course to a significantly new act of composition on the performer's part. The two pieces, then, are complementary. They represent different levels of elaboration at which what are essentially the same materials can be conceived in a musically coherent manner.

A similar kind of transformation from the simple to the elaborate occurs when a composer plans out and realizes a complex musical work such as a symphony. One cannot write a symphony all at once; so part of the skill of composition lies in splitting up what has to be done into a number of 'sub-jobs', each of more manageable length or complexity. If we consider the example of Beethoven (whose compositional process is particularly well documented because he did so much on paper, but whose method of composing may, of course, be untypical for that very reason), then we can distinguish several different types of compositional work in the sketch-books. There are first of all 'idea sketches', often only a few notes long and usually on one stave: in these Beethoven is trying to establish or fix the various motifs or themes from which the work is to be constructed. Then there are 'continuity sketches', consisting of one to three staves, in which extensive sections of the music are drafted, sometimes in the form of a single melodic line and sometimes with the bass-line and important subsidiary lines being included as well. Then there is the 'score sketch', in which different orchestral dispositions of the musical materials are tried out. And finally there is the autograph score, which represents the work in its (hopefully) final form.

It would be easy to rationalize these different aspects of the compositional process by seeing them in terms of an evolution from the simplest way in which the work can be conceived (as a set of characteristic motivic or thematic materials) through increasingly complex representations to the stage at which the final work is achieved; that is to say, the output of the first stage would be the input of the second stage, and so on. But such a rationalization would actually be quite misleading. In the first place, not all these stages are always found (the score sketch, in particular, is rare), nor is it always possible to distinguish them clearly from one another. And more importantly, Beethoven did not use these increasingly detailed representations of the emerging composition in a fixed sequence moving from the simple to the complex: in fact he did not use them in a fixed sequence at all. As Lockwood has convincingly argued,[3] it seems to have been Beethoven's habit to move back from the continuity sketch to the idea sketch when motivic or thematic materials needed refining (for such materials sometimes take a very rudimentary form in the continuity sketches), or to move from the autograph score back to a sketch-book, or even to work on several different types of sketch at the same time. That he should have done this does not necessarily mean that he was encountering unforeseen compositional prob-

---

[3] See e.g. Lockwood 1971: 140.

lems and was having to retrace his steps. Alan Tyson has remarked (1973: 453) that one of the points of sketching is that things look different when they are written down. The idea sketch, the various formats of continuity sketch, and so on represent different manners of writing things down: the emerging composition appears differently in each of them, for each presents it in a different aspect. Each, in other words, represents a different way of imagining the music, and in this sense each is complementary to the others, much as the two versions of Corelli's movement are complementary to one another.

What I want to suggest is that when composers are at work they conceive their music at different levels of elaboration, and that much that is characteristic of tonal compositions is to be explained in terms of these modelling transformations from the simple to the complex. It is presumably for this reason that the same or similar musical formations are often to be found at different levels of compositional structure from the note-to-note level, where the identity or coherence of the formation is of an immediately audible nature, to the largest scale of movemental or even inter-movemental structure, where such formations have a purely imaginative or conceptual significance. And this is the source for much of the divergence between theoretical accounts of musical forms and the way in which listeners experience them that I discussed in Chapter 1; for what is in musicological terms the same formation—say a tonally closed melodic motion—will have a perceptual significance that varies according to the structural level at which it occurs. Thomas Clifton, in his analysis of the basic shapes to be found in Mozart's piano sonatas, comments that as the same shape appears at higher structural levels it is 'transformed from an object of sense to an object of imagination' (1970: 173); that is, it is transformed from something directly perceptible to the listener to something which exists within the composer's imagination but which will probably have reality for the listener only to the extent that he studies the music analytically, with a view to reconstructing the manner in which the composer conceived it. Indeed, the very possibility of Schenkerian analysis, and of other analytical methods such as Réti's (1951, ed. 1965), is predicated on this tendency for composers to conceive entire compositions as single gargantuan melodic gestures, or to shape their musical forms as expansions of the tension–resolution patterns of traditional counterpoint.[4] In working in this way, Western composers reproduce within the imagination of the individual a compositional process such as can extend over centuries of communal playing in the court music traditions of the Far East (Picken 1969: 408), in which pieces from the repertoire come to be played more and more slowly, and with more and more elaboration, so that what was originally a directly audible melodic gesture is gradually transformed into an aspect of formal organization.

II

Though the different levels of elaboration in terms of which composers imagine their music can be arranged in a sequence from the aural to the imaginative or even the conceptual, the music presents itself at each level through a combination of all these attributes. In other words, it is normative that even at the level of formal structure composers do not envisage their music in entirely conceptual terms—without regard for experienced sound—and equally it is normative that they have some imaginative grasp of the emerging composition as they work on note-to-note details at the piano. But before this can be substantiated, we need a clear understanding of just what it would mean to grasp music in purely conceptual or in purely aural terms; and this is conveniently provided by a series of tests carried out by Melissa Howe (1984).

In these tests Howe required her subjects, of whom some were musically trained and some of whom were not, to construct tunes out of what she calls 'tuneblocks'. As Ex. 45 shows, the tuneblocks each consisted of between three and six notes; they were presented to the subjects by means of computer synthesis. The subjects worked individually and could hear any desired tuneblock, or sequence of tuneblocks, by keying in the appropriate numbers on the computer. They were allowed to hear the tuneblocks as often as they liked, and to adopt whatever strategy they preferred in constructing their tunes. Howe found that the subjects who did not have a musical training generally worked on a purely trial-and-

---

[4] See above, p. 98. Rosen gives an illuminating analysis of one of the variations from Haydn's Piano Trio in G minor, H. 19, commenting that this 'witty expansion' of the theme shows that 'sonata form is an immense melody, an expanded classical phrase, articulated, with its harmonic climax three-quarters of the way through and a symmetrical resolution that rounds it off in careful balance with the opening.' (1976a: 87.)

Ex. 45

error basis: they responded to the structural properties of the tuneblocks—such as the cadential quality of the third block—but only when they heard them in appropriate contexts. As Howe explains,

While the final tunes of the novice subjects demonstrated a strong response to block 3 as an appropriate ending, this response appeared to be, for many, dependent upon their actually hearing block 3 in its context as an ending. This dependence on context is reflected in two ways. First of all, many of the novices placed block 3 at the end of a string of tuneblocks seemingly by trial and error. However, once they heard its sound in the closing position, they kept it there. Secondly, 60% of the novices used block 3 in other places in their tunes in addition to the end. They did not respond to the ending properties of block 3 when it was embedded in the body of the tune. These findings suggest that for many of the novices, understanding the structural function of block 3 was dependent upon hearing it in its specific context at the end of the tune. The professionals, on the other hand, demonstrated a more extensive and more abstract understanding of structural function. . . . Unlike the novices, the professionals were not dependent upon hearing block 3 in its context at the end of a tune in order to hear its structural function. (pp. 67–9).

In fact the professionals spent a much longer time than the novices in listening to the tuneblocks individually so as to determine their functional properties—for instance, how suitable a given one would be as a beginning, a middle, or an end. Their categorizations of the tuneblocks according to their functional properties formed the basis of the compositional process through which they created their tunes. The most extreme example of this was provided by one of the professional subjects, named Robert, who 'listened to the blocks individually, and assigned each a label. He then combined the blocks according to their labels, listened to them once, and pronounced his tune complete.' (p. 72.) It is shown in Ex. 46.

When children do group composition in class, they behave very much like the novices in Howe's experiment. They stumble on appropriate musical ideas apparently by chance, but hear their appropriateness and therefore retain them as the composition develops (Loane 1984: 219). Such things do, of course, happen in professional composition, but they form one extreme of the range of what constitutes normal compositional activity; for though composers certainly work empirically at times, for instance when searching for the right sound at the keyboard, they generally have a distinct idea of what they are looking for. There is a story that when Vaughan Williams was studying with Ravel, he worked in a room where there was no piano. Ravel, on discovering this, was horrified (or at least pretended he was) and asked Vaughan Williams how, without a piano, he could possibly find new sounds. Like many composers before and after him, Ravel must have relied on the musical intelligence of his fingers as they explored the keyboard in quest of the desired harmony or the most telling registral placement of a chord; but this kind of directed exploration, in which imagination and even theoretical knowledge are combined with an openness to what is to be heard, is a far cry from the simple trial–and–error of Howe's novices or Loane's children.

As for the kind of musicological calculation by means of which Howe's subject Robert put together his tune, this lies at the other extreme of compositional activity. Robert is an example of what Charles Seeger calls the musicological composer (1977: 128): someone who composes simply in terms of notational symbols without regard for how the music actually sounds. Of course, Robert did listen to the tuneblocks in order to establish his musicological categories, and he checked how his tune sounded before pronouncing it complete; but the sound of the music played no direct role in the actual compositional process. Now in professional composition there are certain situations where music is in effect calculated, without any direct consideration of how it sounds. For instance, there are strict canons in Schoenberg's 'Farben',[5] but everybody hears the music as a study in changing

---

[5] No. 3 of the Five Orchestral Pieces, Op. 16.

Ex. 46

timbres (the 'colours' of the title); indeed, it seems to have taken more than fifty years for anyone to notice that the canons are in fact there, in spite of the strong hint that Schoenberg once dropped regarding their existence.[6] Schoenberg no doubt imagined the music's aural effect: but the canons themselves must have been calculated. Ligeti does something similar in his compositions: as he explains,

> Technically speaking, I have always approached musical texture through part-writing. Both *Atmosphères* and *Lontano* have a dense canonic structure. But you cannot actually hear the polyphony, the canon. You hear a kind of impenetrable texture, something like a very densely woven cobweb. . . . The polyphonic structure does not come through, you cannot hear it, it remains in a microscopic, underwater world, to us inaudible.[7]

I am not, of course, saying that Ligeti does not care about the sound of his music when he does this. But he is manipulating the sound indirectly, using micropolyphonic structures as a means of achieving what is in essence a predetermined effect.[8] One could draw a parallel between these micropolyphonic techniques and the established formulas of orchestration, which have an effect that is

[6] For Max Deutsch's account of this hint see J. A. Smith 1986: 146. For the movement's canonic structure see Burkhart 1974.

[7] This extract from an interview with Ligeti, trans. in *Ligeti in Conversation* (London, 1983), is quoted in Bernard 1987: 209, where further discussion and references may be found.

[8] Bernard, who gives specific examples of these inaudible structures, argues that they do more than realize predetermined effects, because 'without a structure it will not be possible to know precisely what the music *should* sound like' (p. 233). If this is true of Ligeti, it is perhaps less true of other composers using micropolyphonic techniques; see e.g. Lidholm 1968.

sufficiently predictable for it to be possible to apply them without any direct consideration of the acoustic results; perhaps this is why certain composers—such as Liszt in his symphonic poems—have at times been content to leave details of orchestration in their music to collaborators. (Perhaps it also explains Wagner's remark that, by comparison with composition, orchestration is 'already a public process'.[9]) But of course this very fact demonstrates that applying known formulas in such a manner is not the same thing as composition; it is arrangement. And when composers resort to a systematic calculation of possibilities as a means of determining anything more than this kind of arrangement, they generally do it for heuristic purposes, and with a direct and explicit concern for the resulting aural effect.

Perhaps the classic illustration of this is the sketches for Beethoven's song 'Sehnsucht' (WoO 146), which became well known through Nottebohm's study of them and have been more recently examined by Lockwood (1973). Most of these sketches relate to the opening two bars of the voice part (which, as Lockwood points out, largely determine the nature of the song as a whole), and they show Beethoven systematically trying out different possibilities, first for the song's metre and rhythm, and later for its melodic contour. The systematic nature of this process is especially obvious in the case of the melodic contour, for the opening phrase begins on G♯ (the song is in E major) and Beethoven works his way through a number of variants that end first on B, then A, then G♯, then back through A to B, and finally again on A: as Lockwood puts it, 'we can see an almost pedantically systematic alteration of the closing step' (p. 119). It is hardly likely that Beethoven actually bothered to play through what he was writing, and therefore the empirical validation that was involved was probably simply a matter of seeing how each variant worked out and how it looked when written down; but some kind of empirical validation was evidently the purpose of what one can characterize quite literally as a calculus of effects, based on an analytical grasp of the constructive parameters of the music.

The continuity of structure from simple to complex, or from middleground to foreground, that characterizes Beethoven's music and that of the classical composers in general accounts for the exceptional degree of integration which the classical style achieved. As Rosen explains,

The simplest way to summarize classical form is as the symmetrical resolution of opposing forces. If this seems so broad as to be a definition of artistic form in general, that is because the classical style has largely become the standard by which we judge the rest of music—hence its name. . . . Not only . . . does the description fit the large classical form, but . . . the classical phrase as well: in no other style of music do the parts and the whole mirror each other with such clarity. (1976a: 83.)

That is to say, classical composers were able, to a higher degree than perhaps any others, to elaborate the note-to-note details of their music in the full light of its structure at phrase, sectional, and movemental level, and to shape its large-scale organization without losing sight (or sound) of its moment-to-moment detail. This altogether exceptional degree of integration between the small scale and the large, between the aural and the imaginative, was not, however, achieved without cost: the classical style, particularly the early classical style, sacrificed a great deal of the harmonic and textural richness of late baroque music in order to achieve its palpable clarity of design. And as the romantic composers rediscovered baroque music and attempted to encompass within their classically-derived forms some of the harmonic and textural resources of the late baroque style, so the integration between the aural and the imaginative began to break down; or, as one might put it, the modelling transformations that classical composers had employed began to lose some of their reliability and their usefulness.

One symptom of this is the development of fast, scherzo-like music as an at least partially distinct musical type. In the classical repertoire there is, of course, fast music; but it is not essentially different from allegro music, except that it is harmonically less dense and more lightly scored. That is, fast classical music—such as the presto movements of Mozart's piano sonatas—can be played slowly while still making a good deal of musical sense. But from Beethoven's time onwards, a variety of fast music developed which makes less sense when played slowly: in Chopin's scherzos, for instance, or for that matter in most of his faster piano pieces, there are sequences of chords which have no structural significance whatever, and which are meant to be perceived as splashes of colour within slower-moving progressions of structural harmonies. When they are played too slowly, these colouristic chord-sequences are no longer perceived as such: instead they are heard as if they were genuine harmonic progressions, and the result is that the music becomes both texturally clogged and harmonically incoherent. Playing the music too slowly, in other words, turns it into nonsense; and the same applies to a great deal of more recent music, above all, perhaps, to Messiaen's piano works. Whether or not this is of significance to the composer, it is certainly of significance to the performer—especially the amateur performer—because it reduces the value of one of the principal methods of learning up a new piece, which is to decide on fingering, phrasing, and other aspects of interpretation while playing the music in slow motion, and only then to attempt it at the proper tempo. This cannot be done, or at any rate it cannot be done so effectively, if the music does not make aural sense when played at reduced speed. Another point is that amateur pianists have always enlarged their musical horizons by ploughing at reduced speed through music that is technically too demanding for them to be able to play it properly; there is satisfaction to be gained, at least for the player, from struggling through a tricky Mozart sonata (and all Mozart sonatas are tricky), because the music continues to be comprehensible under such conditions—even if its very comprehensibility only serves to highlight the shortcomings of the performance. But there is less satisfaction to be gained from doing the same with Messiaen's *Vingt regards sur l'enfant Jésus*, because the music makes so little sense if it is not played with a reasonably high level of competence. And this only serves to reinforce the division that has grown up from Beethoven's time onwards between the amateur and professional repertoires.

However, as might be expected, what is more important than the decreasing reliability and utility of the transformation from slow to fast is that of the transformation from simple to complex. Whereas it is easy to reduce a classical work to a harmonic skeleton, or to grasp it in terms of its thematic structure (taking the supporting harmonies and textures for granted, or leaving them to be finalized at a later stage), there is much late-nineteenth- and twentieth-century music in which it is hard or impossible to isolate harmonies or themes from the contexts in which they occur; even the viability of a piano reduction becomes questionable in some post-war orchestral and chamber works, in which the particular timbres to which notes are assigned are essential to the music's organization. Music like this cannot really be understood in any simplified form: and as a result the aural awareness and conceptual awareness of music have tended to part company, rather than being closely linked with one another as in the case of the classical style.

A good example of this is the music of Skriabin, which Glenn Gould aptly characterizes as 'a curious blend of determination and spontaneity' (ed. 1987: 164). The foundations of Skriabin's style lie in Chopin and Liszt, but by the time of his later sonatas he was writing at the extreme limits of tonal structure. His first experiments with free atonality were quite different from Schoenberg's: whereas in his atonal piano music Schoenberg relied heavily on motivic coherence to take the place of any explicit tonal organization, Skriabin tended to base his music on a rather small repertoire of chord types, which he used as the source of both melody and harmony. What is noticeable is not just that the same chord types tend to reappear in different pieces, but that they tend to reappear on precisely the same notes and even with more or less the same elaborations. As an illustration, (a) in Ex. 47 shows the second subject from Skriabin's Fifth Sonata, Op. 53, while (b) and (c) show two passages from 'Poème', the first of the *Trois morceaux* Op. 52, in which almost identical musical formations appear, though in quite different musical contexts. (These formations are marked 'x' and 'y'.) The way in which they reappear on exactly the same notes strongly suggests that Skriabin knew them not as Mozart must have known his tunes—as aurally imagined Gestalts which could equally readily be played or written down in any key—but in terms of specific hand-positions at the keyboard, or even of the specific look of the notes on the page. One can imagine Skriabin discovering his chords much as Ravel expected Vaughan Williams to, and remembering them as concretions to be combined with one another in order to form compositions, almost in the manner in which Howe's subjects combined their tuneblocks into tunes. This, then, represents a highly empirical approach to composition in which concrete sounds are manipulated and conjoined on a trial-and-error basis. On the other hand,

Ex. 47

(a)

(b)

(c)

there are other works in which Skriabin's compositional approach represents the opposite extreme: they are constructed or (one wants to say) calculated according to an explicit and rigidly applied system. The best example of this is his Seventh Sonata, which has the historical distinction of being the first piece to require for its analysis, if not a serial note-count, then at least a transposition-count.[10]

But the most striking illustration of the contrast between a highly empirical approach to composition on the one hand, and strict calculation on the other, is to be found in the work of Schoenberg. His freely atonal works were composed empirically, or at least intuitively; there were no rules or theories of atonality, so that in composing such works, as he put it (ed. 1984: 87), the 'composer's only yardstick is his sense of balance and his belief in the infallibility of the logic of his musical thinking'. In other words, everything had to be decided in terms of the individual context, whether by trying out the sound of what was written or

---

[10] Perle 1981: 41–3. However, see Samson 1977: 209.

on the basis of how it looked on the page; and this is presumably why the works of this period, especially *Erwartung*, are notorious for their intractibility in the face of analysis.[11] But Schoenberg himself became dissatisfied with this approach to composition, partly because of what he felt to be the impossibility of writing extended works in this idiom without using literary texts to support them, and partly because, as he explained (and his words are clearly autobiographical),

The desire for a conscious control of the new means and forms will arise in every artist's mind; and he will wish to know *consciously* the laws and rules which govern the forms which he has conceived 'as in a dream'. Strongly convincing as this dream may have been, the conviction that these new sounds obey the laws of nature and of our manner of thinking—the conviction that order, logic, comprehensibility and form cannot be present without obedience to such laws—forces the composer along the road of exploration. (ed. 1984: 218.)

The result of this exploration was, of course, the so-called serial system, in which strict adherence to a single sequence of pitch-classes results in a degree of explicit and conscious calculation almost without precedent in the history of Western music.[12]

III

The purpose of serialism was to provide a rational instrument for large-scale compositional planning which would at the same time procure some control over the music's note-to-note structure; it was meant to ensure, or at least enhance, the imaginative unity of the work, which is why—as Schoenberg himself said—'composition with twelve tones has no other aim than comprehensibility' (ed. 1984: 215). Ever since its inception, serialism has been criticized for being too rational, too cerebral, and Schoenberg attempted to refute this charge by demonstrating the interdependence of emotion and rational thinking. But the most damaging

---

[11] See e.g. Mitchell 1966: 41.

[12] Schoenberg's continuing adherence to romantic values meant that he claimed, at least on occasion, that his use of serial procedures was unconscious or intuitive; in 1949, for instance, he wrote: 'In the last few years I have been questioned as to whether certain of my compositions are "pure" twelve-tone, or twelve-tone at all. The fact is that I do not know. I am still more a composer than a theorist.' (ed. 1984: 91.) But such statements are given the lie by his own sketches, in which he can be seen to plan out serial transformations and manipulations in a thoroughly systematic manner (see Hyde 1983).

accusation that his critics made was that it was impossible for listeners to perceive serial structures, and that serialism therefore neither aided comprehensibility, nor indeed had any perceptual reality for the listener at all.

Did Schoenberg expect or want his listeners to perceive the series, its repetitions, and its transformations as they listened to his music? His own statements on the subject are less than clear. He seems to have inherited Wagner's opinion that it was undesirable for the general public to know too much about the technical means by which musical effects were achieved;[13] accordingly, he wrote, 'I foresaw the confusion which would arise in case I were to make publicly known this method. Consequently I was silent for nearly two years.' (ed. 1984: 213.) What Schoenberg wanted his listeners to perceive was less the serial structure as such than the formal unfolding of a work (Rosen 1976b: 97). However, he frequently used serial structure as a means of articulating or even defining a work's form,[14] and in such cases it is difficult if not impossible to distinguish serial structure and form from one another. In any case, Schoenberg made a number of casual remarks which indicate that he did in fact expect listeners (maybe trained listeners) to perceive serial structure: for example, when referring to occasional reorderings of the series, he observed, 'One could perhaps tolerate a slight digression from this order . . . in the later part of a work, when the set had already become familiar to the ear.' (p. 226.)

Whatever Schoenberg may himself have thought, his followers and commentators have generally assumed that serial structure is only meaningful to the extent that it is perceptible. Alfred Pike, for instance, says that 'the meaning of serialism depends greatly upon its degree of perceptibility or audibility' (1963: 55), while according to Hans Keller 'the aesthetic significance of serialism stands and falls with its audibility.' (1955: 231.) However, there is a great deal of experimental evidence indicating that people cannot, in practice, detect the occurrence of a series or grasp its identity

---

[13] In a letter to Bülow, Wagner complained that Richard Pohl had spoken in public of the resemblances between Wagner's harmonic techniques and Liszt's: 'if friend Pohl babbles this secret to the whole world as a summary review of the *Tristan* Prelude, that's at the very least simply indiscreet, and I can't concede that he was authorized to such an indiscretion.' (Warrack 1979: 96.) Wagner was not questioning the truth of what Pohl had said, merely the propriety of saying it publicly.

[14] e.g. his Piano Piece Op. 33a is cast in a sonata form in which distinct serial partitionings and transformations take the place of keys.

under the different transformations that are employed in serial composition.[15] Schoenberg might have argued that this was a question of familiarization: he wrote in 1941 that his serial works had 'failed to gain understanding in spite of the new medium of organization. Thus, should one forget that contemporaries are not final judges, but are generally overruled by history, one might consider this method doomed.'[16] But this argument is less convincing today than it might have been forty or fifty years ago; and since the time of Schoenberg's first serial compositions there has been no lack of people willing, and indeed eager, to condemn the entire serial system as being contrary to the natural laws of physics and psychology that are embodied in the tonal system, and therefore doomed to failure.

I do not believe that it makes sense to compare the serial system with the tonal system. In so far as there is any such thing as 'the tonal system', it is a theoretical formulation of certain psychological or physiological constraints upon the perception of sounds and their combinations which have been embodied in the historical practice of Western composers—constraints of which the composers have only been aware in the same unreflective manner as that in which ordinary language users can be said to be aware of the principles of grammar. But the so-called serial system is not like this at all. As a matter of fact, Schoenberg records that he personally preferred not to 'call it a "system" but a "method"', and considered it as a tool of composition, but not as a theory' (p. 213). In other words, serialism is a heuristic procedure for the formulation of musical works which a composer consciously chooses to adopt (or not to adopt). And as such it should be compared not to tonality itself, but to the traditional forms that tonal composers adopted.

A classical composer did not simply write a piece of music: he

[15] A summary of these experiments, with references, may be found in Millar 1984; a more recent experiment, which reveals the influence of musical training on the perception of serial invariance, is Krumhansl, Sandell, and Sergeant 1987. One source that Millar does not mention is Pedersen, according to whom 'The controversies that have arisen over serialism have probably resulted from critic and composer alike often failing to distinguish between compositional working techniques and perceptible musical structure. The composer cannot assume that because a technique is logically consistent it will necessarily result in perceptible sound structures. On the other hand, the critic cannot assume that an analysis of the compositional technique will tell one what the musical message is.' (1975: 6–7.)

[16] Ed. 1984: 215. The words 'in spite of' are revealing.

wrote a symphony, a concerto, a sonata, or whatever. In casting his music within such a traditional form, he was giving it a type of organization that was by no means fully perceptible as such. As I tried to show in Chapter 1, classical forms are hardly more successful when regarded as things to be perceived than are serial structures. Indeed, the fact that today's listeners do not, in practice, respond to the large-scale tonal relations on which the classical forms are based has led certain commentators to suggest that classical listeners must have perceived these forms differently from how we to do today: in the course of a discussion of the classical sense of large-scale dissonance Rosen remarks, 'Today, our harmonic sensibilities have become coarsened by the tonal instability of music after the death of Beethoven, and the strength of this feeling is perhaps difficult to recapture.' (1976a: 73.) Alan Walker says more bluntly that 'By the very nature of things tonality is no longer so true for the modern listener whose aural experience of it is not so vivid as that of his classical counterpart.' (1962: 152.) Now statements like this present an epistemological problem because, as Roman Ingarden says, in trying to learn about the music of the past

We must start from communion with the cultural product itself . . . which still somehow exists today. . . . The possibility of our cognizing the contents of works that are directly accessible to us now is the condition of our being able to come to know the past, and not vice versa, as art historians often assume. If by this indirect method we wish to conclude something about past creative processes, say Chopin's when composing his *Revolutionary Etude*, we must make yet another very basic but not obvious assumption that a composition Chopin produced is exactly identical with the work we hear today.[17]

But there is also a more straightforward argument against what Rosen and Walker are saying: this is simply to ask whether the Rosens and Walkers of the twenty-first century would not speak

---

[17] Ingarden 1986: 59–60. Daniel Leech-Wilkinson (1984: 9) has made a similar point ('Analyses of surviving works, while taking careful account of what we know of period techniques, have to proceed from, and to seek to explain, what we currently see and hear in the music. There is no other view available to us'), while Max Meyer asked 'How can we know what Bach or Beethoven or Mozart meant except by experimenting upon ourselves, assuming that the general psychological laws of melody applied to them as they do to us?' (quoted in Esper 1966: 188.)

in precisely the same terms of the irretrievable sensitivity to serial structure that twentieth-century listeners possessed. Rosen is surely correct when he says of the series that 'it is not properly speaking something heard, either imaginatively or practically; it is transmuted into something heard' (1976b: 87); and his words are perhaps equally applicable to the traditional forms of classical music.

How then did Beethoven transmute the forms of his compositions into sound? The traditional wisdom regarding his compositional process, received mainly from Nottebohm, is that he built up his compositions stage by stage, from the smallest motivic fragments to the complete work. For instance, Nottebohm says of 'Sehnsucht' that the music

is not at all the product of a moment, but the result of assiduous, continuous labor. The melody is gathered together from portions of the whole, and is built up in a steady metamorphosis. Only gradually and by means of steady industry do the emerging fragments weld themselves together and group themselves, first into a smaller, then a larger entity.[18]

But, as I mentioned, 'Sehnsucht' is an exceptional case; in general the idea that Beethoven first finalized the motivic or thematic details, then amalgamated them into larger units, and so on is not borne out in the sketches. It has often been pointed out that in his early (and even not-so-early) sketches, the motivic and thematic details often have, as Nottebohm put it, 'little or even nothing of Beethoven's peculiar style and individuality; in fact they are often very ordinary and conventional.' (trans. 1979: 97.) Similarly, Joseph Kerman remarks that 'Beethoven does not start with loose, free, improvisational ideas which are then molded into something more tightly organized. He starts with rigid and even mechanical ideas which are only later smoothed into something more imaginative and fluid.' (1971: 30.) And Robert Winter not only comments on this, but also suggests an explanation for it. Describing the sketches for the String Quartet Op. 131, he says:

The flatness of the thematic material is awesome, but it transmits vividly the impression that Beethoven was not so much drafting themes—the popular assumption concerning his sketching process—as groping

---

[18] Trans. in Lockwood 1973: 121.

towards something more elusive: overall tonal direction. . . . Sketches such as these shed light, then, on the oft-noted banality of many of Beethoven's first jottings. (1977: 116–20.)

What this means is that the early sketches are not really concerned with themes at all: they are concerned with the larger formal context in which the themes are to operate. At this stage the themes are serving primarily as a vehicle for the development of the overall tonal direction, as Winter calls it, of the work as a whole; speaking of the sketches for the 'Eroica' Symphony, Tovey commented on the way in which Beethoven seems to have jotted down 'any cliché that would mark the place where an idea ought to be'.[19] Now Beethoven was, of course, operating within the format of the traditional forms in the course of such sketching. He often devoted a disproportionate number of detailed sketches to the critical points in a traditional form—the first and second subjects, the modulation between the keys of these subjects, and so on—and the larger drafts generally coincide with the sections out of which the forms are built; the traditional forms evidently constituted a starting-point or even a productional mechanism in the compositional process. One can imagine that it was largely through the confrontation with these traditional forms, with the presuppositions that they embody regarding tonal, thematic, textural, and tensional structure, that Beethoven clarified what it was that he wanted in a given work and so moved towards the realization of its specific tonal plan. In Schenkerian terms one would see this overall tonal plan as constituting the real, that is to say functional, form of the work; and it makes sense to suppose that once Beethoven had achieved this, the motivic and thematic details—now having a specific context within which to operate— would fall quickly and easily into place. And this would explain something which Nottebohm was the first to observe: 'in most humans', he wrote (trans. 1979: 98), 'the creative faculty grows slack during work, but with Beethoven it was otherwise, for in him it worked on unimpaired: indeed it often rose to its greatest heights only at the last moment.'

In talking about serial music it has become customary to contrast what George Perle calls 'pre-compositional structure' with the

[19] Quoted in Lockwood 1982: 102.

work of composition as such.[20] By pre-compositional structure
Perle means the various systematic properties inherent in a
particular series: for instance, the transformational relationships
that may hold between the different segments of the series when it
is split up into groups of four or six notes, or relationships of
identity or inversion between different transforms of the series.
Relationships such as these, which a composer can exploit for
purposes of both formal organization and note-to-note structure,
depend on the particular intervallic conformation of a series, and so
vary between one series and another. In other words, the series has
to be designed to allow whatever relationships of this kind the
composer wants in a given work, and it is this process of design that
Perle calls pre-composition—in contrast to the compositional
process as such, which means the particular realization of these
structural possibilities in the finished work. Although Perle does
not intend to imply by this that pre-composition and composition
proper necessarily succeed each other in chronological terms, this
approach does easily lead one to think of the music as serving to
'express' or 'present' the structural relationships inherent in the
series. And accordingly the compositional process comes to be seen
as a matter of realizing in sound what is already implied in the
structural idea of the work.

Such thinking has its origin in Schoenberg's conception of the
musical idea. As formulated in terms of the series, however, it is less
applicable to Schoenberg's music than to that of Webern, who,
according to Adorno, 'realizes twelve-tone technique and thus no
longer composes. . . . His final works are schemata of the rows
translated into notes.' (trans. 1973: 110.) By contrast, Adorno says,
'Schoenberg does violence to the row. He composes twelve-tone
music as though there were no such thing as the twelve-tone
technique.' Here Adorno is referring not so much to certain well-
known instances where Schoenberg deviated from strict serial
ordering as to the way in which the serial structure is, so to speak,
asborbed into the fabric of his music. The series is there in the
String Trio, for instance, or in *A Survivor from Warsaw*, but these
works cannot be understood in terms of the series in the same sense

[20] Perle discussed this concept in a footnote to p. 8 of the 2nd edition (London, 1968) of
his *Serial Composition and Atonality*, which was for some reason deleted in the 5th edition
(Berkeley, 1981). His pre-compositional structure is comparable to what Xenakis (1971:
160–1) calls 'outside-time structure'.

that Webern's Piano Variations can. The series forms the basis of the design of the Piano Variations—in terms not just of its pitches but of its rhythms, dynamics, and textures too. But it does not play the same role in the String Trio or in *A Survivor from Warsaw*; in such works it would make more sense to think of it as something with which the composer engages in a kind of creative dialogue, much as Beethoven evolved his music through the confrontation with the traditional forms and their imperatives.[21] For a composer cannot simply impose his intentions upon a series in the way in which one stamps a design upon a pat of butter; on the contrary, it is characteristic of the series that it creates a kind of resistance, that it 'speaks back' to the composer.[22] Indeed, the mere exercise of trying to mould a composition in terms of notation—to get it down on paper—may be sufficient to elicit this kind of speaking back: I have already quoted Lockwood's account of the far-reaching changes Beethoven made in the autograph score of the Cello Sonata Op. 69, in which 'it was only when he had written down one version of the development in this autograph that he saw how he really wanted the two instruments to be fitted together.'[23] In the same way, the attempt to frame what he wants to write in terms of the series may stimulate a decisive rejection on the composer's part, or equally it may result in the process described by Alexander Goehr (1976: 9) as 'automatic writing', in which whole stretches of music are written out rapidly with a sense of their being 'right' that may be as much visual as aural.

When this happens it does not mean (or at any rate does not usually mean) that the composer is unaware of or unconcerned

---

[21] Adorno remarks: 'In Beethoven's last works barren conventions—through which the compositional stream flows only hesitantly—play approximately the same role as the one performed by the twelve-tone system' (trans. 1973: 120). His extensive discussion of serialism gains weight from his own compositional studies with Berg.

[22] It is perhaps in this light that one is to understand Stravinsky's remarks about the necessity of compositional constraints which can offer a resistance to, as he puts it, the 'inevitable over-rigorousness of the naked will' (1947: 55, 68). For a detailed account of the interaction of compositional restraint and freedom in a complex serial context, see Toop 1984.

[23] See above, p. 116. David Cope has developed an expert system for computer-aided composition which does something rather similar, only at a higher level of technology. The composer enters a motivic idea into the computer, which then generates a complete work on the basis of the structural possibilities inherent in this idea. The computer's compositional choices can be adopted or rejected by the composer, so that the system provides 'an antagonist that develops musical synonyms for fragments of works in progress' (Cope 1987: 30).

about the sound of his music: it means that he is grasping the sound of what he is writing in visual and conceptual terms, hearing with his eyes as much as with his ears. The ambivalence of this situation emerges rather clearly from something that Stravinsky once said to Robert Craft:

Many people today are too ready to condemn a composer for 'not being able to hear what he has written'. In fact, if he is a real composer, he always does hear, at least by calculation, everything he writes. Tallis calculated the forty parts of his *Spem in Alium Numquam Habui*, he did not hear them; and even in twelve-part polyphony such as Orlando's, vertically we hear only four-part music.[24]

The composer, that is to say, does not (or does not necessarily) manipulate sounds as such. Rather, he manipulates notes, motifs, and forms, and it is in terms of these things that his work presents itself to him as sound. The sound of music plays a role in the compositional process that is perhaps comparable to that of its meaning: as Stravinsky said on another occasion, the composer 'perceives, he selects, he combines, and he is not in the least aware at what point meanings of a different sort and significance grow into his work'.[25] These words recall Merleau-Ponty's image[26] of the writer working on the back of his fabric and finding himself suddenly surrounded by meaning; one might perhaps equally think of the composer as working with notes and motifs and forms and finding himself suddenly surrounded by sound.

There is a sentimental idea that the composer simply transcribes what he hears in his 'inner ear'; indeed, Stravinsky himself implied as much when, speaking of his *Rite of Spring*, he said, 'I heard and I wrote what I heard. I am the vessel through which *Le Sacre* passed.' (Stravinsky and Craft 1981: 147–8.) But we should perhaps not interpret these words in too literal a sense: Gilbert Ryle (1973: 235–42) has convincingly demonstrated that such thinking is based

[24] Stravinsky and Craft 1979: 129.
[25] Stravinsky and Craft 1981: 103. In *The Remarkable Musical Life of the Artist in Tones, Joseph Berglinger*, Wackenroder remarks, 'many pieces, whose tones have been put together by their masters like numbers in a ledger or tesserae for a mosaic, merely according to rule, yet meaningfully and in a lucky moment—when rehearsed by instruments these pieces speak out in splendid poetry, full of feeling, although the master in his expert work may have given little thought to the possibility that the genius bewitched in the kingdom of tones would, for initiated ears, so splendidly beat his wings.' (quoted in Dahlhaus 1982: 41.) Schumann says something similar too (quoted in Halbwachs trans. 1980: 181-2).
[26] See above, p. 135.

on a conceptual error, in that so-called mental contents only exist in so far as they are constituted procedurally and directed towards intersubjective realization.[27] And in any case, Stravinsky spoke on another occasion of 'the pleasure that the actual doing of the work affords. . . . Should the impossible happen and my work suddenly be given to me in a perfectly completed form, I should be embarrassed and nonplussed by it, as by a hoax.' (1947: 54.) Accordingly I would maintain that the 'transcription' that occurs when music is written down—getting the music into notational specifics, the 'actual doing of the work' to which Stravinsky refers—is not something that happens after the creative event: rather, I would say, it *is* the creative event, or at least an intrinsic part of it.[28] As it happens, this is borne out by yet another of Stravinsky's remarks. This time he was speaking of the 'Sacrificial Dance' from the *Rite*, which 'I could play, but did not, at first, know how to write' (Stravinsky and Craft 1981: 141). How, one might ask, could a highly literate musician like Stravinsky have found himself unable to write something down when he knew how to play it? The answer presumably revolves around the fact that the *Rite* is not a piano work; it is scored for an exceptionally large orchestra, and the orchestration is not in this instance a matter of mere arrangement but, on the contrary, an essential part of the work's identity. A few sentences later Stravinsky added, 'I always compose the instrumentation when I compose a work'; and from this it follows that until he had determined, as least in outline, the actual notes that the instruments were to play—until, that is, he had got the music more or less into notational specifics—he did not regard a work as really having been composed at all. What he played at the piano before he had figured out how the 'Sacrificial

---

[27] Schoenberg once made the odd remark that 'fantasy, in contradistinction to logic, which everyone should be able to follow, favours a lack of restraint and a freedom in the manner of expression, permissible in our day only perhaps in dreams; in dreams of future fulfilment; in dreams of a possibility of expression which has no regard for the perceptive faculties of a contemporary audience; where one may speak with kindred spirits in the language of intuition and know that one is understood if one uses the speech of the imagination—of fantasy.' (ed. 1984: 274–5.) But would such a disembodied music be music at all? One might conclude that Schoenberg has fallen into the illusion of immanence (p. 90 above) and that his vision of the future is no more than science fiction.

[28] Schenker maintains something similar in his essay 'Let's do away with the phrasing slur', though he arrives at it from a quite different direction: 'the struggle over notation always goes hand in hand with a struggle over the content; but once the content is worked out, then the only possible notation is also immediately present.' (Kalib 1973: ii, 74.)

Dance' could be written down must have been some kind of impression or model or analogue of the music he wanted to write; it cannot have been the 'Sacrificial Dance' itself, for the simple reason that the piece had not yet been composed.

For Stravinsky, then, as for Beethoven, writing down a work was in reality an integral part of the compositional process. The music was not in any simple sense an expression of Beethoven's or Stravinsky's intentions; it was forged out of the confrontation between the composer's intentions and aspirations on the one hand, and on the other the imperatives of notation, the considerations of instrumental playability, and perhaps—*pace* Schoenberg—the requirements of audience-acceptability too. And what is true of Beethoven and Stravinsky is probably equally true of other composers, including Schoenberg himself. Eugen Lehner has recorded that even when Schoenberg was composing serial music, 'no matter what his intention was, when he sat down and the inspiration came, he was just writing music, very much to his astonishment, because it always turned out differently than what he expected'.[29] In transcending whatever intentions or aspirations the composer may have begun with, the work achieves its own existence as something independent of the composer and imbued with a significance that the composer may not himself have been aware of in writing it. Boulez may have had this in mind when he wrote, 'I am convinced that however perceptive the composer, he cannot imagine the consequences, immediate or ultimate, of what he has written, and that his perception is not necessarily more acute than that of the analyst.' (1971: 18.)[30]

It seems to me that the tension between the effect of music and the means by which it is represented—whether in terms of serial structures or tonal forms or even simply notation—plays a positive and perhaps a definitive role in the compositional process. Serialism is the most obvious example of this. Adorno speaks of 'the astonishing contradiction between twelve-tone mechanics and expression' (trans. 1973: 119), while the composer Henri Pousseur writes that 'one cannot impute the fact that one fails to perceive the serial relationships at work within a piece of music to either a lack of culture or to insufficient familiarity. The divergence between

---

[29] J. A. Smith 1986: 193; see also Lehner's remarks on pp. 211–12.
[30] See also Stockhausen's opening remarks in his Foreword to Maconie 1976.

serial procedures and the perceptible result is sought after and exists effectively.' (1972: 99.) And in more general terms Dahlhaus (1983: 56) says: 'the aesthetic rift—the dichotomy between a structure which nobody discerns without laborious analysis and an acoustical façade which nevertheless makes its effect—is a character trait and indeed a constituent of new music. Modern compositions appear simultaneously as paper music and "effect" music.' But I do not think we need to restrict such a characterization to new music. For, as I have said, the same applies to the traditional forms of classical music, and perhaps even more to the 'music games'—to adapt Wittgenstein's phrase—of strict counterpoint. It is in this light that we can understand Schumann's otherwise baffling remark that 'the best fugue is the one that the public takes for a Strauss waltz; in other words, a fugue where the structural underpinnings are no more visible than the roots that nourish the flower.' (Pleasants 1965: 124.) And it is this that renders intelligible the computational and over-determined compositional procedures of composers like Machaut or Isaac, or the glittering display of strict contrapuntal devices that Bach introduced into some of his compositions—compositions that demonstrate their mastery precisely in the fact that the sound of them is really no different from that of Bach's normal compositional style.

A composition, then, exists on two quite distinct, and sometimes apparently unrelated, levels: the level of production and the level of reception. I would suggest that the fact that it can be in some sense grasped, appreciated, or enjoyed on both these levels is one of the defining attributes of a musical composition, as we generally conceive it; it is in this sense that a composition is something different from a free improvisation on the one hand[31] and a purely technical exercise on the other. This means that there is really no compelling reason why we should expect composers to want to narrow or close the gap between these two levels, for example by scrupulously avoiding any type of structural organization that cannot be grasped by a listener in productional terms. After all, there is no evidence to suggest that Machaut or Isaac or Bach was worried if his listeners failed to perceive the contrapuntal

---

[31] Rather than the pre-planned (and to this extent composed) examples of 'improvisation' in C. P. E. Bach's *Essay*, of which Kramer writes: 'The plan and the realization, conceived simultaneously, conceal a tension between the work and its theoretical abstraction that may be said to invigorate all Classical art.' (1985: 553.)

devices in his music, any more than there is evidence that Haydn or Mozart or Beethoven worried that his listeners might fail to perceive a modulation or a recapitulation. Schoenberg, on the other hand, did worry about these things. 'Even someone with absolute pitch', he wrote, 'might mistake the end of the first section of a symphony for the end of the movement if he knew nothing of the structural functions of tonality.' (ed. 1984: 380.) He is referring here to classical music; but his worries are of a thoroughly twentieth-century character, deriving as they do from the assumption that there ought to be a direct correspondence between the formal structure a composer embodies in his music and the way in which it is experienced by the listener.

In an article entitled 'Beyond notation' the composer Trevor Wishart catalogues some of the discrepancies between conventional notation and the experienced sound of music, and speculates about the possibility of replacing conventional notation by computerized languages for digital sound-generation. In such languages, he argues,

total one-to-one correspondence between the notation procedure and the sound itself means that we can use notation to explore the internal architecture of sound. Ultimately, the notation—in fact a set of programmes which generate digital data—becomes a creative tool at a deeper level than the traditional Western notation system. (1985: 325.)

I see no reason to doubt the value of such a language as a means for exploring 'the internal architecture of sound'. But whether it would be equally valuable as a means of composing music is another question. For a language that was in total one-to-one correspondence to the sound—if this is indeed a meaningful concept—would not engage the composer in any kind of creative dialogue: it would function as a purely passive mechanism of transcription. Composition, in other words, would be replaced by mere prediction, by a calculus of effects, of however sophisticated a nature and however astonishing or gratifying its aural results.

4.2   REIFICATION AND EXPLANATION

I

Everyone who has taught aural training must be familiar with the situation where a student is unable to write down a bass-line, not because he cannot write down what he hears, but because he simply cannot hear it. Where a bass-line is played on a different instrument from the rest of the music, or in a substantially lower register, it may be easy enough to pick it out simply by 'filtering out' the other parts; but this may not be possible in the case of homophonic piano music, or even music for string quartet. In such cases, grasping the harmony is the key. The bass-line has to be heard, and seen, as an extension of the harmony; it has to be actively reconstructed by the listener on the basis of his acquired knowledge of the style and structural organization of the music to which he is listening. That is why there is no short cut to writing down bass-lines for the student who finds this a problem.

Although it has to be reconstructed by the listener, the bass-line is at least there in the sense that somebody is actually playing it. But when it comes to perceiving intervals, the whole question of how far the intervals exist in the sound—rather than being created through an appropriate act of listening—becomes problematic. Through aural training, budding musicians learn to distinguish the different intervals used in Western music from one another—a major third, a fourth, and so on. But it can happen that an interval that would be judged to be a major third (perhaps a rather out-of-tune major third) when heard by itself will be heard as a fourth in a given musical context; in experiments musicians have been found on occasion to hear as a C, for example, a note that in objective terms was nearer to a B.[32] In such cases the discrepancy between the way in which a pitch or interval would be heard by itself, and the way in which it is heard in the context of a specific piece of music, makes it obvious that pitch- and interval-classes are imposed forms: they are not 'there' in the sound, but are created through an act of listening which is analytical in the sense that it involves categorizing the sound in accordance with the specific structural context of the music. And, as might be expected, such categorical

[32] See Zuckerkandl 1956: 79–81. 'Objective' here refers to the correlations between frequency and perceived pitch that people make when tones are heard in isolation, as opposed to in a specific musical context. It appears that similar categorical overlaps are to be found in the perception of rhythms; an analysis of recorded performances of the 'Moonlight' Sonata—which a trained listener would presumably hear in accordance with the rhythmic specifications of the score—revealed overlaps between the different rhythmic categories, 'sometimes to the extent that, for instance, some of the longest performed quarter notes were in fact longer than some of the shortest performed half notes' (Gabrielsson 1985: 61).

perception—hearing this note as a B or a C, hearing this interval as a major third or a fourth—requires specific training: there is evidence that trained musicians perceive musical sound in categorical terms in a way in which, or to an extent to which, untrained listeners do not.[33] That is to say, a musically trained listener who is trying to listen for the bass-line, or to identify the intervals in a melody, is perceiving what he hears in terms of categories that may have little or no perceptual reality for the untrained listener—a listener who may be just as capable as a trained one of responding to the music's aesthetic content, but proves upon examination to be incapable of making the simplest discriminations as to which of a pair of notes is the higher, or as to which of a pair of intervals is the larger.[34] In other words, people can and do enjoy music without being able to make what are, in terms of musicological representation, the most elementary and basic perceptual judgements.

It is normal, at least in Western (or Westernized) musical cultures, for any listener—whether trained or untrained—to 'see' music as moving in space; the opening of Wagner's *Rheingold* Prelude emerges from the depths, while swirling clouds of sound rise and fall in Ligeti's *Atmosphères*. But the means of musicological representation that are specific to Western musical culture render this spatial metaphor more precise and more intersubjective in its application, or, as one might say, they rationalize it. What this essentially means is that in being experienced in terms of these representations, sound is mapped on to a topographical matrix whose co-ordinates are pitch and time; and the intersections between these two dimensions define the note, which is the basic

---

[33] e.g. experiments conducted by Roberts and Shaw (1984) show that untrained listeners are much poorer than trained ones at distinguishing the various categories of triads, while Blechner's studies (1978) of harmonic perception indicate that the listener's level of experience 'can affect both the level and pattern of performance, and that significant patterns of results may be masked by the procedure of data averaging that has been common in studies of categorical perception'. This may possibly tie in with the findings of brain lateralization studies, which have yielded different results for trained and untrained listeners in melody recognition tasks; it has been suggested that 'the "crossover" of laterality in music recognition occurs because the musicians adopt an analytic strategy whereas the non-musicians adopt a holistic strategy.' (Sloboda 1985: 264.)

[34] For a discussion of this with further references see Serafine 1988: 62–3. On the basis of an extensive series of experiments she concludes that good performance in tests of pitch discrimination 'is not highly related to higher-level cognitive processes in music. What it may represent, however, is a kind of analytic auditory acuity' (p. 230).

sound-event in terms of which Western music is rationalized. Now I have said that the categories in terms of which musicians evaluate pitch and time exist only by virtue of acts of perception that embody culture-specific knowledge; and the same applies to the note itself. Musical sounds do not contain notes in the same sense that lemons contain pips: rather, notes are imaginative entities which have a history and a geography of their own.

If one were to write a 'history of the note',[35] it would begin (at least in the West) with the neume, which was the unit in terms of which Gregorian chant came to be notated. Neumes do not correspond in a one-to-one manner with notes as we would conceive them or write them today; rather, each one incorporates several notes, as we would see them. (A comparison of the two notations in Ex. 48 will demonstrate this.[36]) That is, the minimal sound-event of the Gregorian chant, as it is represented in neumatic notation, is defined not by what we would call a single pitch and a single rhythmic value, but rather by a single melodic motion that encompasses a number of pitches and rhythmic values; it is for this reason that Thomas Clifton writes of Gregorian chant that 'The notation itself is wonderfully expressive. . . . The neume . . . not only provides a visual clue to the way the tones themselves are rhythmically grouped in performance, but also graphically demonstrates that a certain passage through space is implicit in the notion of "interval".' (1983: 145.) The neume, in other words, is less analytical than our contemporary concept of the note; it is embedded in a larger musical context, which it presents holistically, as a single Gestalt. It is also embedded in the text of the chant; in neumatic notation, as Leo Treitler explains (1982a: 244), 'The essential melodic phenomenon . . . was the

---

[35] Cf. Sloboda 1985: 248–52. A much fuller account of the neume, along with a consideration of the fundamental attributes of musical notation, will be found in Treitler 1982a.

[36] Ex. 48a shows p. 31 of the Cantatorium of St Gall (Stiftsbibliothek St Gallen, Cod. 359), which dates from the late 9th cent. (see Parrish 1959: 17–18.) The neumes written above the words do not designate specific intervals, so there is no way of knowing precisely how this chant was sung at St Gall. Ex. 48b shows the *Liber usualis* version of the gradual 'Domine Deus virtutum' (ll. 5–7), which is based on a collation of later MSS in which intervals are specified. The 2 versions are compatible as far as the asterisk on the final syllable (the rest of the melisma is not in the St Gall MS). The shorter slurs in Ex. 48b are equivalent to the single neumes; the initial S-like neume over 'Dom' corresponds to the notes G–B–A in Ex. 48b, the following 5 dots are single notes, the next neume corresponds to C–A–B, etc.

Ex. 48a

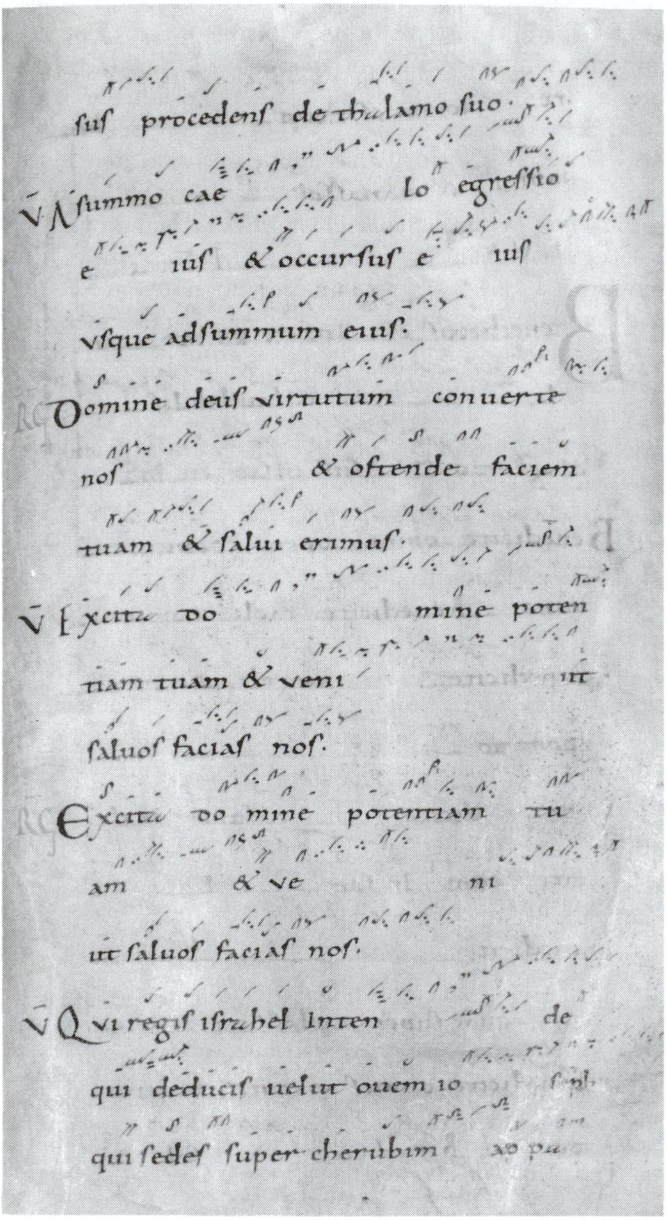
sus procedens de thalamo suo.
V A summo cae lo egressio
e ius & occursus e ius
usque ad summum eius.
Domine deus virtutum converte
nos & ostende faciem
tuam & salui erimus.
V Excita do mine poten
tiam tuam & veni ut
saluos facias nos.
Excita do mine potentiam tu
am & ve ni
ut saluos facias nos.
V Qui regis israhel inten de
qui deducis uelut ouem io seph
qui sedes super cherubim ap pa

Ex. 48b

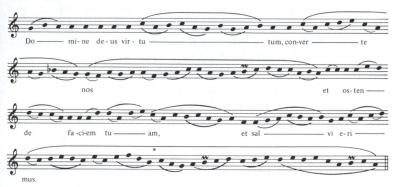

Do —— mi- ne de- us vir - tu ———————— tum, con-ver ———— te

nos   et   os- ten ——

de   fa -ci-em   tu ——— am,   et sal ————— vi e- ri ——

mus.

movement of the voice in declaiming a syllable of text'. And the history of the note from the eighth century, when the neume developed, to the twentieth has been a history of increasing abstraction from context, both textual and musical. As conceived by the Ars Nova composers of the fourteenth century, for example, the note represents an intermediate stage in that, while it corresponds to a single pitch and a single rhythmic value, the interpretation of these values depends upon the prevailing melodic and rhythmic modes, as well as upon the practice of *musica ficta*.

Of course, the values that are embodied in the note as we conceive it today, as regards both pitch and time, are still tied to context; the difference between the present-day note and that of the fourteenth century is merely one of degree. In being more independent of context, and consequently more flexible in its application and more fine-grained in its resolution, the present-day note provides a more versatile calculus of compositional possibilities than was the case with its fourteenth-century counterpart. (At least, this is true of today's conventional notation; contemporary graphic scores such as Cage's *Aria*, in which the note is not presented as a singularity but embedded within a larger musical gesture, represent in this sense something of a regression.) That is to say, it presents musical sounds in terms of a distinctly different, and greatly enlarged, repertoire of possibilities as regards their specification and combination; and this means that one cannot properly appreciate the manner in which fourteenth-century music was conceived by the composer if one approaches it purely through the medium of modern transcriptions. There can be something peculiarly arbitrary or even eccentric about the appearance of a medieval composition transcribed into modern notation, which may not reveal itself in the sound of the music when it is played—and this is perhaps to be put down to the fact that modern notation presents the sounds of the music in a relatively abstract manner, rather than in terms of the concrete possibilities of specification and combination through which they presented themselves to the composer. To the extent that the notation is an intrinsic part of the musician's productional engagement with the music, one should perhaps not regard as authentic any performance of medieval music in which the players read from modern notation.

Notation, then, is not simply a technology for communicating musical sounds or ideas: from a productional point of view, musical sounds and ideas are only constituted as such by virtue of a cognition in which means of notation play a predominant role.[37] Like a number of other writers, mainly ethnomusicologists, I would argue that a musical culture is essentially a cognitive entity, in other words that to define a musical culture means defining 'the things a people must know in order to understand, perform and create acceptable music in their culture'.[38] If this is the case, then ear training forms the basic means by which the identity of a musical culture is maintained; for however such training is done—whether through the formalized classes of the twentieth-century college or conservatory, or through the apprentice sitarist's imitation of what his teacher plays—it teaches the student how to co-ordinate the sound of music with the repertoire of cognitive representations that is specific to his culture. And it is these cognitive representations that give music its historical continuity. For if musical cultures are defined in terms of patterns of ear training, then they may be seen to have considerable powers of endurance; one might reasonably maintain that contemporary Western music and that of the Baroque period belong to what is more or less the same musical

[37] Serafine goes as far as to suggest that 'Most probably, the development of notation . . . brought about the isolation of separate pitches. . . . Notation and the idea of discrete steps appear to have developed in synchrony.' (1988: 61–2.) Halbwachs makes the same point in a more general manner: 'Musical language is not some instrument invented after the fact to fix and communicate to musicians what certain among them have spontaneously imagined. On the contrary, it is this language that has created music.' (1980: 176–7.)

[38] Feld 1974: 211. See also Herndon 1974: 246, Marshall 1982: 165, and Serafine 1988.

culture, in that the basic patterns of ear training on which they depend are largely coextensive. It is not these patterns that are subject to rapid change, nor the repertoire of sonic events or forms which they make available to the composer; it is the manner in which these events or forms are combined with one another in the service of an aesthetic programme, an ideology, or a musical fashion. Classical, romantic, neo-classical, and neo-romantic are styles of music, not musical cultures, just as were the fashionable musics that succeeded one another on an almost annual basis during the 1920s.[39] Each depends on essentially the same means of musical representation, and hence on essentially the same pattern of ear training.

II

It is through conceiving sounds as objects—objects which can, in Stravinsky's words,[40] be perceived, selected, and combined with one another—that musicians overcome the essential passivity of a purely aural response to music; and this is the precondition of a musical culture's very existence.

A musical culture is a tradition of imagining sound as music. Its basic identity lies in its mechanism for constituting sounds as intentional objects, from the level of a single note to that of a complete work.[41] This means that the ubiquitous discrepancies between the manner in which musicians conceive music and that in which listeners experience it are endemic to musical culture. Indeed, they define it. Stravinsky once said, 'when I compose an interval I am aware of it as an object . . . as something outside me, the contrary of an impression.' (Stravinsky and Craft 1979: 17.) After all, a composer cannot perceive, select, and combine mere impressions of intervals: in order to perceive, select, or combine intervals he has to conceive them as objects. But for a listener the interval is not an object; it is, as Stravinsky put it, an impression. There is in this way a fundamental contradiction between the way in which the composer conceives music and the way in which the

[39] Schoenberg lists 'Machine Music', 'New Objectivity', 'Music for Every Day Use' (*Gebrauchsmusik*), and 'Play Music' or 'Game Music', as well as neo-classicism (ed. 1984: 52).

[40] See above, p. 212.

[41] And also in the extent to which these intentional objects can be specified independently of a particular social context. This consideration is less important in the case of Western art music than in that of most non-Western musics, however, and is not pursued further here.

listener experiences it, and the same, of course, applies to the formal level at which a composer sees his piece as a structurally integrated whole—a level of structure which may have little if any reality for the listener. If it were not for this contradiction between the composer's conception and the listener's experience, there would be no possibility of the kind of compositional engagement with sound that I described in the first half of this chapter, an engagement which is predicated upon the composition being conceived as an object and not an impression.

Fundamental as this contradiction may be to musical composition and to musical culture, it can create both practical and theoretical problems for the musician. It may be helpful at this point to make a comparison between the spatial metaphor in terms of which musical sounds are constituted as objects and the medical metaphor within which clinical psychiatry operates. Just as musical notation represents sounds as imaginary objects, so psychiatry represents abnormal mental conditions as imaginary diseases. Alasdair MacIntyre (1958: 16) has pointed out that Freud originally trained as a neurologist, and hence 'What Freud in fact does is to bring a scheme of explanation derived from neurology to the phenomena which his psychological studies had forced on his attention.' (p. 23.) Or to put it another way, 'Freud thought of the mind on the analogy of the brain' (Coulter 1979: 116); he treated it as a quasi-physical object, and ascribed abnormal mental conditions to quasi-physical causes, much in the manner that physical symptoms (for example, coming out in spots) can be ascribed to physical causes (say an allergy to prawns). Freudian concepts such as the unconscious, the ego, and the mechanisms of repression all have this reified aspect; as MacIntyre puts it, 'while Freud illuminatingly describes a good deal of behaviour as unconsciously motivated, and describes too how the recall of events and situations of which we had become unconscious may have a therapeutic role, he wishes to justify not just the adverb or the adjective but the substantive form: the unconscious.' (1958: 71.) And the same applies to the ego, the id, and so forth.

Now Wittgenstein put forward an influential critique of Freudian theories, in which he accepted the therapeutic value of psychiatric practice while at the same time rejecting the entire Freudian concept of causation. In essence his argument was that neither the traumatic experiences that were recalled through psychoanalysis, nor Freud's reified unconscious, ego, and id, had any real existence at all: they were no more than imaginary constructions on the part of the psychiatrist. But these constructions were valid to the extent that they allowed the patient to come to terms with his predicament on the one hand and made possible the detailed description of individual cases on which the practice of psychiatry depends on the other.[42] (Applying this to music, we would say that the musician's reified intervals, sonata forms, and so forth are imaginary constructions which are valid to the extent that they enable the musician to create aesthetic pleasure for the listener.) Jeff Coulter (1979: 116) puts Wittgenstein's point more trenchantly and indicates some of the dangers that arise as a result:

I believe that Freud's model constitutes a psychological iconography of the most bizarre and reifying kind in the history of the subject, but that it is quite intelligible as a metaphorical construction designed to come to terms in general with the common experiences of socialization and conduct. It comes to grief only because it encourages psychology to seek and construct fictitious explanations rather than allow its conceptualizations to be constrained by the logic of ordinary concepts and the limits of generality in theorizing about human behaviour in its specifically human aspect.

It is the contention of the anti-psychiatry movement centred around R. D. Laing that the practice of clinical psychiatry has actually become ineffective or counter-productive in so far as the psychiatrist's reifying theories have led him to view his patient as a case-study, a bundle of symptoms, rather than as a person.

The essence of the intellectual fallacy known as reification is that something is mistakenly believed to have a real existence when it is in fact purely an artifice of representation.[43] Thus such concepts as the unconscious, the ego, and the id are perfectly valid as means of representing the reality of mental disorder, but to impute any real existence to them is (at least according to the anti-psychiatrists) to fall into an error whose social consequences can be devastating. It seems to me that the fallacy of reification is just as entrenched in much theoretical thinking about music. I have already mentioned some examples of reification. Seashore's idea that the artistic value

---

[42] For further discussion of this see Scruton 1979: 147 and MacIntyre 1958: 72.

[43] See S. J. Gould 1984: 250 ff. for a particularly clear discussion of reification in connection with intelligence testing.

of musical performance inheres in its expressive deviations from notational norms[44] is such an example, because it imputes a psychological reality to notational values—values which are brought into being only in the representation of musical sound. The same applies to Petzold's approach to musical listening in terms of the 'elements' of melody, rhythm, timbre, and so forth;[45] these are artefacts of musical explanation, and there is no reason to assume that they correspond in any direct manner to psychological processes or structures. But what is perhaps the most significant example of the reification of the listening process is to be found in Schoenberg's theoretical writings.

When Sartre says that 'What is successive in perception is simultaneous in the image',[46] he is treating the image as a representation of the reality that is directly grasped in perception. Now there is an obvious similarity between this and Schoenberg's statement that a composer conceives his work in spatial terms but that 'In writing the work down, space is transformed into time. For the hearer this takes place the other way round; it is only after the work has run its course in time that he can see it as a whole—its idea, its form and its content.'[47] However, there is a striking difference of emphasis, in that Schoenberg regards the musical work as an essentially timeless entity: what happens during the time of performance, he implies, does not define or constitute the work as such, it merely communicates it from composer to listener.[48] Indeed he spelt this out when, in 1940, he told Dika

[44] See above, pp. 156–7. Iser writes at some length on the 'reification of structure basic to the deviationist theory' as it applies to literature (1978: 89), and the same critique could be extended to the theories that explain stylistic changes in music in terms of deviation from norms (p. 147 above).

[45] See above, pp. 163–4.

[46] See ch. 2, n. 13 above.

[47] See above, p. 40.

[48] See Riemann's similar remark, trans. in Slatin 1967: 68. This Schopenhaurian notion of musical time is also to be found in Keller (1965: 116), who links it with Freud, and Schenker, according to whom the background is timeless and its temporal presentation a purely psychological necessity. This leads Schenker to a conception of the relationship between the musical master-work and its performance which is close to Schoenberg's; my argument regarding Schoenberg and the reification fallacy could equally well have been directed at Schenker, who 'predicated his notion of totality not upon perceptual mechanisms in the observer, but upon the work of art itself. Wholeness stems from a central generative force to which everything else is subordinate.' (Solie 1980: 150.) This 'central generative force' is just as reified as Freud's unconscious mind. In saying this I do not wish to question the heuristic value of Schenkerian analysis, but only the idea that its findings can attain some kind of objective validity.

Newlin that 'Music need not be performed any more than books need to be read aloud, for its logic is perfectly represented on the printed page; and the performer, for all his intolerable arrogance, is totally unnecessary except as his interpretations make the music understandable to an audience unfortunate enough not to be able to read it in print.' (Newlin 1980: 164.) This basic conception of the relationship between the work and its performance is deeply embedded in Schoenberg's thinking about music. For instance, in 1923 or 1924 he wrote of performance that

The highest principle for all reproduction of music would have to be that what the composer has written is made to sound in such a way that every note is really heard, and that all the sounds, whether successive or simultaneous, are in such relationship to each other that no part at any moment obscures another, but, on the contrary, makes its contribution towards ensuring that they all stand out clearly from one another. Every composer of any experience arranges his notes in that way. . . . It is the precondition of all music making. (ed. 1984: 319.)

The idea that every note should be made to sound implies, again, a conception of the work not as an aural experience, but as some kind of formal structure, or even configuration of notes, that is to be communicated as such to the listener through the act of performance.

Now this is perfectly reasonable if regarded as the statement of an aesthetic viewpoint. As such, it embodies a preference for the clean, rather dry textures that not only Schoenberg but also many other composers favoured in the 1920s, by way of reaction against the post-Wagnerian style of orchestration that was general up to the First World War. It embodies the ideal of objectivity that characterizes the music of this period. At a deeper level, it perhaps also ties in with Schoenberg's Krausian conception of the work of music as a moral rather than a perceptual entity; for this conception naturally leads to the composition being seen as something that has an intrinsic, revealed significance, in other words as a kind of text (and this 'fundamentalist' approach is even more characteristic of Boretz's and Babbitt's explicitly text-based conception of music, which I discuss in the next section). However, Schoenberg presents what he is saying not as the expression of a specific aesthetic viewpoint but as a general truth applicable to all music, which it obviously is not; as Dahlhaus says, 'Anyone trying to apperceive every detail in Wagner's "Magic Fire Music" or in many pieces by

Debussy hears aesthetically incorrectly.' (1983: 55.) And the separation Schoenberg is making between the structural content of music on the one hand and its aural presentation on the other leads him to make some rather bizarre statements when he tries to interpret the listening process in terms of it.

For instance, Schoenberg frequently says that if a composer wishes his music to be comprehended by the general public, he must repeat everything many times, so that 'were I prepared to be as discursive as one must be, in order to be widely comprehensible, my works would all last 10 or 12 times as long, and a piece which now lasts 10 minutes would play for two hours, while a whole day would not suffice to get through a longer one.' (ed. 1984: 104.) Again, he remarks (p. 327) that

At the first performance of works whose ideas are not superficial, correct tempi can, for the most part, not be taken at all, because this would make everything too hard to understand, and too unusual. Thus I could not understand Mahler's First Symphony until I heard it under a mediocre conductor who got all the tempo relationships wrong. All the tensions were alleviated, banalized, so that one could follow.

It seems to me that there is something extremely strange, not to say perverse, about the idea that a listener can only understand a work when it is played so badly that everything becomes banal—unless, of course, one thinks of this 'understanding' not in the sense of an aesthetic response, but in terms of aural training. It is indeed easier to follow harmonies, grasp themes, and track forms when a work is played much too slowly, or when it is repeated ten or twelve times; and to view musical performance as the communication of musical structures is precisely to view listening from an aural-training perspective. Now it is understandable that Schoenberg, as a composer, would want to grasp Mahler's music in production-orientated terms. But that is not why most people listen to it; it is not why people put on concerts of Mahler's music. Schoenberg, in other words, is hopelessly caught in a confusion between musical and musicological listening.

It would be possible to argue that Schoenberg is guilty of reification, in that the musical idea or structural content that is communicated through performance, and that he regards as constituting the highest musical reality, is more properly regarded as a mere representation of the aesthetic experience in which the work is unfolded; except that, as I have said, this position is a perfectly tenable one provided that it is intended as an aesthetic stance and not a generally valid theory. What is, however, beyond doubt is that Schoenberg's approach to musical listening, in leading certain of his followers to formulate a theory of subconscious perception in music, resulted in a clear instance of the reification fallacy.[49] It is obvious that listeners find it hard, if not impossible, to perceive musical structures in the way Schoenberg says they should when they listen to music. On the other hand, if the aesthetic response to music comes about, as Schoenberg says it does,[50] only through the listener's comprehension of these structures, then this leads to the unwelcome or even absurd conclusion that few listeners, if any, are capable of responding aesthetically to music. One way out of this dilemma is to suppose that, while a listener might not consciously perceive a certain structural relationship (could not identify it, could not say it was there), he might nevertheless perceive it subconsciously.

The origin of this idea perhaps lies in a remark that Schoenberg himself made in his *Theory of Harmony* that 'of the acoustic emanations of the tone nothing is lost. . . . The more remote overtones are recorded by the subconscious'.[51] Some forty years later, Anton Ehrenzweig (1953: 110–12) adopted the same approach to the perception of serial structures, suggesting that while serial transformations might not appear to be related in terms of surface perception, nevertheless their relationships were grasped by the 'depth mind';[52] it was presumably similar thinking that led Hans Keller (1953: 56) to declare that 'Everything that is recognizable on paper is recognizable "by the ear alone" '. And the

---

[49] It is possible to distinguish two concepts of subconscious perception in music, one modelled on Freud and the other on psycholinguistics. I have touched on the latter in my book on analysis (1987a: 220–2); this discussion should be read in the light of Serafine's remarks (1988: 63–4) regarding the perceptual reality of phonemes.

[50] See above, p. 180.

[51] Trans. 1978: 20–1. Far-fetched as this idea may be, something of the sort was already implied by the venerable theories explaining scale formation in terms of ratios derived from the lower overtones—overtones that are not, after all, heard as such under normal conditions (Serafine 1988: 21).

[52] Alan Walker (1962: 65 ff., 143) followed up this idea in a series of tests in which he showed that listeners sometimes recognize that a transformational relationship exists between two sets, without being able to say exactly what this relationship is; he took this as evidence that they were perceiving it subconsciously.

same idea was applied to musical analysis by Rudolph Réti, according to whom it is not a precondition of a motif's significance 'that it must be heard and understood as a motivic utterance by the listener. The unnoticeable influence that it may exert on the listener as a passing subconscious recollection—in fact, *its theoretical existence in the piece*—suffices.' (1951: 47.)

The fallacy of such thinking is not just that it replaces the experience of music with a subconscious mechanism that is as reified as anything Freud ever conceived, and in consequence relieves the composer and the analyst from any obligation to consider the manner in which the music is actually heard; it is that it describes as the subconscious perception of a relationship what is in reality not the perception of a relationship at all. Schoenberg was perfectly correct in saying that one perceives the more remote overtones; but one perceives them as timbre and not as overtones, and the perception of them as timbre is a conscious perception and not a subconscious one. In the same way, one's experience of a serial piece may be in some manner influenced by a transformational relationship of which one is not consciously aware; but in that case one is not perceiving it as a transformational relationship.[53] And as for Réti, I would argue that the unnoticeable influence of his motifs is in reality no influence at all.

The worst thing about this sort of obscurantist thinking is that it makes the listener's experience of music seem mysterious and problematical. But the experience of music is not, in itself, problematical at all; it is, in a sense, the one thing we can be sure of. The problems lie in correlating what we hear with what we think, know, or imagine.

---

[53] Dahlhaus writes: 'The opinion . . . that the structure of a work has to be apperceived consciously in order to be effective is a prejudice. . . . Logical elements can be apprehended half-consciously. . . . A hearer of dodecaphonic music feels the density of the nexus without conscious awareness of the system of tonal relations. Nobody is so dull as to misinterpret twelve-tone music, with all its external ruggedness, as an improvisation. The impression of strictness and logic prevails, even if one does not know the premises.' (1983: 55; cf. Schoenberg's remarks about motivic structure, as paraphrased in Newlin 1980: 229.) There is some truth in what Dahlhaus says, at least in the case of Schoenbergian serialism; but the impression of logic is just an impression of logic, not a subconscious perception of logical structure. It is, in other words, not a matter of structure but of style. And, after all, some serial music (I am thinking of the total serialism of the 1950s) sounds very much as if it were being improvised.

III

A good deal of influential theoretical and compositional thinking during the past twenty years has turned on the distinction Schoenberg made between musical structure and acoustic realization. Indeed, the distinction has become more rigorous. As I mentioned in Chapter 3,[54] Schoenberg himself seems to have vacillated as to how far the musical idea which the work was meant to communicate could be framed in notes. But for the theorists who worked in the shadow of Nelson Goodman and his *Languages of Art*, such as Benjamin Boretz,[55] there could be no doubt about this: the score defines the musical work, and therefore what happens in performance is simply that the formal structures embodied in the score are communicated to the listener by means of their acoustic realization. That is to say, the sounds are logically quite distinct from the music: Boretz writes—and he is doing little more than repeat what Schoenberg told Dika Newlin—that 'we need not *ever* construct sounds to construct music, regardless of their indispensability in its transmission, for once we have extracted their full burden of significant relational information . . . we have no further *musical* use to put them to.' (1970: 63.) Viewed in this light, musical analysis becomes a matter of discovering or demonstrating the formal integration that exists among the structural elements of the work as they are presented in the score; and composition becomes a matter of designing integrated formal structures, for instance through the application of set theory, which are subsequently realized in sound.[56] Now as I suggested in the case of Schoenberg, such an approach (or for that matter any other approach) is perfectly valid if regarded as a compositional heuristic, that is to say as a mechanism for creating new and possibly interesting sound-combinations to be validated empirically through listening; it is just this that is implied by Milton Babbitt's statement that 'every musical composition justifiably may be regarded as an experiment' (1972: 148), and there is no doubt that this was, in its time, a liberating attitude from the composer's point of view. But I would argue that such an approach is not valid if

---

[54] See ch. 3, n. 68 above.

[55] See in particular Boretz 1972. Goodman's identification of the work with the score has been widely criticized; see e.g. Kivy 1984: ch. 6.

[56] This is what Seeger called 'musicological composition' (see p. 197 above).

it is regarded as a means of making generally valid predictions about the manner in which music is experienced by the listener, or—what is worse—if it is applied as a criterion of aesthetic value.

The degree to which a work can be shown to possess structural integration is, in fact, widely assumed to be an index of the work's value.[57] Boretz sees such integration primarily in terms of hierarchical organization, and implies that composers such as Schoenberg abandoned free atonality in favour of serialism because of the lack of hierarchical depth that free atonal works evidence when they are analysed (1973: 177–8); he asks what possible reason we could have for caring for a piece of music if it could not be shown to be in some way structurally integrated (p. 189). Again, Allen Forte and Steven Gilbert outline the kind of structural features that can be found in variations when they are analysed by Schenkerian methods, and then comment, 'the extent to which these things may or may not be present is, of course, an index of the quality of the composition' (1982: 326). The 'of course' takes it for granted that aesthetic value can be determined by theoretical means. Hans Keller also spells out this assumption when he says, referring to his own analytical methods (which, incidentally, have little in common with either Schenker's or Boretz's), that 'the looser the manifest integration, the stricter the demonstrable latent unification. I use this criterion as one of my critical tools for objective evaluation.' (1965: 97.)

Now Boretz, Forte and Gilbert, and Keller could, if they wished, maintain that the aesthetic value of a piece of music is simply a function of the score's formal structure. It would follow from this that aesthetic value has nothing to do with the listener in any direct sense; his job is simply to cope with what he hears as best he can. This position, which in some ways resembles the nineteenth-century concept of art-religion which I mentioned in Chapter 3, is a perfectly logical one, for it involves no internal contradiction. But it is not a very helpful or interesting position, because it merely prescribes an artificial definition of aesthetic value. And that is not the same as explaining why, in real life, people value Beethoven more highly than Dittersdorf, or find the 'Eroica' Symphony more satisfying than the 'Battle Symphony'.

---

[57] For explicitly psychological formulations of this see Swain 1986, particularly his comparison of the finale of Schubert's 6th Symphony with the 2nd movement of Beethoven's Quartet Op. 59 No. 1 (pp. 137–44), and Lerdahl 1988: 255–6.

Boretz and the rest, however, make it clear that they do in fact want to explain such things; they are not simply telling people what works they should value—on the grounds that the theory says so—but offering explanations as to why the master-works are in fact valued as such. This means that their theories are not simply concerned with the formal patterns created by the notes in musical scores. They are also, however indirectly, concerned with people's psychological responses to what they hear. In other words, they imply some kind of significant correlation between the formal structures of the score and the listener's experience of the music. What, then, is the nature of this correlation?

As Boretz sees it (1970: 60), the basic units of musical structure are the 'qualia' of pitch and temporal ordering. These qualia represent the smallest values or increments that possess structural significance within a given musical system—for instance, in terms of twelve-tone serialism, the smallest significant increment of pitch is the tempered semitone. Now these values or increments must obviously be perceptible if the larger structures of the music are to be successfully communicated to the listener; it would not do to have a serial system in which pitches a hundredth of a semitone apart represented distinct classes of structural significance, just as it would not do if all the pitches in the music were so high that only bats could hear them. But within these general psychoacoustical constraints (Babbitt 1972: 178–9), the assumption seems to be that if the qualia of significant structure are perceptible in themselves, then any larger structure formed through combining them ought to be perceptible too. Admittedly, Boretz is at pains to emphasize (at least in his later writings) that the results of his deductive theories need to be validated perceptually (e.g. 1977a: 242). Babbitt, however, seems to have no such qualms. He writes, for instance, that the transforms of a series S 'require for the perception of their relation to S merely the ability to identify interval classes' (1962: 120), and there is a simple logic underlying this statement: serial structures—indeed any musical structures— are constructed out of intervals, and hence can be perceived by anyone who can recognize these intervals. Such an approach reduces the whole issue of musical perception to the level of ear-training drill.

But this is, of course, a wholly illegitimate generalization, from the kind of identification of individually presented intervals that goes on in the aural-training class or the psychological laboratory to the entirely different perceptual context that is constituted by a piece of music. So it is not surprising that the facts do not confirm Babbitt's prediction. As I have already mentioned,[58] experiments show that in practice people find it hard or impossible to perceive the kind of relationships he describes. And what little empirical evidence is available would suggest that the same applies to other predictions that have been made, on the basis of formal theories of musical structure, about the manner in which music is experienced. For instance, working on the basis of Allen Forte's very influential application of set theory to music (1973), Robert Morris has developed a computational 'rationale for the selection of sets that insure predictable degrees of aural similitude' (Morris 1980: 446), and this has been tested empirically by Cheryl Bruner. Her conclusion is that Morris's system does not succeed in its aim, because 'the perception of similarity among contemporary pitch structures seems to be tied to the context in which the structures are presented.' (1984: 38.) Or to put it another way, formal classifications of pitch–class content do not suffice to specify the context within which musical sounds are heard as similar or dissimilar, coherent or incoherent.

I have described the kind of formalism represented by Babbitt's remark about serial transformations as being based on an illegitimate generalization from the way in which pitches or intervals are perceived individually to the manner in which they are perceived in a musical context. For a strict formalist, a musical context is constituted by a specific combination of pitches or intervals; formal theories of analysis and composition are precisely about the ways in which pitches or intervals may be combined to create musical structures. But the whole notion of combining pitches or intervals is actually somewhat problematic. If the manner in which a pitch or an interval is perceived depends on the context—so that a given pitch may be heard in one context as a B and in another as a C, or a given interval heard in one context as a major third, and in another as a fourth[59]—then combining pitches or intervals is not in fact a simple matter of combination at all, because it changes the context and so modifies the things that are

---

[58] See n. 15 above.
[59] See above, p. 217.

being combined. And more generally, if the result of combining pitches or intervals in complex formations, such as the massive chords of Ligeti's *Atmosphères*, is that nobody hears the individual pitches or intervals, then the act of combination has actually eliminated what was combined: for a pitch or an interval (as opposed to a frequency or a relationship of frequencies) can only exist to the extent that someone perceives it as such.

The solution to this apparent conundrum is that when we speak of combinations of pitches or intervals, we are not speaking directly of any psychoacoustical reality. What we are doing is drawing a comparison between the psychoacoustical reality of musical perception within a given context and the judgements of pitch or interval that would be made were the music's constituent sounds to be heard individually; that is to say, we are modelling the experience of music in terms of the musicological categories embodied in ear training. In short, to borrow Scruton's words, we are making use of 'a complex system of metaphor, which is the true description of no material fact'.[60] And the same argument that applies to the basic elements of musical structure, as it is conceived in theoretical terms—that is, to pitches and intervals—also applies at the larger level of motifs, phrases, and periods. Combining these things is not a simple arithmetic process, for like pitches and intervals they are modified (or at least their significance is) when they are combined with one another, or with other elements of musical structure; as Keller puts it, 'a motif or phrase or period can only acquire and accumulate meaning in the course of a composition if it does not remain what it is; in order to evince musical logic it must develop into something else and yet remain itself' (ed. 1987: 116). Indeed, Keller regarded this as the essential difference between conceptual and musical logic. But in the absence of any clearly demonstrable or generally accepted axioms of musical logic (or for that matter of any compelling reason to believe that such axioms might exist), it is perhaps best to regard the notion of musical 'logic' as itself a metaphorical construction, that is, one that is based on an analogy between formal reasoning and musical structure.

A formal model of music, it seems to me, should be valued in the same way as any other metaphorical construction: for its

[60] See above, p. 24. For a related argument see Boretz 1977*b*: 107–8.

usefulness, for its heuristic value, and perhaps for the intellectual satisfaction that it affords, but not for its truth.[61] To clarify this, we can consider the nature of the basic intervallic categories on which formal theories of music are based. To model musical structures in terms of intervals or interval-classes involves regarding each interval or interval-class—the semitone, for instance, or the whole tone—as a category of structural significance in music. That is, any elaboration of such a model must be predicated on the assumption that the intervals between the third and the fourth of the major scale, or the leading-note and the tonic, or the fifth and the flattened sixth, are in some sense equivalent. Now this is a very useful assumption in certain ways: beginners grasp the different scales in terms of their patterns of semitones and whole tones, harmony students grasp complex chromatic harmonies in terms of their particular intervallic formations, and pianists memorizing a new piece probably make use of representations formulated in these terms too. But these are no more than representations of a reality that is itself more complex. Experiments have repeatedly shown that musicians such as singers and violinists, who are not tied down to a fixed set of intervals (as keyboard players are) consistently vary the size of their intervals; indeed, most singers and violinists are perfectly aware that they do this. However, there is no generally accepted rationale for how it should be done; people make these adjustments 'by ear'. Empirical studies have not, as yet, revealed the basis of the practice. But they have demonstrated that no explanation in terms of a fixed intervallic scale will match the facts; violinists do not play in just intonation, or mean-tone intonation, or Pythagorean intonation, any more than they play in equal temperament. In other words, they determine their intonation in accordance with the individual musical context.[62]

---

[61] For a further discussion of this point, with references, see Lewis 1987: 28.

[62] See Boomsliter and Creel 1963. Certain methodological limitations of their experiments—in particular the visual feedback provided by the 'Search Organ'—mean that their particular contextual explanation of preferred intonation has to be regarded as purely provisional; but their results do clearly indicate that musicians do not adopt fixed intonations, and this is in any case confirmed by other studies (for a survey with references see Ward 1970: 414–22). I wonder if the whole concept of intonation may not in fact be too restrictive to provide an adequate account of what happens in performance; in a psychological sense, elements like vibrato, glissandos, and portamenti could conceivably play as structural a role as discrete pitches and intervals.

What this means is that the semitone, as such, has no objective reality in what singers and violinists actually do. When we talk about semitones we are dealing in approximations. We are lumping together, for convenience, the large or perhaps indefinite number of specific intervallic values that musicians actually adopt in specific musical contexts. In other words, the semitone, like the other intervals or interval-classes on which formalized music theory is based, is a representation of a phenomenon, and not the phenomenon itself. V. V. Sadagopan is making the same point when he describes the *śruti* of North Indian music as 'a pointer and not a measure':[63] it provides a guide to the performer but it does not tell him exactly what is required. So it is a feature of both Indian and Western music that the precise intervallic values required in performance are not given in theory; they have to be determined by the performer in the light of the particular musical context. But this does not mean that such values are of no aesthetic importance. Quite the contrary: audiences and critics alike ascribe a special significance to them, and this is very probably just because they are not rationalized, so that through his intonation a violinist directly demonstrates his sensitivity (or lack of it) to the demands of the musical context. He reveals his capacity for intuitive judgement. And the same applies to such other aspects of music as rubato, dynamics, and articulation, none of which are rationalized to any high degree within the culture of Western art music.

There is a general issue of some importance here. Music theorists, analysts, and historians have a tendency to assume that

---

[63] Ed. 1983: 85. Sadagopan's distinction between 'pointer' and 'measure' can be brought to bear upon the hoary issue of low-integer-ratio (LIR) intervals. It seems clear that 'the ear is good at making octave judgements' (Dowling 1982*b*: 23), and the almost universal use of octaves, together with fifths and other LIR or near-LIR intervals, suggests that the perception of such intervals is in some way privileged, maybe for reasons connected with the physiology of the ear (for a general discussion with references see Burns and Ward 1982: 255–6). But this does not necessarily mean that there is anything special about LIR intervals in a specifically musical sense; it might just be that musical styles tend to favour the use of intervals that cluster round LIR values because the latter provide convenient 'pointers' to the precise intervals demanded by the context, and in this case there would be no special reason to assume that these precise intervals have anything to do with integer ratios. There is a parallel with the building industry: when metrication was introduced in the UK, architects tended to adopt metric modules in their designs where they had previously used imperial ones. In other words, the dimensions of buildings began to cluster round integer metric values, whereas before they clustered round integer imperial values. But obviously this was just a matter of convenience; neither metres nor feet and inches are privileged in any functional sense.

only those aspects of music that a given culture rationalizes are of aesthetic significance. Now all musical cultures rationalize certain aspects of their musical production, while leaving others open to determination by ear in the light of the specific musical context. The pattern of rationalization varies between different cultures: for instance, whereas in Western classical music note-to-note structure is highly rationalized but the precise values of intervals are not, in Iranian classical music it is just the other way round. The primary formal unit of Iranian classical music is the *dastgāh* (Nettl 1983: 109–10), which resembles the *raga* of North Indian music in that it rationalizes intervallic values to a rather high degree and in a relatively context-sensitive manner, while leaving note-to-note structure effectively up to the discretion of the performer (that is why one speaks of Indian and Iranian music being improvisatory). But the fact that the note-to-note structure is not rationalized surely does not mean that nobody cares what the performer does provided he plays in tune; it simply means that the Iranians are not accustomed to thinking about note-to-note structure in terms of detailed intersubjective representations. Christopher Marshall (1982: 170) makes this distinction rather clearly in his account of the Debarčani, a Yugoslav peasant community whose language has a highly developed terminology for timbre and tempo but altogether lacks other concepts that we would consider to be of equal or greater musical importance:

I found no indication that the Debarčani are aware of scale, ambitus, or interval width as aspects of form in their music, for example. This does not mean that such parameters do not exist in the objective sound of the music, or that the Debarčani could not make distinctions within these parameters if taught to do so by an outsider; it means merely that their normal course of thought does not lead them to consider these things.

I would argue that the failure to distinguish between what a given culture rationalizes and what is of musical significance in its productions necessarily leads to a fundamental misunderstanding as to the nature of the musical enterprise. As good an example of this as any is an interpretation of Machaut's music, and of medieval polyphony in general, that has gained some currency in recent years. There was in the fourteenth century no rationalized conception of the harmonic aggregates created by the several voices of a polyphonic composition, or at any rate of the manner in

which the harmonies should be linked together to form progressions. Because of this, some modern commentators have assumed
that the harmonic formations that result from such polyphony
must have been fortuitous, and it has even been suggested that in
order to hear Machaut's music in a truly authentic manner one
ought to perceive each part independently in its relationship to the
cantus firmus, rather than hearing them all together.[64] It is hard to
imagine quite how this could be done; but in any case, as Daniel
Leech-Wilkinson (1984: 10) contemptuously remarks,

Is it conceivable that a composer of the calibre of Machaut was unable to
imagine a piece of music; that, rather, he had to assemble it a line at a time
according to a set of rules (which, incidentally, he honoured more in the
breach than the observance) in the hope that the result would sound
acceptable? And must we therefore assume, as has been usual, that he and
his contemporaries somehow managed to perceive polyphony principally in a single horizontal dimension, remaining largely insensitive to
vertical coincidences? So simplistic a view of medieval polyphony could
never adequately explain the complexity of much of the surviving music.

Leech-Wilkinson's critique equally applies, *mutatis mutandis*, to the
attacks that are sometimes levelled against serial music on the
grounds that, as Richard Kell writes (1985: 303), 'Each voice is
strictly regulated, but, though care may be taken over contrapuntal interweaving . . . the harmonies made by the counterpointing
are fortuitous.' Are we to believe that, after inventing serialism, the
author of the massive and punctilious *Theory of Harmony* ceased to
care about the harmonic structure of his music and instead adopted
an attitude of Cage-like impassivity towards whatever harmonies
his system generated?[65] So facile an identification of the systematic
with the significant, and hence of the non-systematic with the
fortuitous, not only leads to a failure to appreciate the complexity
of Schoenberg's serial music, but also betrays a thoroughly
inadequate conception of the relationship between compositional
theory and practice.

[64] This notion, put forward by F. J. Bashour, is documented and criticized in
Leech-Wilkinson 1984: 25–6. For another critique of such thinking see Blackburn 1987, esp.
pp. 221–4.

[65] Adorno (trans. 1973: 83) traces this idea back to Ernst Kurth. Stravinsky said of his
own serial work, 'I can create my choice in serial composition just as I can in any tonal
contrapuntal form. I hear harmonically, of course, and I compose in the same way I always
have.' (Stravinsky and Craft 1979: 24–5.)

IV

It was Schoenberg's belief—a belief which he inherited from Hanslick—that, in music, practice precedes theory; or, as he put it, 'Schemes of musical arrangement, even if they exist a priori, should only be discovered after they have been used.'[66] By this he meant that composers work not only on the basis of formalized knowledge, but also through an intuitive awareness of relationships that have not as yet been embraced by theory. (Hanslick expressed the same idea by saying that the composer works 'through the unconscious application of pre-existent conceptions of quantity and proportion, through subtle processes of measuring and counting; but the laws by which the latter are governed were demonstrated only subsequently by science' (trans. 1957: 110).) For instance, Schoenberg argued, composers used dissonances before theoretical explanations of them were developed, just as he himself used harmonies built on fourths in some of his early works without having any rational understanding of the principles governing their use (trans. 1978: chapters 3, 21). He also believed that, by the time such things have been rationalized in theoretical terms, they lose their 'power to convey a thought worthy of expression. Therefore every composer is obliged to invent, to invent new things, to present new tone relations for discussion and to work out their consequences.' (ed. 1984: 269.)[67] In this way the irrational had, in Schoenberg's eyes, an essential role to play both in the compositional process and in the historical development of music: it was, in fact, the cutting edge of musical evolution.

Whatever one makes of Schoenberg's theory, it remains the case that each musical culture rationalizes only a few selected aspects of its musical production: considerations of cognitive economy dictate that it could not be otherwise. And what this means is that, if it is to achieve any measure of direct intersubjective intelligibility, any cultural representation of music must constitute a thoroughly incomplete specification of the intended musical experience. As I argued in Chapter 2, such representations only

[66] Quoted in Rufer 1969: 168. This trans. of the original German is by Humphrey Searle; in Leo Black's trans. it becomes 'Schemes of musical organization, too, should be invented only after one has used them, even if they were conveniently in existence before.' (Schoenberg ed. 1984: 267.)

[67] The historicism of Schoenberg's approach to musical style also has a source in Hanslick (trans. 1957: 64–5).

make sense when they are interpreted in the light of culture-specific knowledge and actualized as real or imagined sound. They are understood, that is to say, precisely to the extent that they are experienced as music; and this is just what the entire enterprise of formal music theory makes impossible. A formal analysis is a kind of mechanism whose input is the score, and whose output is a determination of coherence or an aesthetic judgement. In other words, it purports to establish or explain what is significant in music while circumventing the human experience through which such significance is constituted; to borrow a phrase from Coulter, it aims at 'deleting the subject'.[68] Indeed, according to Leonard B. Meyer (whose analytical theories can be described as a formalism expressed in psychological terms) it is even possible to operationalize the subject's emotional responses to music in terms of its formal structure, for, as he states,

Once the norms of a style have been ascertained, the study and analysis of the affective content of a particular work in that style can be made without continual and explicit reference to the responses of the listener or critic. That is, subjective content can be described objectively. (1956: 32.)

To the extent that it aims at an objective formulation and explanation of the experience of music, formal analysis functions in much the same manner as psychoanalysis. Both types of analysis are supported by a highly deterministic theory that explains the subject's experience in terms of what are assumed to be real causes—the patient's case history and mental mechanisms in the one case, and the structure of music as defined in terms of the score in the other. But in both cases it is possible to argue that these so-called causes are not in reality causes at all, because they have no existence outside the act of analysis; they are explanatory metaphors or fictions.[69] Now this is not to deny their validity: it is

[68] Coulter (1979: ch. 3) uses this phrase in the course of a critique of Chomsky's psychology of language—a critique which is equally applicable to certain trends in music theory.

[69] On the concept of causation in a Freudian context see Scruton 1979: 110–11, 139, 198; in Scruton's terms, a musical analysis does not uncover *causes* of the listener's experience but rather provides *reasons* for experiencing it in a given manner. It is perhaps worth mentioning a quite different type of explanatory fiction that was common in 19th-cent. musicology, and that is still to be encountered in Schoenberg's and Schenker's writings: this is the idealized history of music as it must have existed in primordial times, the purpose of which is almost invariably to clarify some aspect of contemporary music (see Allen 1962: 306).

to qualify it. MacIntyre (1958: 79) says that 'Freud's indispensable terms are "unconscious" and "repression" used descriptively; except in so far as illuminating description may count as a kind of explanation, their place as explanatory terms is highly dubious.' I would maintain that precisely the same applies to music: not only formalized theory, but also all other thinking or talking about music, consists of metaphors or fictions that become highly dubious or downright bogus if they are regarded as being explanatory in any scientific sense, but that are at the same time indispensable in their descriptive function. As Wittgenstein pointed out, the foundation of psychiatry as a discipline lies in Freud's terminology, because it established for the first time the possibility of describing abnormal behaviour in a manner that was both detailed and intersubjectively comprehensible: without this psychiatry would not exist as a profession, drawing upon a body of shared knowledge vastly in excess of anything a single practitioner could learn solely through his own experience. In the same way, musical culture depends for its very existence on the availability of intersubjective representations for music, because a musical culture, like any other, is in essence no more and no less than a body of knowledge shared between culture-members.

The psychoanalyst helps his patient come to terms with his predicament through rationalizing it in terms of his past experiences; the music analyst renders a new work intelligible by interpreting it in terms of familiar structural prototypes. In both cases understanding results, to use Pandora Hopkins's phrase,[70] from comparing the unfamiliar with the familiar. And to say this is to liken such descriptions, or explanations, to myths. For it is the function of a myth to render natural phenomena or psychological conditions negotiable, so to speak, through formulating them in terms of the experiences that are familiar to any member of the culture in which the myth originates; and this means that the content of a myth, like that of a ritual, can only be grasped when it is enacted by someone who has lived through those experiences and is accordingly possessed of the appropriate cultural knowledge. In other words, mythopoeic explanation takes place entirely within a culture: it explains things to culture-members in terms of culture-specific knowledge. It is by virtue of being in this sense

---

[70] See above, p. 140.

internal to a culture that mythopoeic explanation is the opposite of scientific explanation. For, whether or not it is achieved or even achievable, one of the defining aims of a scientific explanation is to achieve a generality and a validity that transcend the bounds of any given culture. And if I am correct in likening musical explanations to myths, then this is precisely what no explanation that is formulated in terms of the concepts of music theory can do: the theory of music is grounded in the experience of the individual, and for this reason objectivity is neither a feasible nor a desirable aim for accounts of music based on music-theoretical concepts.

I do not wish to argue that music cannot be a valid topic for scientific study. I am merely saying that, just as a musicological study of music should be musicological and therefore not scientific, so a scientific study of music should be scientific and therefore not musicological. This does not mean that scientists should ignore what musicians know about music; on the contrary, it is hard to imagine that any scientific study of musical productions could be viable which did not take into account the culture that gave rise to them, and this means taking into account just such knowledge. But, as Ian Cross says (1985: 3), the scientific study of music 'should not necessarily follow music theory. . . . Music theory, as a codificatory body of knowledge and pro-cedures, should form part of the object of the study.' In other words, it is up to the psychologist or the social scientist, and not the music theorist, to study music scientifically.

References

Abraham, Gerald (1939), *This Modern Stuff: an Introduction to Contemporary Music*. London.
—— (1974), *A Hundred Years of Music*. London.
Adorno, Theodor W. (trans. 1973), *Philosophy of Modern Music*. New York. [*Philosophie der neuen Musik*, Tübingen, 1949, trans. A. G. Mitchell and W. V. Bloomster.]
—— (trans. 1976), *Introduction to the Sociology of Music*. New York. [*Einleitung in die Musiksoziologie: Zwölf theoretische Vorlesungen*, Frankfurt, 1962, trans. E. B. Ashton.]
Allen, Warren Dwight (1962), *Philosophies of Music History: A Study of General Histories of Music 1600–1900*. New York.
Anderson, Emily (1961), trans. and ed., *The Letters of Beethoven*. London.
Arom, Simha (1976), 'The use of play-back techniques in the study of aural polyphonies'. *Ethnomusicology*, 20: 483–519.
Aschenbrenner, Karl (1981), 'Music criticism: practice and malpractice'. In Kingsley Price (ed.), *On Criticizing Music: Five Philosophical Perspectives*, Baltimore, 99–117.
Babbitt, Milton (1962), 'Twelve-tone invariants as compositional determinants'. In Paul Henry Lang (ed.), *Problems of Modern Music*, New York, 108–21. [Originally pub. in *Musical Quarterly*, 46 (1960): 246–59.]
—— (1972), 'Twelve-tone rhythmic structure and the electronic medium'. In Benjamin Boretz and Edward T. Cone (eds.), *Perspectives on Contemporary Music Theory*, New York, 148–79. [Originally pub. in *Perspectives of New Music*, 1/1 (1962): 49–79.]
Bach, Carl Philipp Emanuel (trans. 1949), *Essay on the True Art of Playing Keyboard Instruments*. New York. [*Versuch über die wahre Art das Clavier zu spielen*, Berlin, 1753, 1762, trans. and ed. W. J. Mitchell.]
Bailey, Kathryn (1983), 'Webern's Opus 21: creativity in tradition'. *Journal of Musicology*, 2: 184–95.
Baily, John (1985), 'Musical structure and human movement'. In Peter Howell, Ian Cross, and Robert West (eds.), *Musical Structure and Cognition*, London, 237–58.
Bamberger, Jeanne (1976), 'The musical significance of Beethoven's fingerings in the piano sonatas'. *The Music Forum*, 4: 237–80.
Bernard, Jonathan W. (1987), 'Inaudible structures, audible music: Ligeti's problem, and his solution'. *Music Analysis*, 6: 207–36.

Blackburn, Bonnie J. (1987), 'On compositional process in the fifteenth century'. *Journal of the American Musicological Society*, 40: 210–84.

Blacking, John (1973), *How Musical is Man?* Seattle.

—— (1987), '*A Commonsense View of All Music*': *Reflections on Percy Grainger's Contribution to Ethnomusicology and Music Education.* Cambridge.

Blechner, M. (1978), 'Musical skill and the categorical perception of harmonic mode'. *Dissertation Abstracts International*, 39: 1931-B.

Blom, Eric (ed. 1977), 'An essay on listening and performance'. In A. L. Bacharach and J. R. Pearce (eds.), *The Musical Companion*, London, 697–745.

Blume, Friedrich (1972), *Classic and Romantic Music: A Comprehensive Survey*, trans. M. D. Herter Norton. London.

Boomsliter, Paul, and Creel, Warren (1963), 'Extended reference: an unrecognized dynamic in melody'. *Journal of Music Theory*, 7: 2–22.

Boretz, Benjamin (1970), 'Sketch of a musical system (Meta-Variations, Part II)'. *Perspectives of New Music*, 8/2: 49–111.

—— (1972), 'Nelson Goodman's *Languages of Art* from a musical point of view'. In Benjamin Boretz and Edward T. Cone (eds.), *Perspectives on Contemporary Music Theory*, New York, 31–44. [Originally pub. in *Journal of Philosophy*, 67 (1970): 540–52.]

—— (1973), 'Meta-Variations, Part IV: analytical fallout (II)'. *Perspectives of New Music*, 11/2: 156–203.

—— (1977*a*), 'Two replies'. *Perspectives of New Music*, 15/2: 239–42.

—— (1977*b*), 'What lingers on (, when the song is ended)'. *Perspectives of New Music*, 16/1: 102–9.

Botstein, Leon (1987), 'Wagner and our century'. *19th-Century Music*, 11: 92–104 [review].

Boulez, Pierre (1971), *Boulez on Music Today*. London. [*Penser de la musique aujourd'hui*, Mainz, 1963, trans. S. Bradshaw and R. R. Bennett.]

Bradley, Ian L. (1972), 'Effect on student musical preference of a listening program in contemporary art music'. *Journal of Research in Music Education*, 20: 344–53.

Bruner, Cheryl L. (1984), 'The perception of contemporary pitch structures'. *Music Perception*, 2: 25–39.

Burkhart, Charles (1974), 'Schoenberg's *Farben*: an analysis of Op. 16, No. 3'. *Perspectives of New Music*, 12: 141–72.

Burns, Edward M., and Ward, W. Dixon (1982), 'Intervals, scales and tuning'. In Diana Deutsch (ed.), *The Psychology of Music*, New York, 241–69.

Cage, John (1966), *Silence*. Cambridge, Mass.

Carpenter, Patricia (1967), 'The musical object'. *Current Musicology*, 5: 56–87.

Clarke, Eric F. (1985), 'Structure and expression in rhythmic performance'. In Peter Howell, Ian Cross, and Robert West (eds.), *Musical Structure and Cognition*, London, 209–36.

Clayton, Anthony M. H. (1985), 'Co-ordination between Players in Musical Performance'. Ph.D. thesis, University of Edinburgh.

Clifton, Thomas (1970), 'An application of Goethe's concept of Steigerung to the morphology of diminution'. *Journal of Music Theory*, 14: 165–89.

—— (1976), 'Music as constituted object'. In F. Joseph Smith (ed.), *In Search of Musical Method*, London, 73–98.

—— (1983), *Music as Heard: a Study in Applied Phenomenology*. New Haven.

Collingwood, R. G. (1938), *The Principles of Art*. Oxford.

Cone, Edward T. (1962), 'Analysis today'. In Paul Henry Lang (ed.), *Problems of Modern Music*, New York, 34–50. [Originally pub. in *Musical Quarterly*, 46 (1960): 172–88.]

—— (1971), ed., *Hector Berlioz: Fantastic Symphony*. New York.

—— (1974), *The Composer's Voice*. Berkeley.

—— (1987), 'On derivation: syntax and rhetoric'. *Music Analysis*, 6: 237–55.

Cook, Nicholas (1987a), *A Guide to Musical Analysis*. London and New York.

—— (1987b), 'Diana Deutsch (ed.): *Music Perception*'. *Music Analysis*, 6: 169–79 [review].

—— (1987c), 'Structure and performance timing in Bach's C major Prelude (WTC 1): an empirical study'. *Music Analysis*, 6: 257–72.

—— (1987d), 'Musical form and the listener'. *Journal of Aesthetics and Art Criticism*, 46: 23–9.

—— (1987e), 'The perception of large-scale tonal closure'. *Music Perception*, 5: 197–205.

Cooper, Martin (1961), *French Music from the Death of Berlioz to the Death of Fauré*. London.

Cope, David (1987), 'An expert system for computer-assisted composition'. *Computer Music Journal*, 11/4: 30–46.

Copland, Aaron (1961), *Music and Imagination*. Cambridge, Mass.

Coulter, Jeff (1979), *The Social Construction of Mind: Studies in Ethnomethodology and Linguistic Philosophy*. London.

Creel, Warren, Boomsliter, Paul C., and Powers, Samuel R., Jr. (1970), 'Sensations of tone as perceptual forms'. *Psychological Review*, 77: 534–45.

Crickmore, Leon (1968a, b), 'An approach to the measurement of music appreciation'. *Journal of Research in Music Education*, 16: [a] 239–53, [b] 291–301.

Cross, Charlotte M. (1980), 'Three levels of "idea" in Schoenberg's thought and writings'. *Current Musicology*, 30: 24–36.

Cross, Ian (1985), 'Music and change: on the establishment of rules'. In Peter Howell, Ian Cross, and Robert West (eds.), *Musical Structure and Cognition*, London, 1–20.

Dahlhaus, Carl (1982), *Esthetics of Music*. Cambridge. [*Musikästhetik*, Cologne, 1967, trans. W. M. Austin.]

—— (1983), *Analysis and Value Judgment*. New York. [*Analyse und Werturteil*, Mainz, 1970, trans. S. Levarie.]

—— (1987), *Schoenberg and the New Music: Essays by Carl Dahlhaus*, trans. D. Puffett and A. Clayton. Cambridge.

Davies, John Booth (1978), *The Psychology of Music*. London.

Davies, Stephen (1983), 'Attributing significance to unobvious musical relationships'. *Journal of Music Theory*, 27: 203–13.

Deliège, Irène (1987), 'Grouping conditions in listening to music: an approach to Lerdahl and Jackendoff's grouping preference rules'. *Music Perception*, 4: 325–59.

Deutsch, Diana (1975), 'Two-channel listening to musical scales'. *Journal of the Acoustical Society of America*, 57: 1156–60.

—— (1982a), 'Grouping mechanisms in music'. In Diana Deutsch (ed.), *The Psychology of Music*, New York, 99–134.

—— (1982b), 'The processing of pitch combinations'. In Diana Deutsch (ed.), *The Psychology of Music*, New York, 271–316.

Dowling, W. Jay (1982a), 'Melodic information processing and its development'. In Diana Deutsch (ed.), *The Psychology of Music*, New York, 413–29.

—— (1982b), 'Musical scales and psychophysical scales: their psychological reality'. In Robert Falck and Timothy Rice, *Cross-Cultural Perspectives on Music*, Toronto, 20–8.

—— (1984), 'Development of musical schemata in children's spontaneous singing'. In W. R. Crozier and A. J. Chapman (eds.), *Cognitive Processes in the Perception of Art*, North-Holland, 145–63.

—— and Harwood, Dane L. (1986), *Music Cognition*. Orlando.

Dunsby, Jonathan, and Whittall, Arnold (1988), *Music Analysis in Theory and Practice*. London.

Durant, Alan (1984), *Conditions of Music*. London.

Edmonston, W. E., Jr. (1969), 'Familiarity and musical training in the esthetic evaluation of music'. *The Journal of Social Psychology*, 79: 109–11.

Ehrenzweig, Anton (1953), *The Psycho-analysis of Artistic Vision and Hearing: An Introduction to a Theory of Unconscious Perception*. London.

Esper, Erwin (1966), 'Max Meyer and the psychology of music'. *Journal of Music Theory*, 10: 182–99.

Evans, Martyn (1985), 'The Participant Listener'. Ph.D. thesis, University College, Cardiff.

Feld, Steven (1974), 'Linguistic models in ethnomusicology'. *Ethnomusicology*, 18: 197–217.

Fétis, Francis James [François Joseph] (1842), *Music Explained to the World*. Boston. [Trans. of *Musique mise à la portée de tout le monde*, Paris. 1830.]

Flowers, Patricia (1983), 'The effect of instruction in vocabulary and listening on nonmusicians' descriptions of changes in music'. *Journal of Research in Music Education*, 31: 179–89.

Forte, Allen (1973), *The Structure of Atonal Music*. New Haven.

—— and Gilbert, Steven E. (1982), *Introduction to Schenkerian Analysis*. New York.

Francès, Robert (1984), *La Perception de la musique*. Paris.

Franklin, Peter (1985), *The Idea of Music: Schoenberg and Others*. London.

Gabrielsson, Alf (1985), 'Interplay between analysis and synthesis in studies of music performance and music experience'. *Music Perception*, 3: 59–86.

Geringer, John M., and Nelson, Janice K. (1980), 'Effects of guided listening on music achievement and preference of fourth graders'. *Perceptual and Motor Skills*, 51: 1282.

Goehr, Alexander (1976), *Musical Ideas and Ideas about Music*. London.

Gombrich, Ernst H. (1969), *Art and Illusion: A Study in the Psychology of Pictorial Representation*. Princeton.

Gotlieb, Heidi, and Konečni, Vladimir J. (1985), 'The effects of instrumentation, playing style and structure in the Goldberg Variations by Johann Sebastian Bach'. *Music Perception*, 3: 87–101.

Gould, Glenn (ed. 1987), *The Glenn Gould Reader*, ed. T. Page. London.

Gould, Stephen Jay (1984), *The Mismeasure of Man*. Harmondsworth.

Gourlay, Kenneth A. (1984), 'The non-universality of music and the universality of non-music'. *The World of Music*, 26/2: 25–37.

Haack, Paul A. (1980), 'The behavior of music listeners'. In Donald A. Hodges (ed.), *Handbook of Music Psychology*, Lawrence, Kan., 141–82.

Halbwachs, Maurice (trans. 1980), *The Collective Memory*. New York. [*La mémoire collective*, Paris, 1950, trans. F. J. Ditter and V. Y. Ditter.]

Hampshire, Stuart (1969), *Modern Writers and Other Essays*. London.

Hanslick, Eduard (trans. 1957), *The Beautiful in Music*. Indianapolis. [*Vom musikalisch-Schönen*, Leipzig, 1854, trans. G. Cohen.]

—— (trans. 1963), *Music Criticisms 1846–99*, trans. and ed. H. Pleasants. Harmondsworth.

Hantz, Edwin Charlton (1982), 'Towards a Psychology of Tonal Music'. Ph.D. thesis, University of Michigan.

Hawkins, John (ed. 1875), *A General History of the Science and Practice of Music*. London. [Originally pub. London, 1776.]

Heartz, Daniel (1980), 'The Great Quartet in Mozart's Idomeneo'. *The Music Forum*, 5: 233–56.

Heingartner, A., and Hall, F. (1974), 'Affective consequences in adults and children of repeated exposure to auditory stimuli'. *Journal of Personality and Social Psychology*, 29: 719–23.

Herndon, Marcia (1974), 'Analysis: the herding of sacred cows?' *Ethnomusicology*, 18: 219–62.

—— and McLeod, Norma (1982), *Music as Culture*. Darby.

Herriot, Peter (1974), *Attributes of Memory*. London.

Hopkins, Pandora (1966), 'The purposes of transcription'. *Ethnomusicology*, 10: 310–17.

—— (1982), 'Aural thinking'. In Robert Falck and Timothy Rice (eds.), *Cross-cultural Perspectives on Music*, Toronto, 143–61.

Howe, Melissa Theresa (1984), 'Recognition of Structural Function in Tonal Music by Professional and Novice Musicians'. Ph.D. thesis, University of Boston.

Hyde, Martha M. (1983), 'The format and function of Schoenberg's twelve-tone sketches'. *Journal of the American Musicological Society*, 36: 453–80.

Ihde, Don (1976), *Listening and Voice: A Phenomenology of Sound*. Athens, Ohio.

Ingarden, Roman (1986), *The Work of Music and the Problem of its Identity*. Berkeley. [*Vtwór muzyczny i sprawa jego tożsamości*, Warsaw, 1966, trans. A. Czerniawski.]

Iser, Wolfgang (1978), *The Act of Reading: A Theory of Aesthetic Response*. Baltimore. [Trans. of *Der Akt des Lesens, Theorie Ästhetischer Wirkung*, Munich, 1976.]

Jarocinski, Stefan (1976), *Debussy: Impressionism and Symbolism*. London. [*Debussy, a impresionizm i synmbolizm*, n. p., 1966, trans. R. Myers.]

Jorgensen, Estelle R. (1987), 'Percy Scholes on music appreciation: another view'. *British Journal of Music Education*, 4: 139–56.

Kalib, Sylvan (1973), 'Thirteen Essays from the Three Yearbooks "Das Meisterwerk in der Musik" by Heinrich Schenker: An Annotated Translation'. Ph.D. thesis, Northwestern University.

Kaplan, Max (1966), *Foundations and Frontiers of Music Education*. New York.

Kell, Richard (1985), 'What Schönberg left out'. *Music Review*, 46: 302–5.

Keller, Hans (1953), 'First performances and their reviews'. *Music Review*, 14: 55–9.

—— (1955), 'The audibility of serial technique'. *Monthly Musical Record*, 85: 231–4.

—— (1965), 'The chamber music'. In H. C. Robbins Landon and Donald Mitchell (eds.), *The Mozart Companion*, London, 90–137.

—— (ed. 1987), *Criticism*, ed. J. Hogg. London.

Kerman, Joseph (1971), 'Beethoven's early sketches'. In Paul Henry Lang (ed.), *The Creative World of Beethoven*, New York, 13–36. [Originally pub. in *Musical Quarterly*, 56 (1970): 515–38.]

Kessler, Edward J., Hansen, Christa, and Shepard, Roger N. (1984), 'Tonal schemata and the perception of music in Bali and in the West'. *Music Perception*, 2: 131–65.

Kikkawa, Eishi (1987), 'The musical sense of the Japanese'. *Contemporary Music Review*, 1/2: 85–94.

Kirkpatrick, Ralph (1984), *Interpreting Bach's Well-Tempered Clavier: A Performer's Discourse of Method*. New Haven.

Kivy, Peter (1984), *Sound and Semblance: Reflections on Musical Representation*. Princeton.

Konečni, Vladimir J. (1984), 'Elusive effects of artists' "messages"'. In W. R. Crozier and A. J. Chapman (eds.), *Cognitive Processes in the Perception of Art*, North-Holland, 71–93.

Kramer, Richard (1980), 'On the autograph of Beethoven's Quartet in F major, Opus 59 No. 1'. In Christoph Wolff (ed.), *The String Quartets of Haydn, Mozart and Beethoven: Studies of the Autograph Manuscripts*, Cambridge, Mass., 223–65.

—— (1985), 'The new modulation of the 1770s: C. P. E. Bach in theory, criticism, and practice'. *Journal of the American Musicological Society*, 38: 551–92.

Krenek, Ernst (1962), 'Extents and limits of serial techniques'. In Paul Henry Lang (ed.), *Problems of Modern Music*, New York, 72–94. [Originally pub. in *Musical Quarterly*, 46 (1960): 210–32.]

Krumhansl, Carol L., Sandell, Gregory J., and Sergeant, Desmond C. (1987), 'The perception of tone hierarchies and mirror forms in twelve-tone serial music'. *Music Perception*, 5: 31–78.

Leech-Wilkinson, Daniel (1984), 'Machaut's *Rose, lis* and the problem of early music analysis'. *Music Analysis*, 3: 9–28.

Le Huray, Peter, and Day, James (1981), eds., *Music and Aesthetics in the Eighteenth and Early-Nineteenth Centuries*. Cambridge.

Lerdahl, Fred (1988), 'Cognitive constraints on compositional systems'. In John Sloboda (ed.), *Generative Processes in Music: The Psychology of Performance, Improvisation, and Composition*, Oxford, 231–59.

—— and Jackendoff, Ray (1983), *A Generative Theory of Tonal Music*. Cambridge, Mass.

Lester, Joel (1970), 'Revisions in the autograph of the Missa Solemnis Kyrie'. *Journal of the American Musicological Society*, 23: 420–38.

Levy, Janet M. (1982), 'Texture as a sign in classic and early romantic music'. *Journal of the American Musicological Society*, 35: 482–531.

Lewis, Christopher (1987), 'Mirrors and metaphors: reflections on

Schoenberg and nineteenth-century tonality'. *19th Century Music*, 11: 26–42.

Liang, Mingyue (1985), *Music of the Billion: An Introduction to Chinese Musical Culture*. New York.

Lidholm, Ingvar (1968), ' "Poesis" for orchestra'. In I. Lidholm and B. Wallner (eds.), *Three Aspects of New Music*, Stockholm, 55–80.

Ligeti, György (1965), 'Metamorphoses of musical form'. *Die Reihe* (Eng. version), 7: 5–19. [Originally pub. as 'Wandlungen in der musikalischen Form', *Die Reihe*, 7 (1965); trans. C. Cardew.]

Lippman, Edward A. (1986), *Musical Aesthetics: A Historical Reader, from Antiquity to the Eighteenth Century*. New York.

Loane, Brian (1984), 'Thinking about children's compositions'. *British Journal of Music Education*, 1: 205–31.

Lobe, J. C. (trans. 1897), *Traité pratique de composition musicale*. Leipzig. [Trans. of *Lehrbuch der musikalischen Komposition*, i, Leipzig, 1850.]

Lockwood, Lewis (1970a), 'On Beethoven's sketches and autographs: some problems of definition and interpretation'. *Acta Musicologica*, 42: 32–47.

—— (1970b), 'The autograph of the first movement of Beethoven's Sonata for Violoncello and Pianoforte, Opus 69'. *The Music Forum*, 2: 1–109.

—— (1971), 'Beethoven's unfinished piano concerto of 1815: sources and problems'. In Paul Henry Lang (ed.), *The Creative World of Beethoven*, New York, 122–44.

—— (1973), 'Beethoven's sketches for "Sehnsucht" (WoO 146)'. *Beethoven Studies*, 1: 97–122.

—— (1982), ' "Eroica" perspectives: strategy and design in the first movement'. *Beethoven Studies*, 3: 85–105.

McAdams, Stephen (1984), 'The auditory image: a metaphor for musical and psychological research on auditory organization'. In W. R. Crozier and A. J. Chapman (eds.), *Cognitive Processes in the Perception of Art*, North-Holland, 289–323.

MacIntyre, Alasdair C. (1958), *The Unconscious: A Conceptual Analysis*. London.

McMullen, Patrick T. (1980), 'Music as a perceived stimulus object and affective responses: an alternative theoretical framework'. In Donald A. Hodges (ed.), *Handbook of Music Perception*, Lawrence, Kan., 183–93.

Maconie, Robin (1976), *The Works of Karlheinz Stockhausen*. London.

Marshall, Christopher (1982), 'Towards a comparative aesthetics of music'. In Robert Falck and Timothy Rice (eds.), *Cross-Cultural Perspectives on Music*, Toronto, 162–73.

Marx, Leo (1967), *The Machine in the Garden: Technology and the Pastoral Ideal in America.* New York.

Meibach, Judith (1984), 'The Society for Musical Private Performances: antecedents and foundation'. *Journal of the Arnold Schoenberg Institute,* 8: 159–76.

Merleau-Ponty, Maurice (trans. 1964), *Signs.* Evanston, Ill. [*Signes,* Paris, 1960, trans. R. C. McCleary.]

Meyer, John A. (1982), 'The Concerto'. In Gerald Abraham (ed.), *The Age of Beethoven 1790–1830* (New Oxford History of Music, viii), London, 206–54.

Meyer, Leonard B. (1956), *Emotion and Meaning in Music.* Chicago.

—— (1967), *Music, the Arts, and Ideas: Patterns and Predictions in Twentieth-Century Culture.* Chicago.

—— (1973), *Explaining Music: Essays and Explorations.* Chicago.

Millar, Jana K. (1984), 'The Aural Perception of Pitch-Class Set Relations: A Computer-Assisted Investigation'. Ph.D. thesis, North Texas State University.

Miller, George A. (1956), 'The magic number seven, plus or minus two: some limitations on our capacity for processing information'. *Psychological Review,* 63: 81–97.

Mitchell, Donald (1966), *The Language of Modern Music.* London.

Morris, Robert (1980), 'A similarity index for pitch-class sets'. *Perspectives of New Music,* 18: 445–60.

Mursell, James L. (1937), *The Psychology of Music.* New York.

Nettl, Bruno (1983), *The Study of Ethnomusicology: Twenty-nine Issues and Concepts.* Urbana.

Newlin, Dika (1980), *Schoenberg Remembered: Diaries and Recollections (1938–76).* New York.

Norton, Bruce (1975), 'Victor Zuckerkandl: "Man the Musician" '. *Journal of Aesthetics and Art Criticism,* 33: 354–6 [review].

Nottebohm, Gustav (trans. 1979), *Two Beethoven Sketchbooks: A Description with Musical Extracts.* London. [*Ein Skizzenbuch von Beethoven aus dem Jahre 1803,* Leipzig, 1880, and *Ein Skizzenbuch von Beethoven,* Leipzig, 1865, trans. J. Katz.]

Nyman, Michael (1976), 'Hearing/Seeing'. *Studio International,* 192: 233–43.

Parakilas, James (1984), 'Classical music as popular music'. *Journal of Musicology,* 3: 1–18.

Parrish, Carl (1959), *The Notation of Medieval Music.* New York.

Pedersen, Paul (1975), 'The perception of octave equivalence in twelve-tone rows'. *Psychology of Music,* 3/2: 3–8.

Perle, George (1981), *Serial Composition and Atonality: an Introduction to the Music of Schoenberg, Berg and Webern.* Berkeley.

Petzold, Robert G. (1969), 'Auditory perception by children'. *Journal of Research in Music Education*, 17: 82–7.

Picken, Laurence (1969), 'Tunes apt for T'ang lyrics from the *Shō* part-books of Tōgaku'. In *Essays in Ethnomusicology: A Birthday Offering for Lee Hye-ku*, Seoul, 401–20.

Pike, Alfred (1963), 'Perception and meaning in serial music'. *Journal of Aesthetics and Art Criticism*, 22: 55–61.

Pleasants, Henry (1965), trans. and ed., *The Musical World of Robert Schumann: A Selection from his Own Writings*. London.

Pollard-Gott, Lucy (1983), 'Emergence of thematic concepts in repeated listening to music'. *Cognitive Psychology*, 15: 66–94.

Pousseur, Henri (1972), 'The question of order in new music'. In Benjamin Boretz and Edward T. Cone (eds.), *Perspectives on Contemporary Music Theory*, New York, 97–115. [Originally pub. as 'La question d'ordre dans la musique nouvelle', *Revue belge de musicologie*, 20 (1966): 136–52; trans. D. Behrman in *Perspectives of New Music*, 5/1 (1966): 93–111.]

Prince, Warren F. (1974), 'Effects of guided listening on musical enjoyment of junior high school students'. *Journal of Research in Music Education*, 22: 45–51.

Radocy, Rudolf E., and Boyle, J. David (1979), *Psychological Foundations of Musical Behavior*. Springfield.

Randall, J. K. (1972), 'Two lectures to scientists'. In Benjamin Boretz and Edward T. Cone (eds.), *Perspectives on Contemporary Music Theory*, New York, 116–26. [Orignally pub. in *Perspectives of New Music*, 5/2 (1967): 124–34.]

Réti, Rudolph (1951), *The Thematic Process in Music*. New York.

—— (ed. 1965), *Thematic Patterns in Sonatas of Beethoven*, ed. D. Cooke. London.

Roberts, Linda A., and Shaw, Marilyn L. (1984), 'Perceived structure of musical triads'. *Music Perception*, 2: 95–124.

Rosen, Charles (1976a), *The Classical Style: Haydn, Mozart, Beethoven*. London.

—— (1976b), *Schoenberg*. London.

—— (1980), *Sonata Forms*. New York.

Rosner, Burton S., and Meyer, Leonard B. (1986), 'The perceptual roles of melodic process, contour and form'. *Music Perception*, 4: 1–39.

Rothstein, William (1984), 'Heinrich Schenker as an interpreter of Beethoven's piano sonatas'. *19th Century Music*, 8: 3–28.

Rufer, Josef (1969), *Composition with Twelve Notes Related only to One Another*. London. [*Die Komposition mit zwölf Tönen*, Berlin, 1952, trans. H. Searle.]

Rushton, Julian (1983), *The Musical Language of Berlioz*. Cambridge.

Ryle, Gilbert (1973), *The Concept of Mind*. Harmondsworth.

Sadagopan, V. V. (ed. 1983), *Spirals and Circles: An Organismic Approach to Music and Music Education*, ed. S. Bharatl. Melkote.

Samson, Jim (1977), *Music in Transition: A Study of Tonal Expansion and Atonality, 1900–1920*. London.

Sartre, Jean-Paul (1972), *The Psychology of the Imagination*. London. [Trans. of *L'imaginaire*, Paris, 1940.]

Schenker, Heinrich (ed. 1972), *Beethoven: die letzten Sonaten. Sonate As dur Op. 110*, rev. Oswald Jonas. Vienna.

—— (trans. 1979), *Free Composition*. New York. [*Der freie Satz*, Vienna, 1935, trans. E. Oster.]

—— (trans. 1987), *Counterpoint*. New York. [*Kontrapunkt*, Vienna, 1910–22, trans. J. Rothgeb and J. Thym.]

—— (trans. 1988), 'Three essays from the *Neue Revue* (1894–7)', trans. J. Dunsby *et al.*, *Music Analysis*, 7: 133–41.

Schoenberg, Arnold (ed. 1969), *Structural Functions of Harmony*. London. [2nd edn., rev. L. Stein.]

—— (trans. 1978), *Theory of Harmony*. London. [*Harmonielehre*, Vienna, 1911, trans. R. E. Carter.]

—— (ed. 1984), *Style and Idea: Selected Writings of Arnold Schoenberg*, ed. L. Stein, with trans. by L. Black. Berkeley.

Schulz, J. R. (1825), trans., 'An unpublished letter of Mozart'. *Harmonicon*, 3: 198–200.

Schumann, Robert (trans. 1971), 'A symphony by Berlioz'. In Edward T. Cone (ed.), *Hector Berlioz: Fantastic Symphony*, New York, 220–48.

Schutz, Alfred (ed. 1964), 'Making music together: a study in social relationship'. In A. Brodersen (ed.), *Alfred Schutz: Collected Papers II. Studies in Social Theory*, The Hague, 159–78. [Originally pub. in *Social Research*, 18 (1951): 76–97.]

—— (ed. 1976), 'Fragments on the phenomenology of music', ed. F. Kersten. In F. Joseph Smith (ed.), *In Search of Musical Method*. London, 5–71.

Scruton, Roger (1979), *The Aesthetics of Architecture*. London.

—— (1983), 'Understanding music'. *Ratio*, 25: 97–120.

Seashore, Carl E., and Metfessel, Milton (1925), 'Deviation from the regular as an art principle'. *Proceedings of the National Academy of Sciences*, 11: 538–42.

Seeger, Charles (1977), *Studies in Musicology 1935–75*. Berkeley.

Serafine, Mary Louise (1988), *Music as Cognition: The Development of Thought in Sound*. New York.

Shaffer, L. Henry (1981), 'Performance of Chopin, Bach and Bartok: studies in motor programming'. *Cognitive Psychology*, 13: 326–76.

Shaw, George Bernard (1899), *The Perfect Wagnerite: A Commentary on the Ring of the Niblungs*. Chicago.

Shepard, Roger N. (1982), 'Structural representations of musical pitch'. In Diana Deutsch (ed.), *The Psychology of Music*, 343–90.

Shono, Susumu (1987), 'The role of listening in *gagaku*'. *Contemporary Music Review*, 1/2: 19–43.

Slatin, Sonia (1967), 'The Theories of Heinrich Schenker in Perspective'. Ph.D. thesis, Columbia University.

Sloboda, John A. (1982), 'Music performance'. In Diana Deutsch (ed.), *The Psychology of Music*, New York, 479–96.

—— (1983), 'The communication of musical metre in piano performance'. *Quarterly Journal of Experimental Psychology*, 35-A: 377–96.

—— (1984), 'Experimental studies of music reading: a review'. *Music Perception*, 2: 222–36.

—— (1985), *The Musical Mind: the Cognitive Psychology of Music*. Oxford.

—— and Gregory, A. H. (1980), 'The psychological reality of musical segments'. *Canadian Journal of Psychology*, 34: 274–80.

—— and Parker, David H. H. (1985), 'Immediate recall of melodies'. In Peter Howell, Ian Cross, and Robert West (eds.), *Musical Structure and Cognition*, London, 143–67.

Slonimsky, Nicolas (1965), *Lexicon of Musical Invective*. New York.

Smith, Alan (1973), 'Feasibility of tracking musical form as a cognitive listening objective'. *Journal of Research in Music Education*, 21: 200–13.

Smith, J. David (1987), 'Conflicting aesthetic ideals in a musical culture'. *Music Perception*, 4: 373–91.

Smith, Joan Allen (1986), *Schoenberg and his Circle: A Viennese Portrait*. New York.

Solie, Ruth (1980), 'The living work: organicism and musical analysis'. *19th Century Music*, 4: 147–56.

Solomon, Maynard (1981), 'On Beethoven's creative process: a two-part invention'. *Music & Letters*, 61: 272–83.

Stoffer, Thomas H. (1985), 'Representation of phrase structure in the perception of music'. *Music Perception*, 3: 191–220.

Stravinsky, Igor (1947), *Poetics of Music in the Form of Six Lessons*. New York. [*Poétique musicale*, Cambridge, Mass., 1942, trans. A. Knodel and I. Dahl.]

—— and Craft, Robert (1979), *Conversations with Igor Stravinsky*. London.

—— —— (1981), *Expositions and Developments*. London.

Subotnik, Rose Rosengard (1981), 'Romantic music as post-Kantian critique: classicism, romanticism and the conception of the semiotic universe'. In Kingsley Price (ed.), *On Criticizing Music: Five Philosophical Perspectives*, Baltimore, 74–98.

Sudnow, David (1978), *Ways of the Hand: The Organization of Improvised Conduct.* London.

Swain, Joseph P. (1986), 'The need for limits in hierarchical theories of music'. *Music Perception*, 4: 121–47.

Thayer, Alexander Wheelock (ed. 1921), *The Life of Ludwig van Beethoven*, ed. H. E. Krehbiel. New York.

Thomson, Virgil (1939), *The State of Music.* New York.

Toop, Richard (1984), 'Stockhausen's "Klavierstück VIII" '. *Contact*, 28: 4–19.

Treitler, Leo (1967), 'On Patricia Carpenter's "The musical object" ', *Current Musicology*, 5: 87–93.

—— (1980), 'History, criticism and Beethoven's Ninth Symphony'. *19th Century Music*, 3: 193–210.

—— (1982a), 'The early history of music writing in the West'. *Journal of the American Musicological Society*, 35: 237–79.

—— (1982b), ' "To worship that celestial sound": motives for analysis'. *Journal of Musicology*, 1: 153–70.

Tyson, Alan (1971), 'Stages in the composition of Beethoven's Piano Trio Op. 70 No. 1'. *Proceedings of the Royal Musical Association*, 97: 1–19.

—— (1973), 'Sketches and autographs'. In Denis Arnold and Nigel Fortune (eds.), *The Beethoven Companion*, 443–58.

Vetter, Roger (1981), 'Flexibility in the performance practice of Central Javanese music'. *Ethnomusicology*, 25: 199–214.

Walker, Alan (1962), *A Study in Musical Analysis.* London.

Ward, W. Dixon (1970), 'Musical perception'. In Jerry V. Tobias (ed.), *Foundations of Modern Auditory Theory: I*, New York, 407–47.

Warrack, John (1979), 'The musical background'. In Peter Burbidge and Richard Sutton (eds.), *The Wagner Companion*, London, 85–112.

Watkins, Anthony J., and Dyson, Mary C. (1985), 'On the perceptual organization of tone sequences and melodies'. In Peter Howell, Ian Cross, and Robert West (eds.), *Musical Structure and Cognition*, London, 71–119.

West, Robert, Howell, Peter, and Cross, Ian (1985), 'Modelling perceived musical structure'. In Peter Howell, Ian Cross, and Robert West (eds.), *Musical Structure and Cognition*, London, 21–52.

Westernhagen, Curt von (1976), *The Forging of the 'Ring': Richard Wagner's Composition Sketches for 'Der Ring des Nibelungen'.* Cambridge. [*Die Entstehung des 'Ring'*, Zurich, 1973, trans. A. and M. Whittall.]

White, Eric Walter (1979), *Stravinsky: The Composer and his Works.* London.

White, Pamela C. (1984), 'Schoenberg and Schopenhauer'. *Journal of the Arnold Schoenberg Institute*, 8: 39–57.

Winter, Robert (1977), 'Plans for the structure of the String Quartet in C sharp minor, Op. 131'. *Beethoven Studies*, 2: 106–37.

—— (1982), *Compositional Origins of Beethoven's Opus 131*. Ann Arbor.

Wishart, Trevor (1985), 'Beyond notation'. *British Journal of Music Education*, 2: 311–26.

Wittgenstein, Ludwig (ed. 1966), *Lectures and Conversations on Aesthetics, Psychology and Religious Belief*, ed. C. Barrett. Oxford.

Xenakis, Iannis (1971), *Formalized Music: Thought and Mathematics in Composition*. Bloomington.

Yung, Bell (1984), 'Choreographic and kinesthetic elements in performance on the Chinese seven-string zither'. *Ethnomusicology*, 28: 505–17.

Zuckerkandl, Victor (1956), *Sound and Symbol: Music and the External World*. Princeton.

Index